Britney

THE UNAUTHORIZED BIOGRAPHY

Sean Smith is one of the UK's leading celebrity biographers, whose bestselling books have been translated throughout the world. His subjects include Cheryl Cole, Victoria Beckham, Robbie Williams, Kylie Minogue and Jennifer Aniston. Described by the *Independent* as a 'fearless chronicler', he specializes in meticulous research, going 'on the road' to find the real person behind the star image.

Britney

THE UNAUTHORIZED BIOGRAPHY

SEAN SMITH

PAN BOOKS

First published 2005 by Sidgwick & Jackson

This edition first published in paperback 2009 by Pan Books
an imprint of Pan Macmillan, a division of Macmillan Publishers Limited
Pan Macmillan, 20 New Wharf Road, London N1 9RR
Basingstoke and Oxford
Associated companies throughout the world
www.panmacmillan.com

ISBN 978–0–330–51274–9

Copyright © Sean Smith 2005, 2009

The right of Sean Smith to be identified as the
author of this work has been asserted by him in accordance
with the Copyright, Designs and Patents Act 1988.

1 3 5 7 9 8 6 4 2

A CIP catalogue record for this book is available from
the British Library.

Typeset by SetSystems Ltd, Saffron Walden, Essex
Printed and bound in the UK by CPI Mackays, Chatham ME5 8TD

Contents

Introduction

Is it really just five years since I first travelled to the Deep South to begin my journey through the life of Britney Spears? On that very first visit I discovered there were two Britneys, squaring up to each other like two boxers preparing for the big fight. In one corner was *the* Britney Spears we all know, the world's most successful young singer, a smouldering sexpot and multi-millionairess, and an iconic figure for a generation. In the other was a natural fun-loving girl making mistakes in her life just like everybody else does.

I wasn't being a genius in psycho-analysis; it was obvious. *The* Britney was on Broadway at ten, a star of the Mickey Mouse Club when she was eleven and a number one recording artist on both sides of the Atlantic when she was not yet eighteen and unable to buy a drink or have sex in most states of the US.

The contrast with the little girl with a strong Christian upbringing, working studiously in the classroom on the back lot of Disney, could not have been sharper. Chuck Yerger, who taught Britney back then – as well as Justin Timberlake and Christina Aguilera – told me stories of a youngster with a crucifix earring in each ear, 'raising her little face to the heavens and imploring the Lord to help with a difficult question'. She would then leave his class and go to a lesson in how to smile (drop your lower lip down to show a maximum number of teeth).

Many people I have spoken to about Britney over the years have voiced the same opinion – Britney was very malleable. She had an unshakeable belief that adults would not steer her wrong. This worked brilliantly when she was learning a new dance step or being moulded into a singing sensation by Jive Records. It worked less well in preparing her for serious disappointments and failures in real life. It seems that Britney has a chronically under-developed instinct for survival.

She responded badly to the dual blows in 2002 of the break-up of her parents' marriage and her split with Justin Timberlake, who she always believed would be the man with whom she would spend the rest of her life. I was told they lived like an 'old married couple' in Los Angeles and that is exactly what Britney had wanted. The lines between the professional Britney and the private one suddenly became blurred, with the singer walking off stage in Mexico City and bursting into tears during a Diane Sawyer television interview. It was not until 2008 that Britney herself finally admitted the traumatic effect of losing Justin: 'When he was gone, it was like "What am I supposed to do with myself?"'.

After Justin, and without the direction and security she was used to, Britney, still only twenty, went off the rails in spectacular fashion, culminating in her notorious fifty-five-hour marriage in Vegas to childhood friend Jason Alexander. For the first time the private Britney was trying to break free of the constraints of her professional life. She was fighting for control and, as a result, making haphazard, ill-considered decisions that would plague her for the next five years. And her relationship with her mother, Lynne, for so long of primary importance in keeping Britney grounded, started to crack.

Her hasty marriage to Kevin Federline, a dancer, would have an even more dramatic effect on her life. Almost overnight she became a wife and mother, but the failure of her marriage and the subsequent custody battles involving her two children were the catalysts for her distressing breakdowns – of February 2007 when she shaved off all her hair, and the beginning of 2008 when she was hospitalized for her own safety.

Britney now recognises that she married for the wrong reasons: 'I didn't follow my heart. I did it for the idea.' Britney, in my opinion, was just acting out the life she had always envisaged for herself and the right man – marriage and a couple of kids playing in the yard. It was the life many of her contempories had followed in Kentwood, Louisiana. Britney was twenty-three when she had her first child, Sean Preston, which was by no means young in southern terms. Her younger sister, Jamie Lynn, was just seventeen when she first gave birth.

Britney's private meltdown was, of course, anything but private, and was played out in front of the constant gaze of the persistent paparazzi. Back in 2005 a respected and serious photographer in LA told me he was worried about what was happening with the Britney posse and feared something bad might occur. I described her then as the Princess Diana of Malibu. What I didn't know was that this was how Britney was beginning to see herself, declaring, 'Princess Diana got killed by one of these people. They're crossing the line.'

For the last few years, just getting through each day has been difficult for Britney. Rumours that she was diagnosed as being bi-polar and that she requires daily medication have been neither confirmed nor denied. That's exactly as it should be. The private Britney needs to be just that – a private person getting on with her life and rebuilding her relationship with her family and sons, whom she loves to bits.

But Britney's professional recovery has been breathtaking in its speed and effectiveness. *The* Britney Spears is in rude health. I am not at all surprised – being Britney Spears, the star, is easy for her. She's been doing it all her life and it's just like getting back on a bicycle. Her career is relentlessly golden. I have been asked many times if I think Britney's comeback will be a success and my reply is always the same. She doesn't need to make a come-back because she hasn't gone away.

First Impressions

April 2005: 'Britney Spears? Nobody round here likes her,' declared the slightly surly waitress. When she walked away with my order of blackened chicken, the owner of the restaurant, an affable character with the air of someone who had seen it all, announced, 'Some folks get real jealous of success.' I nodded in agreement. The fact that the teenage waitress had never met Britney was immaterial. She had an opinion. Everyone round here in McComb, Mississippi or down the road in Kentwood, Louisiana, had an opinion about the most famous person to come from around these parts.

This is a strange country. When we read that Britney Spears is a 'typical southern miss', or some such fanzine platitude, we tend to skim over it without having the slightest idea of what that means. Perhaps we think she is someone stepping out of the pages of *Gone with the Wind* who goes to the prom with Rhett Butler. The average British person would believe that, because English is our shared main language, we are all kindred spirits and that going to Mississippi and Louisiana is rather like going to Cornwall. I found it far more foreign than France, Italy, Spain or anywhere else in Europe.

I went down to breakfast at my hotel on my first morning in McComb. I was my usual bleary-eyed self so, spotting an empty table out of the corner of my eye, I stumbled over and sat down hoping that someone would take pity on me and bring me coffee. After a minute I put on my glasses and looked around the room. It was a large breakfast area divided by a rectangular table, an island in the middle containing all the buffet items for a feast. Everybody sitting on the other side of the buffet was black. On my side of the buffet, we were all white. There were no free tables on the black side of the room so I was stuck on the white. There is no segregation any more so this had just been natural choice as people had drifted in.

My first interview that day was with someone who had known Britney as a child. We arranged to meet at an office in a street past downtown McComb. I found it easily, parked up and went to meet her. The first thing she did was apologize for my having to come to this neighbourhood. Apparently I had driven through the black quarter, something of which I had been completely unaware.

I decided to look up Britney's private school on a computer in the library and discovered the number of black pupils enrolled there. Nil. But there is no segregation. Since 1970 it has been illegal. My whole time in McComb I never saw a mixed race couple enjoying a drink together in a bar, eating dinner in a restaurant or just walking down the street hand in hand. The only thing obviously shared by all races was a love of calorie-laden Southern cooking.

McComb, Mississippi, seldom or never features in the story of Britney Spears. Kentwood is always given the plaudit as home town and it is true that her family home is ten miles away, over the state line in Louisiana, but she was actually born in McComb. Her father was born in McComb and her grandfather. Her school is in McComb, as is Wal-Mart and the shopping mall with her favourite boutiques and accessory shops. Her first serious boyfriend lived in McComb. The football game on a Friday night was in McComb, and when she comes home she goes to watch her kid sister play basketball in McComb.

That first boyfriend, Reg Jones, told me that one day they had been talking about the beautiful black actress Halle Berry and the conversation drifted on to mixed race relationships and what their parents might think if they became involved in one. Britney had told him that she didn't have a problem marrying a black guy, if the opportunity arose and she liked him. I thought that sounded good in theory.

Back at the library one of the members of staff was a lovely blonde girl (a typical Southern miss) who told me that one of her friends was on the basketball team at Parklane Academy with Britney. She also had an aunt who had arranged the Christmas flowers at Britney's mother's house. I popped over to Wal-Mart and one of the assistants told me that, in the flesh, Britney's mother was way prettier than her famous daughter. Another told me that Britney would pop in with her younger sister and they would go through the make-up together, trying on lipsticks before departing with a really downmarket brand.

There was no escaping Britney. I went into Ruby Tuesday's opposite the mall and, while I was waiting for my table, spotted a photograph of Britney on the wall. It was taken from her school year book and showed her posing next to a boy with a bad haircut. It was recognizable as Britney but she had long, curly, mousy brown hair. The picture was captioned *Junior High Most Handsome and Most Beautiful*. While I was in the restaurant having the first cheeseburger of my visit to the South, I heard the staff saying that there was a tornado warning, which struck me as amusing until I saw the lightning and heard the first roars of thunder. I was trapped, unable even to reach my car a few yards from the entrance.

I asked one schoolfriend of Britney's what young people did for entertainment here. 'We have bonfire parties,' she said. I asked her what that was exactly. 'Well, we light a bonfire and then we all sit around it drinking beer.' That evening, I went to a karaoke night in McComb. The girls, predominantly blonde-haired in blue jeans, sang LeAnn Rimes' songs while the men wearing big western-style hats wailed Hank Williams. Nobody sang a Britney song.

Everywhere you look there's a church. They are all immaculate. Britney's old house is just a few yards from one. And her family church in Kentwood is huge. It even it has its own mini van and visitor centre.

Nyla's Burger Basket in Osyka is Britney's favourite local restaurant. It's a small and friendly place by the side of Highway 61 between McComb and Kentwood. The restaurant achieved nationwide recognition in the US when it was revealed as Britney's favourite home-town restaurant. The walls are a homage to her. I thought how weird it must be for Britney coming to eat here. This is home but she munches her burger staring at giant-sized pouting posters of her professional self.

By luck I sat at the next table to two men having lunch, both of whom knew the Spears family. They told me that everyone was related to each other in the neighbourhood. They were charming, friendly and polite. These were easy folks to get along with, happy to shake your hand and call you sir. One of them told me he had been doing some electrical work up at Britney's mother's house when Britney had been staying there. She was sitting on the floor, drawing a picture for her sister. Britney had addressed him: 'How are you today, Sir?' She is still very respectful at home. She has never lost the graciousness of Southern manners. Perhaps she was a typical Southern miss after all.

'They are good people,' my new confidant observed. 'We remember them before they were rich.' He told me that Lynne Spears would not think twice about spending $10,000 on a car but would be delighted if she could get a bargain at the Super Dollar store where she paid $20 instead of $30.

I was told how much her new husband Kevin liked it at Britney's home. They always stayed at Serenity, the name of her mother's house, but would come down to Nyla or the Sonic Burger Bar in Kentwood. 'She comes here for serenity,' he laughed.

I was warming to Britney's private world. Britney Spears, it seemed, was a small-town girl. A glance around the walls backed up what I had been told about everyone being related. A clipping from a newspaper revealed that even the Mayor of Kentwood, Bobby Gill, is related. His grandmother and Britney's great grandfather were sister and brother. The walls also displayed a handwritten note Britney had sent the proprietor, Nyla Price, which said, 'Take care and keep cooking the best food in the world.'

The woods around here are deathly quiet. I was invited to a barbecue at a house in the woods. I spent the evening drinking beer and aimlessly throwing golf balls into the trees for an energetic dog which would fetch them back and drop them at my feet. It was slow and peaceful – serenity indeed.

ONE

Roots

At their first dance recital Britney and her cousin Laura Lynne Covington wore pink frou-frou dresses and white ribbons in their hair. Laura Lynne giggled the whole way through like an ordinary little girl. Britney, however, was deadly serious.

Kentwood, Louisiana, used to be a town you passed through. Now it is a town you pass by. Cars speed along the busy interstate Highway 55 between New Orleans and Jackson, Mississippi, just a mile from the centre but there is precious little reason to get off at Exit 61 unless you want to see the home town of Britney Spears. Those expecting to see a thriving little place celebrating their most famous daughter will be sorely disappointed. Even the local museum is downbeat and almost apologetic in its presentation of Britney's life.

In truth, Kentwood does not really have a centre but past the Sonic drive-in restaurant and the Super Dollar store there is a traffic light where photographers congregate if they know Britney is visiting her mother, who lives six miles straight across at the lights, or her father, who is two or three miles to the left just off

Highway 51, which used to be the main route through town before the interstate took over.

A few hundred yards along 51 is a disused gas station with a sign hanging outside that bears the legend Granny's Seafood Deli. The premises are now dusty and neglected. The granny in question was Lexie Pierce, great grandmother of Britney Spears and a local legend. It was here on any given Saturday that the menfolk of the family would be washing crawfish, the local favourite. In the UK it's called crayfish, a kind of miniature lobster. In these parts a 'crawfish boil' is a family occasion, a treat for a birthday or a family party.

In a side street on the other side of the highway is the Kentwood Museum, a small building with a very large American flag, where visitors can admire Britney memorabilia. Here the story of Britney Jean Spears begins, not in her own exhibit, but in the other part of the museum, the military room, where the curator Hazel Morris is devotedly putting together a history of the men of Kentwood at war. She has gathered together weapons and guns from the Second World War and the Korean conflict of a few years later.

On the walls are pictures of the town's veterans in their uniforms. One of them is Sgt Barney Bridges, a handsome young Southerner, who was stationed near London during the Second World War. He was one of the GIs who, according to cockney comic Tommy Trinder, were 'overpaid, overfed, oversexed and over here'. While he was here he met a vivacious girl, Lillian Portell, fresh out of her teens, at the Royal Opera House, which in wartime was a dance hall where everyone could let off steam to the sounds of a big band, a welcome release from the constraints of war. Lillian, an electrician's daughter from East Finchley, loved to go out dancing with her sister Joan, who was with her that evening.

Joan recalls, 'Barney was a nice-looking man and he was wearing his uniform. He was very Southern. Sometimes I could understand what he said and sometimes I couldn't.' Barney and Lillian started a whirlwind wartime romance which ended with their marrying at the All Saints Church in East Finchley.

'My mother was dreadfully upset,' says Joan. She herself was dismayed when her sister left to start a new life in Louisiana: 'I thought I would never see her again.'

That proved not to be the case, although the only time Lillian came back to the United Kingdom during the next thirty years was when their father died in 1953. Joan believes Barney would not let her sister visit because he was worried she would never want to go back to Louisiana. Lillian and Barney had three children, Barry, Sandra and Lynne, mother of Britney Spears. Joan did manage to go over to the US herself three times to visit. She was impressed with the large farm but discovered that, despite sharing a common language, the Deep South was quite foreign to her.

Barney, she felt, was very 'domineering' while the devout Christianity was very strict and formal. Grace, she remembers, was said before and after every meal. Churchgoing was compulsory. 'Lillian was always a bit of an outsider,' she says.

Barney had died three years before Britney was born and, sadly, Lillian died in 1993, before Britney became a superstar. She did, however, live long enough to witness her granddaughter joining the cast of Disney's *Mickey Mouse Club*, the biggest event in Kentwood history for a generation.

The English branch of the family has flourished and Britney has many cousins living in and around Northolt and Greenford in

West London. Contact between the two branches is, however, very sporadic. Britney's mother Lynne has sent Joan flowers and her aunt Sandra keeps in touch. Joan has never met Britney. Some of her family did go backstage at Britney's first UK concert but that is the only contact. Britney may be one-quarter English but a deeply Christian farming community on the Louisiana–Mississippi border might just as well be on the moon.

On another wall of the Kentwood Museum is a picture of a swarthy young man who fought in the Korean War. He is June Spears, Britney's paternal grandfather and the only surviving grandparent. The Spears 'clan' is one of the biggest in the area and practically everyone is a relation. June, more usually a female first name, is a family name throughout the Spears clan. Papaw June, as he is known, has the physical characteristics that both Britney's father and brother possess. He is not particularly tall but he is formidably wide – a stocky and muscular man who can strike fear into young Southern boys.

On one occasion, Britney's teenage boyfriend Reg Jones went to collect her from Papaw June's house. He was with a friend, Rick Newman, and both of them wore their hair quite long. Papaw June was very polite while they were visiting but when it was time to leave he declared, 'Let me tell you one thing, son. You can come in here this time but the next time you come in here with hair like that I'm going to cut it off. Get that shit off your head!'

Reg laughs, 'He was very to the point.'

That straightforward nature is something Papaw June's son Jamie inherited. Like many couples in the area, he met his future wife Lynne when they were both at high school. Lynne was eighteen when they married, had her son, Bryan, when she was twenty-one and longed for a daughter. She would later explain in her book *Heart to Heart* that everyone in the family seemed to be having boys. When Britney Jean Spears was born on 2 December 1981, she was ecstatic that, at last, she had an 'adorable baby girl to dress up like a little doll!' Brittany – as in the name of Georgia-born actress Brittany Murphy – is a popular name in the South but Lynne decided to spell it the way it sounded, especially when pronounced with a local Louisiana drawl.

The very first mention of Britney Spears in a newspaper came in the *Kentwood News* when she was 'Baby of the Week'. She was, according to the article, an 'active, precious bundle of joy'. By a twist of fate that original piece was written by the same Hazel Morris who is now responsible for the Britney exhibit in the town museum.

The young Spears family settled down to life in Kentwood. Technically the population of Kentwood is a miserly 2,656, according to the 1998 census, but that is misleading. The houses away from the centre are spread out and scattered as might be expected in a farming community, one which was thriving when Britney was born. Tangipahoa Parish, of which it is part, has a population of 100,000. This is open countryside but not a prosperous one. The average income is less than $20,000, which in sterling is about £11,500. After Britney Spears, the most important export is Kentwood Spring Water and every visitor to the Britney exhibit at the museum gets a free bottle as a reminder that this is not just the home town of a famous pop star.

Statistics can always be manipulated, but an analysis of Kentwood shows a significantly higher black population (66 per cent) than the state average, household income significantly below state average, house prices below state average, number of college students below state average and the percentage of population with a bachelor's degree or higher also significantly below state average. The overall picture is of a relatively poor, under-educated, predominantly black town. It is all relative, however, and Kentwood has pretty, tree-lined avenues with spotless gardens and no visible signs of any ghetto. Figures for 2001 reveal no murders, no rapes and only two robberies. No wonder people feel relaxed about going out and leaving their homes unlocked.

The most telling figure in revealing a town in gentle decline is the one relating to new homes being built in Kentwood. There are barely any. When Britney built a new $4.5-million Tudor-style mansion, Serenity, for her mother Lynne, she single-handedly revived the fortunes of local tradesmen. When she was a young child her father Jamie worked in the construction business and was thriving. At the end of the 1980s, however, work was becoming scarce and he had to travel further and further afield to find jobs, putting an enormous strain on family life. The Interstate Highway 55 afforded easy access to Wal-Mart and the other larger stores in McComb, a much bigger town just across the Mississippi border. A flying visit to Wal-Mart needed to take little more than an hour out of a Kentwood resident's day.

Those harder times when money became tight were in the future for the first few years of Britney's life. The family home off Highway 51 was nicely situated a few hundred yards from Greenlaw Baptist church on the one side and Skinny's Bar on the other. It was a very comfortable middle-class Southern home. When you pulled into the driveway the first thing you saw was a basketball hoop where her brother Bryan, who is four years her senior, would shoot hoops with his pals. At the end of the carport you could stroll on to a deck out the back of the house. Most visitors went that way into the kitchen, which had a dining-room area within it where they ate their meals. The kitchen led into a pretty living room, reflecting Lynne's personal taste – a beige carpet, a white leather recliner and a blue sofa with big magnolia leaves on it.

Behind the sofa was the family piano where Britney would practise her singing while everyone else was trying to watch television. The room was big enough for Britney, who was always very little as a child, to show off her ability at back flips, tumbling across the living room floor.

The other door in the kitchen led to a long hallway. Britney's room was on the right opposite a bathroom, Bryan's room was at the far end across from Lynne and Jamie's room. When Britney's younger sister Jamie Lynn arrived she would sleep in Lynne's room, which worked out well because by this time Jamie was spending a great deal of time working away and only coming home at weekends. The furniture in the house was nothing out of the ordinary but the overriding impression for visitors was that it was a 'comfortable' home.

From an early age, Britney's small bedroom was stuffed full of dolls. Her mother collected them for her – a passion they could share which cemented the bond between them. The original furniture is now on display at the Kentwood Museum, donated by her father. Some of the dolls are there, as well as her day bed, assorted teddy bears and pictures, some dresses she wore in her talent-contest days and, on the wall, the ubiquitous child's prayer, 'Now I lay me down to sleep . . .'

Britney has admitted that, when she was a little girl, she liked to line up all her dolls and all her teddy bears in the bathroom as if they were her audience. Then she used to stand in front of the big mirror they had on the wall and pretend she was a superstar. From an early age she became fascinated with how she looked when she sang or danced. She was Madonna and Whitney Houston rolled into one and she was bigger than both of them. The camera has loved Britney from a very tender age because she has been transfixed with how she looks in a pose.

Renowned singing teacher Bob Westbrook, who gave her singing lessons when she was a pubescent member of *The Mickey Mouse Club*, recalls, 'She stared in the mirror the whole time. Most of the children who turned up for lessons treated them as an extension of their schoolwork. They were being taught a subject in a relaxed, easy way – not Britney. She treated the whole thing as a performance. She was so intense. If I sweated for any student, I sweated for her.'

Britney, it seems, became two people almost before she could walk. She was the sweet little girl, all frills and bows, a living embodiment of the cutesy dolls neatly arranged around her bedroom. She was also a miniature professional, totally driven, focused on the dream of being a superstar. From time to time throughout her life, the two Britneys have collided in their battle for supremacy, rendering her shattered.

One of the great myths of entertainment, the Hollywood view of showbusiness, is that happy accidents do happen. Britney would be a Southern belle, all peaches and cream, singing to herself as she ordered a soda. The man in front would be a record producer who would discover her on the spot and invite her to make a record. This fantasy world is what drives thousands of hopeful but hopeless wannabes to try and win *Pop Idol*, *American Idol* or *The X Factor*. They may have the dream but as kids they watched TV and played football or computer games. In contrast, the great majority of today's major stars have literally sweated blood to get their chance. Robbie Williams was rehearsing pantomime dance steps while his mates played football in the park; Kylie Minogue was eleven when she landed her first television role; Justin Timberlake was taking singing lessons from Bob Westbrook when he was eight.

Britney Spears was two years old when she had her first dance lesson in Kentwood. A lady called Renee Donewar ran a dance school in the town of Hammond, about thirty miles away, but once a week she would come up to Kentwood and put little girls through their ballet paces in a room she rented. It is a scene re-enacted in thousands of towns and villages throughout the world every day: little tots in tutus frolicking about. Many little girls take ballet or dancing lessons but not many take it as seriously as Britney. She won the Best Attendance prize in class and would get quite stroppy if others were not as dedicated as she was.

Renee Donewar confirmed, 'She was always a perfectionist – when there was a new step she was always the first to get it.' That characteristic of educated feet has never left Britney throughout her career. Britney's earliest memories of dancing classes all involve her cousin Laura Lynne Covington, the daughter of Lynne's sister Sandra. The two cousins are the same age and have remained the closest of friends throughout their lives. The two sisters would dress their daughters up in matching outfits, especially for dancing where they wore the same frilly dresses with white ribbons for their hair. They even had matching night shirts with teddy bears on them. The family photo albums are filled with pictures that would now make the cousins cringe with embarrassment.

Laura Lynne has been a constant in Britney's life. She and

Britney's other closest friends from Kentwood, Jansen Fitzgerald and Cortney Brabham, are a reminder of her real self. They do normal things like go to college and get married. Britney rewards their loyalty with her own. Together they have formed a tightly knit coterie from little girls to young women.

Ms Donewar was the first of many to recognize that Britney always wanted to be a star. She was, however, just a tiny girl being happily indulged by her parents. Amateur psychologists could have a field day with the root causes of childhood ambition. She may have been following the Southern tradition of a daughter who loved her daddy and wanted to please him. Or she may have been acting out the fantasy life of an intelligent mother who recognized a big world outside Kentwood, Louisiana. Perhaps she just loved the delight on people's faces as they praised her and told her how cute she was and how very talented. Later she would have to justify the sacrifices the family made to allow her to pursue the American dream. She would push herself to the limits and beyond. While still a young schoolgirl she was on an exhausting timetable that included being driven ninety miles, three days a week, for a dancing lesson.

Throughout her early life, Britney was always more of a dancer than a singer. Even today, her live performances are as much about showcasing her skill and agility moving around the stage as they are about her vocal talents. She was such an athletic little girl that for a while it looked as if a career in gymnastics was far more likely than one in showbusiness. Five nights a week she would be in the gym. An interest that started with Britney doing flips in the living room soon escalated into something far more serious. Her father Jamie, who would indulge his daughter's slightest wish, built her a balance beam in the living room, which proved a bit of a distraction when everyone was trying to watch television. Locally she began entering competitions and was doing so well that her father suggested she should go to a special camp run by Olympic coach Bela Karolyi about fifty miles north of Houston, Texas.

Karolyi had become the most acclaimed coach in the sport when he was in charge of the all-conquering Romanian team of the 1980s, which included the great Olympic champion Nadia Comaneci. He defected to the US in 1981, quickly establishing himself as a force in his adopted country. He set up this special training camp on a 500-acre ranch where Olympic stars Mary Lou Retton and Dianne Durham were among the earliest residents. Karolyi seemed able to take girls that barely came up to one's knee and turn them into serious, dedicated sportswomen. These tiny girls flipping and twisting somersaults in the air were seriously scary.

Even to be considered promising enough to spend a week at the camp was a tremendous compliment to Britney's ability. Karolyi acknowledged that she was 'one of the little girls who excelled'. It held the prospect of years of top sport. She had already been placed first in her own junior grade at state level but now it was the time to step everything up a notch. The future would be more training, more dedication and more competition. This was not little girls having fun, it was ruthless sport for budding anorexics and Britney later revealed that the world it opened up for her was not one she wanted at all. There was no Laura Lynne by her side, giggling away and raising everyone's spirits. She did not mind the hard work – that has never been something Britney shirks – it was the single-minded seriousness of it all: 'I started to cry when I had to go to gymnastics. I had been good at gymnastics because it was fun. I missed that and I didn't want to do it any more.'

It would not be the last time that Britney became thoroughly fed up with the performance treadmill. To her great credit, however, her mother Lynne decided that it was not just a phase like hating maths or Brussels sprouts. She realized that it had all 'got way too much' for her daughter Britney and it was time for singing and dancing to take centre stage once more. Despite her precocious ability, she was, after all, just a little girl.

'Kentwood was in their hearts.'

TWO

Supplication

Britney used to take the school bus from her home in Kentwood to Parklane Academy in McComb. One morning a teacher asked them to put up their hands if they had any news. Britney raised her hand. 'My mama's pregnant,' she announced.

To be respectful is the Southern way. Britney, however, was more than just respectful in the company of adults. She was humble, keen to please and trusting. Chuck Yerger, who later would be her tutor at Disney, observes that she was completely unquestioning in that trust. 'It struck me that she had an unshakeable faith that adults would never steer you wrong and that you should always do as you were told. If the teachers from her Christian school had told her to write her name a certain way on a sheet of paper, or to write in blue rather than black ink or that her margins should be exactly three-quarters of an inch on the right-hand side, then her entire self was invested in making sure she did exactly that.'

The Christian school in question was Parklane Academy in McComb, a small private school founded in 1970. This was the year that racial integration became law and it is no coincidence that a number of private schools sprang up almost immediately. Parklane Academy has no black pupils, although it does have an open admissions policy. One former classmate of Britney's explains, 'It's not that they don't accept other races. They just never had any. I mean it's open to anyone, it's just always been all white.' Even when money was very tight for the Spears family they still found the cash for the school fees. They were not especially high and parents paid less for a second child at the school. Britney's elder brother Bryan was already enrolled, which reduced the cost of sending Britney to Parklane to approximately $150 a month. But on top of that parents had to pay for literally everything else, including books, which practically doubled the cost. To send Britney to an all-white, private Christian school cost a minimum of $3,000 a year which, combined with the cost of sending Bryan there, put a substantial dent in the family's ailing finances.

Britney was at Parklane on and off from first grade right through to ninth grade, that is from the age of six to fifteen. It was quite often more off than on as she spent time first in New York and then in Orlando, pressing on with a show-business career from an early age. 'She was always just coming or going,' recalls Kelly Burch, who was a member of Britney's basketball team. Britney was a very useful basketball player despite her small stature. Kelly observes, 'She was just a natural at it. She played point guard and was a constant player in the games.' By coincidence Justin Timberlake was also a point guard on his school's basketball team and the sport was an enjoyment the future lovers would share.

The Parklane campus is quite small but is dominated by the football field of the Parklane Pioneers. The school day began at

8 a.m. with a 'devotional' when the class teacher would read something from the Bible for ten or fifteen minutes. Parklane's school motto is 'Excellence in Christian education' and the mission statement declares that the school exists to 'challenge young Christian men and women to love others as themselves'. To further endorse this message the school's website displays a cross which opens up to display the word 'love'. Kelly explains, 'They tried to instil in us Christian values and beliefs.' Every year the school held a special 'Christian Emphasis Week' in which speakers would come in and address the children about topics embracing the importance of moral values, the difference between right and wrong and what they needed to do to be 'saved'. The younger pupils also had to recite the Pledge of Allegiance to the American Flag every morning. From time to time a speaker from the True Love Waits campaign would come to the school and address pupils. The campaign founded by Southern Baptists in the early 1990s preached sexual virtue to teenagers. The True Love Waits commitment says: 'Believing that true love waits, I make a commitment to God, myself, my family, my friends, my future mate, and my future children to be sexually abstinent from this day until the day I enter a biblical marriage relationship.' It would be very easy to speculate that Britney was all attention on the days the campaign visited. Certainly it might explain her preoccupation with her own chastity a few years later.

In many ways, although Parklane was very zealous in its pursuit of fundamental Christian principles, it was merely reflecting what the children were already learning in their home environment. Darlene Hughes, Britney's third-grade teacher, confirms, 'She came to school with these values.' Britney's own family heritage was strongly Southern Baptist and very strict. Religion filtered through the teaching of Parklane but not in a way that these Southern children thought was in any way unusual or against the norm. Arithmetic problems, for instance, were devised within a religious framework along the lines of – Jesus was dispensing 5,000 fish equally to a crowd of one hundred men and women. How many fish did each person receive?

Intriguingly, one of Britney's school friends, Lindey Hughes Magee, could not recall that sort of teaching at all and was very surprised when she looked up an old exercise book. On the very first page she opened was a Bible pictograph – a graph which uses pictures to make comparisons. It began: 'Answer these questions about the Bible pictograph: 1. On which day were the most Bibles sold? 2. How many more Bibles were sold on Saturday than on Tuesday?'

Nor was this a one-off. Turning the page she came across 'Pastor Jones had a special offering to raise the $5,000 his church still owed on the church organ . . .'

By far the most contentious element of the school curriculum at Parklane was creationism. This is an extreme view of world history which believes it to be fact that God created the world in seven days. It does not tolerate evolutionary theories or Darwinism. This is what Britney, and all her school friends, were taught as children and reveals the strength of the Christian element in her upbringing. This is not a Christmas carol concert with a little Sunday school thrown in. 'Bible Belt' is a phrase that trips a little too lightly off the tongue. Britney's exposure to the good book, while commonplace in the Southern Baptist community, nevertheless deeply colours the person she is.

All her life, Britney has had to try and reconcile her devout

Christian upbringing and schooling to a music business with a reputation as one of the most amoral, or immoral, you could choose. Britney's adult sexy image would sit very uneasily among certain of the more fervent Christian supporters of Parklane – to such an extent in fact that the school is reputed to have turned down a considerable donation from Britney, which would have been worth several million dollars.

Chuck Yerger's abiding impression of Britney is of a young girl with a crucifix in each ear raising her little face to the heavens and imploring 'the Lord' to help with a difficult question in a test paper. Britney never had any real trouble with her academic studies at Parklane or at Disney. She was conscientious if a little uninspired. Mrs Hughes remembers that she received mostly A grades with a few Bs thrown in. Her school did not interfere with her singing and dancing lessons outside school and that was the main thing.

Britney is not especially bright but, like many stars, she is smart about what she cares about. Justin Timberlake, who is particularly intelligent, handed Britney a classic double-edged compliment: 'That's the greatest thing about Britney; even when she doesn't understand, she understands that she doesn't under-stand because she has such a big heart.'

Britney's religious beliefs are very real and honest. In her early interviews as a chart phenomenon she would often reveal that she wrote in her special prayer journal every night. It was true. Her first serious boyfriend, Reg Jones, confirms that this was the case – at an age when teenage hormones are flying around and when hiding the fact that you were a closet smoker from your parents would be a major concern.

It is very easy to regard thanking God at every opportunity as a slightly cheesy Southern trait, reeking of insincerity. Britney's belief in God and her respect for Him was part of her life before she could walk. In the notes for her first album ... *Baby One More Time*, Britney's first acknowledgement is to 'thank God for the blessing of song'. For her second album, *Oops! ... I Did It Again* (two glimpses of the Spears midriff) she thanks God for 'the most incredible adventure anyone could ever wish or dream for – praise to You!' On *Britney*, her third album (twelve navel flashes) she thanks 'the Almighty Creator from up above for giving me so many beautiful gifts'. *In the Zone* (three pictures of the Spears midriff) she thanks 'the Lord for blessing me with so many precious gifts'. It is not difficult to imagine the principal emotion invoked by trying to appease childhood indoctrination – guilt.

As a school, Parklane deserves considerable credit for allowing Britney to develop her career as a child performer. She never encountered any opposition to the pursuit of her dream. Her mother was well liked and respected and her elder brother was an excellent young sportsman. As a result Lynne and Jamie had no hesitation in enrolling Britney's young sister Jamie Lynn at the school.

Unsurprisingly, Britney's first public performance was at her family's church in Kentwood, the First Baptist on Avenue E. It is an imposing, red-brick, double-storey building with a visitor centre and a minibus parked outside bearing the logo Kentwood First Baptist. Churches are everywhere in the Deep South. It isn't called the Bible Belt for nothing and you cannot drive five miles in any direction without coming across a church. Even though Britney could have lobbed pebbles into Greenlaw Church from her backyard, her family's church had always been the First Baptist a few miles away.

The very first Baptist church in the United States was established in 1639 in Providence, Rhode Island, but the faith did not grip the South until the late eighteenth and nineteenth centuries, when it spread rapidly through the black population. The black Baptist churches of the South played an important role in the development of the Civil Rights movement, especially in the Sixties, when the Reverend Martin Luther King, Jr was the leading voice advocating social change. He had himself been the son of a Baptist minister. Going to church was a fundamental part of life for practically every family in this area of the South. It was part of the fabric of Britney's life. Darlene Hughes observes, 'You wake up on Sunday and go "Thank you God for this day, I'm going to go to your House."'

Britney was four years old when she got up in front of the congregation at the First Baptist and sang 'What Child Is This?' at a Christmas service. It was a well-known Christian song sung to the tune of the school favourite 'Greensleeves'. She was already in the church junior choir and would sing every weekend when her family attended. Even so, she was petrified at her first solo. It was all very well belting out a Madonna song in front of the dolls and bears in the bathroom at home, but this was entirely different. She was so nervous that she sang the entire song with her head cocked to one side but nobody noticed. Everybody was enthralled by what a powerful pair of lungs this little girl possessed.

In the Spears household they were already well aware of that. Britney was an all-dancing, all-singing bundle of energy. Lynne's friends would come round and hear her singing in the bathroom and believe it was just the radio playing loud. Her brother was forever shouting at her to keep the noise down. Britney had a natural singing voice but she was also especially good at imitating her heroes like Whitney Houston, Madonna and Mariah Carey. When Lynne drove her to dance classes they would crank the radio up and Britney would sing along the whole time, making sure she was out-singing the stereo. Singing teacher Bob Westbrook observes, 'She had a big belt voice as a kid.' Lynne always played pop on the radio so Britney grew up on a diet of chart songs and not the usual local favourites like Dolly Parton and Loretta Lynn or music from the Christian stations.

Britney has always said that the first time her mother realized that her daughter could really sing was when she heard her singing a Sinead O'Connor song while jumping around on a trampoline in the backyard. She would bounce especially high when she had to hit a high note. It was almost a eureka moment when Lynne realized that her little girl had perfect pitch. She whizzed Britney round to her teacher to show her. At the age of six, Britney entered her first talent contest at the Kentwood Dairy Festival. She wore a top hat, brandished a cane and she won. From that time on she mopped up in local talent contests. When she was eight Lynne took her to Baton Rouge for the Miss Talent Central States Competition, where she competed against girls from four states – Texas, Alabama, Mississippi and Louisiana. She danced, sang and showed off her gymnastic abilities with some trademark tumbling. She was the overall winner for all categories.

At Parklane Academy, Britney entered into the spirit of the school musical. She played a school marm in a show called *Give Thanks America* and then in the third grade she sang a solo, 'Lavender Blue', in a revue put together by the music teacher

Mary-Ellen Chamberlin, who was impressed: 'Her voice was so much more mature than the other children her age.' This was the first time Britney was watched by her younger sister, Jamie Lynn, although she was just a baby and spent the whole performance enjoying a bottle while Lynne watched her daughter.

Britney was in demand at the school, singing the national anthem at Grandparents Day on more than one occasion. Darlene Hughes recalls she sang the 'Star Spangled Banner' with such power and feeling that some of the audience thought she was miming or lip-synching, as it is now more commonly known: 'She was awesome. She was so dynamic and forceful that some of the people didn't even believe it was her singing.' Britney also performed at fundraisers. Mrs Hughes still has the video she shot of Britney performing four numbers at a fish fry in the school cafeteria. A fish fry, like a crawfish boil, is very popular in the South. It is exactly what it sounds and familiar to anyone from the UK who has been to the Caribbean for a holiday. All sorts of shapes and sizes of fish are fried up and served, although in Britney's neighbourhood this was usually catfish and served with French fries, hushpuppies and coleslaw. Hushpuppies are a Southern speciality – cornbread balls flavoured with chopped spring onions, deep fried and served hot. One of the songs was a duet with another girl of the Naomi Judd ballad 'Love Can Build a Bridge', which she performed when she lost the *Star Search* talent final on television. Mrs Hughes has kept every last scrap of Britney's school memorabilia, having always had a sense that the young girl she taught as an eight-year-old was destined for great things. She laughs, 'Did I see this coming or not!'

Local talent contests, singing at school and in the bathroom were indications of the possibility that Britney had something special. But lots of children within their local community are thought of as special, whether in entertainment, sport or art. Then when they move from the small pond to the lake they quickly disappear with the realization that they are not really that special at all.

Britney was set to find out whether she had any future beyond the Kentwood Dairy Festival when a girl from dance class told her that there was an open-call audition for *The All New Mickey Mouse Club* in Atlanta, Georgia. Britney desperately wanted to go and kept on at her mother to drive her the 450 miles for the try-out. Eventually Lynne agreed, even though it would be an expensive journey that might lead to nothing but disappointment.

The All New Mickey Mouse Club had begun in 1988 but was only available on cable on the Disney Channel. The original show, however, had been an institution of American broadcasting in the late 1950s. When Disneyland opened in 1955, Disney put together an all-singing, all-dancing group of children and called them 'Mouseketeers'. It turned one young teenager into a household name. She was Annette Funicello and she became the sweetheart of a generation of teenagers as she grew up from an innocent fourteen-year-old to a more pneumatic seventeen-year-old. At the age of eighteen, her much publicized measurements were 36–24–36. Parents loved her because she projected the classic Disney image of wholesomeness. She played down what film critics described as a 'formidable bustline' to continue to trade on that image after the show was cancelled in 1959. She made a number of very tame beach movies in the 1960s in which she often paraded in a swimsuit, but never had a serious dramatic role. Her popularity remained undimmed. She was also one of the first-ever stars to become known and universally identifiable by one name – Annette.

She was a guest star when *The Mickey Mouse Club* enjoyed a brief revival in 1977 and again on the latest version in 1990. She gave it continuity and stature. Sadly, she was diagnosed with multiple sclerosis at the age of 45.

Britney wanted to be Madonna, not Annette, but the principle that a TV show could make a career was quite clear. More than 2,000 children travelled to Atlanta to try and catch the eye of the chief talent scout, Matt Casella. He literally saw thousands of children the length and breadth of the country. He knew exactly what he was looking for – an average kid with extraordinary talent. One of the youngsters he found the year Britney auditioned was Tony Lucca in Detroit.

Tony had no experience and had to be talked into auditioning by his sister. He recalls, 'I had never really auditioned before and I was chewing gum and he said "Do you want to spit your gum out?" and I said "No, I'm cool, I can speak and chew gum at the same time." And he just laughed.' Matt Casella was a superb judge of whether a boy or girl was the right blend of all-American child for the show. He was looking for poster kids, children that could be identified as the ideal American offspring – the child that every parent with a young delinquent wished was theirs. He wanted small-town versions of Mickey Rooney and Judy Garland whose chirpiness was infectious and who could put on a show five minutes after thinking of the idea.

Matt wanted to find kids whose smile could light up a room. That might have been problematical for Britney before she embarked on some serious dental work. She started going to see local dentist Sue Le Blanc when she was eight, telling her she needed a beautiful smile because she was going to be in show-business. She had to wear a retainer, a horrid red object with a key that had to be tightened at night to help persuade the teeth to grow in the right direction. Britney was always mislaying hers, including leaving it on the table of the school cafeteria where she had been having lunch. It was thrown out with the trash from where she had to retrieve it later in the day. The retainer was a precursor to the heavy-duty braces which all American children seem to wear as part of the growing process. A little discreet whitening when she was a teenager on the verge of stardom and Britney's smile was a Hollywood dazzler.

Britney had very little time to impress Matt Casella with or without her smile. It was rather like an audition for *The X Factor*. She sang 'Sweet Georgia Brown' while executing a breathtaking display of running, jumping, dancing and flipping.

Casella had an instinct which would prove extremely fortunate for Britney's career. He has made no secret of the fact that from the very first he knew Britney was 'a one-in-a-million kid' by the way she could switch on a light and change from a shy little girl into a confident (still little) performer: 'I could not believe this child was nine. I don't know where her mother had brought her to prior to these auditions but she had so much experience. She just came in and got tens all across the board – for singing, dancing and acting. She was a triple threat!'

For a man as respected as Matt Casella to single her out was the biggest indication yet for Lynne and Jamie that they had something special on their hands. Britney made a shortlist of six at the open day, an astonishing achievement for someone so young. Casella was keen for her to go through but in the end she lost out because the programme's executives felt she was too young and would upset the balance of the show. The intake that year, which included Tony Lucca, were all about five years older than Britney. It was a setback but Matt Casella was not giving up on her.

There is one golden rule involved in the world of child performers: the mother must be OK. If the mother is a nightmare, then show the child the exit door. Tony Lucca observes, 'The bottom line is that the main ingredient in the audition process was the parental interview. I don't care what you hear, they auditioned the kids but they interviewed the parents. A lot of talented kids fell by the wayside over the years in the audition process because the parents didn't check out.'

Lynne Spears always checked out. The image of a pushy woman forcing her child into the spotlight to line the coffers of the family bank vault is one that all mothers of talented youngsters are vulnerable to, and often justifiably so. Some stars have had high-profile disputes with their mothers, usually over career and money. There is no evidence of that nature involving Britney and her mother. Lynne has never been her manager nor, since Britney reached the age of fifteen, has she been her constant companion, perched on her shoulder like a vampire bat. She has given Britney time and space to develop while retaining a quiet authority, suggesting until quite recently that she was the power in the Spears' household.

She is petite, raven-haired and very pretty. In that regard she takes after both her parents. At the Wal-Mart store in McComb, where she is still a regular, a shop assistant who often serves her observes, 'She is way prettier than Britney.' She grew up in a male-dominated, strongly Christian household and radiates patience and thoughtfulness. Britney's father Jamie is strong, physically fit and a man's man. He is a rugged Southern man displaying many of the qualities that Britney also goes for in the men in her life. One attribute, which might not be so attractive, is the very masculine habit of constantly chewing tobacco and spitting it out.

Lynne, conversely, was an elementary schoolteacher who took great care in plotting how to ensure Britney made the very best of her precocious talents. By no means the least of her accomplishments was keeping that dream alive during the worst times for her family.

She freely admits that the family had a terrible financial struggle just to put food on the table. She told the VH1 documentary *Driven*: 'I had to rob from Peter to pay Paul. I was late on things.' Even in this Southern backwater singing and dancing lessons were expensive and that was on top of school fees. Britney's brother Bryan suffered from asthma as a child, which resulted in some horrendous medical bills for his mother and father. On one occasion he had a seizure and had to be airlifted to hospital in New Orleans, which was very expensive. The family phone was cut off and their boiler broke down when they could not afford to have it repaired. For two winters they huddled round tiny petrol heaters. Britney had to get used to wearing hand-me-downs but she was never less than a well-presented little girl. She also became adept at searching through the sales racks and the charity shops for bargains. She has never lost that appetite for spending time hunting for clothes, even now when she can afford any item in any shop.

Perhaps having another baby when Britney was nine allowed Lynne to keep her feet on the ground back in Kentwood while

Britney lived the high life all over the world. Jamie Lynn helped bridge the generation gap between Britney and her mother that can lead to such discord between a teenage daughter and her mom. Mrs Gay Austin, the mother of Britney's teenage boyfriend Reg Jones says, 'Lynne was always very genuine.' Other classmates of Britney confirm that Lynne is a 'sweet lady'. When Bryan brought home his footballing gang, Lynne would always be there, being a 'mom', fixing sodas and snacks.

At every stage of Britney's development Lynne is praised for how she conducted herself. Darlene Hughes found her 'dedicated'. She was prepared to uproot herself and turn her life upside down not once but twice so that Britney could pursue the American dream. New York agent Nancy Carson, who would regularly see her after she had struggled up to her office with Jamie Lynn in a pushchair, remarks, 'I think it was hard for her at times. I am sure she missed home but I think they were determined to let Britney have this opportunity.'

Lynne was never a nuisance to people involved in Britney's career. She generally trusted that the best was being done. She did, however, possess an inner steel and would make the decisions for Britney. When Britney, for instance, thought she might try out for cheerleading because her girlfriends did it and her boyfriend was in the football team it was Lynne who persuaded her otherwise. She convinced her that all that hollering was not going to do her singing voice any good.

Only Lynne knows how much of Britney's dream was her own dream. She would write poetry about her daughter with cloying titles like 'My Little Star' in which the sentiment is one of a mother finding fulfilment in her daughter's quest for success.

Lynne was no monster mom but she kept her eye on the ball. Her fulfilment as a mother is something that Britney is seeking to emulate in her own life.

'Do not worry about anything. Instead pray about everything.'

THREE

New York Stories

Her agent, Nancy Carson, would tease young Britney about saying 'yes ma'am' all the time to her, as it betrayed her Southern origin: 'It was a dead giveaway. I used to tell her "Don't keep saying yes ma'am" and she would nod her head seriously and reply, "yes ma'am".'

Nancy Carson has been a Broadway institution for more than twenty-five years. From her chaotic office in a building on the corner of West 57th Street and Seventh Avenue she devotes long hours every day to promoting an ever-changing squadron of young hopefuls. She has the precious gift of treating her child clients in an unpatronizing way, answering every telephone call with the same friendly but businesslike greeting: 'Hello, it's Nancy.' She knows how to dispense bad news as well as good without crushing fragile egos. Most of all she knows talent when she sees it. Her battered, old-fashioned box of contact cards still contains the details of the famous and not so famous who took the lift eight floors to the Carson-Adler office – Matt Damon, Ben Affleck, Mischa Barton, Cynthia Nixon and Britney Jean Spears all took their first steps to stardom here.

The first Nancy heard of the little girl from Louisiana was when she took a phone call from Matt Casella's assistant Jean, who told her that the parents of a talented youngster would be getting in touch with her. Nancy immediately sat up and took notice: 'I knew Matt and he rarely sent me anybody. But he just has a great eye and knows stars. I generally listen to him.'

Soon afterwards Lynne Spears was on the phone asking what they should do about Britney. Nancy was very non-committal and suggested writing her a letter about their daughter and including some material if they had it. She was aware the Spears family lived a long way from New York so did not want to suggest right away that they travel to the city to see her.

Jamie Spears sat down and wrote the letter to Nancy Carson on 25 January 1991. His tone was unpushy and polite. Nancy, who kept the letter, recalls, 'It said Britney really wanted to do this and she had a lot of energy and enthusiasm. At first they thought maybe gymnastics was a good thing for her but that it wasn't fulfilling her. He just wrote that they would love my opinion and asked me to look at the video.'

The video was rough and ready but it had Nancy purring with anticipation. It began with Britney in a little white dress with white boots and white ribbons in her hair performing the old musical standard 'Shine on Harvest Moon'. It could have been pure cornball but Nancy immediately noticed the precociousness of Britney's performance, particularly in the use of her hands: 'It was not something a child of this age was taught.' Next up was 'Cry', a heart-wrenching Johnnie Ray classic from the fifties which nine-year-old Britney, now in a denim top, sang with a big mouth and pleading eyes. At this point, nine times out of ten Nancy would have turned the tape off, having decided whether it was worth taking a chance on the child. But she was transfixed by Britney.

The third number was aimed at showing off Britney's dancing prowess and was filmed in the old dancing studio in Kentwood. Now dressed in a white leotard she sang 'Somebody Loves Me' and did a series of tumbles rather like a girl's gymnastic floor exercise. 'It was very raw,' observes Nancy. In the background she could spot Lynne, obviously pregnant, trying to encourage her daughter. A much more accomplished version of the Prince song 'Nothing Compares 2 U' followed. Nancy thought it a good choice for Britney, one that showed off her voice. The ethereal Irish singer Sinead O'Conner had enjoyed a number one hit on both sides of the Atlantic with her version the previous year and that was the style Britney chose to imitate.

The first performance video of Britney Spears ended with her singing 'This is My Moment'. It was strangely unimpressive after what had gone before. 'It wasn't very good at all,' scoffs Nancy. 'It's off pitch.' That unsentimental view of her last number speaks volumes for the honesty Nancy Carson brings to her appraisal of the young Britney. She does not have time to waste on a maybe. She needs to be sure a child has quality before she takes her on. She had seen enough to call up the Spears family straight away and say that she would love to meet them if they would come to New York.

Back in Kentwood, Jamie and Lynne were faced with the expense of taking their daughter to New York. Britney was beside herself with the excitement of it all. She demanded to know if there were cows in New York City. Lynne was now heavily pregnant, which meant that flying was problematic. In any case, her parents knew they could not afford to fly up there from New

Orleans. It was a $400 fare per person. So they decided to turn it into a family jamboree by rail, courtesy of Amtrak. It was quite a crowd – Lynne, Jamie, Bryan, Britney, Jamie's sister Jeanine, her little girl Tara and Jamie's buddy Hunter. The train journey lasted twenty-six hours.

Eventually, Jamie, Lynne and Britney arrived at the office of a real, live Broadway agent. Nancy recalls that first meeting, 'I liked her just as much in person as I did on the tape. She was a very nice child, kind of a little shy but very polite. It was always "Yes ma'am, no ma'am." '

'I could tell right from the start that Britney desperately wanted to be here. After I spent some time with Britney, I had her mom and dad come in. They just wanted me to tell them honestly if I thought their daughter had what it took to make it professionally. I told them that maybe they should come up to New York and spend a summer and let Britney study dance and voice up here and maybe some acting. I could get some auditions and she could get a feel for training and working on that level. I told them that while I could see she was good, I also thought she needed some professional training.'

In effect, what Nancy was suggesting was a summer camp. But instead of one where the kids would be in the middle of the woods enjoying sports and fresh air, this would be one set amid the crowded sidewalks and big yellow taxis of Manhattan. Nancy had no doubt that if it was up to Britney herself then she would move to New York in a moment. But Lynne and Jamie explained at that first meeting that finances were tight. Nancy could not make the decision for them so advised that they go home to Kentwood and think about it: 'I always say to parents "Don't sell the farm because nothing may come of it".'

In the case of the Spears family there was definitely no farm to sell. The seven-strong visiting party were staying in one hotel room and walking everywhere to avoid cab fares. It happened to be a rainy week in Manhattan which meant everyone got soaked as they only had one umbrella between all of them. Nancy, however, was confident that she would be seeing them again.

Britney's little sister Jamie Lynn was born in McComb on 4 April 1991. While her mother rested at home Britney was back at Parklane, where she was nominated to sing the 'Star Spangled Banner' at Grandparents Day. Lynne was not up to making the ten-mile journey to the school so she called Darlene Hughes and asked her to stand in for her. Darlene laughs, 'It's my favourite Britney story. Her daddy was bringing her but Lynne wanted me to get someone to cover my classroom so that I could go and be the mama that morning. I fluffed her hair and tied her bow and she got up to sing. Suddenly she looked at me at the side and came running over to me, put her hand in her mouth, stretched out and popped her retainer in my hand. You know a child's comfortable with you when they'll hand you their retainer!'

At the end of May, Lynne felt fit enough to make the journey to New York for Britney's 'summer camp'. The contrast with the wide empty roads of Kentwood and McComb could scarcely have been greater. Over the next eighteen months, whenever they left home, Britney and her mother were Broadway nomads, moving from small apartment to small apartment, depending on word of mouth to hear about sub-lets at peppercorn rents which would pop up when other families temporarily left New York for work opportunities. Britney, however, did not mind the change of lifestyle, at least not at first. She was a little girl on an adventure and threw herself into her new world with all the gusto of a child on a day trip to the seaside. As she had promised, Nancy fixed her up with classes in the Broadway neighbourhood. First up was a respected voice teacher called Gene McLaughlin who taught Britney how to use her muscles, how to breathe and the placement of her voice. McLaughlin, who was a very popular figure, sadly died of AIDS in the mid nineties. 'During the AIDS disaster I lost many friends,' observes Nancy, wistfully.

She also sent Britney to Robert Marks, a vocal coach, who worked on material and on presentation. An avuncular New Yorker, Marks thought Britney sang well but not correctly. He was, however, impressed by the tiny girl's professionalism. She always had her music ready and gave the impression she knew what she wanted. It is a view echoed time and again by Britney's instructors. For dancing, Britney went to the Broadway Dance Centre where she attended classes run by black choreographer Frank Hatcher whose much copied style is based on an artist selling their performance. He is particularly noted for his work in jazz dance where individual interpretation is so important. He later recalled that Britney was a 'little professional'. She may have been little but she acted like a little grown up.

Nancy echoes that view. 'She was a little sponge. She just absorbed it so well and learned so much. Her dance skills had just leapt ahead, so had her singing. She was just in a whole different place.'

At the end of 'summer camp', Britney made another video, which Nancy also kept. The improvement in Britney from the first video to the second is exceptional. She displays enormous poise. Dressed in a black swimsuit, she belts out Whitney Houston's 'One Moment in Time' and dances around a studio. 'She was so improved,' recalls Nancy. 'She was such a tiny girl, very small for her age, but her conformation was phenomenal. Brilliant.'

Britney left New York to return to Kentwood having had her first real taste of the bright lights and the big city, but would she want to return? During her first visit Nancy had secured her a couple of small commercials for cars and barbecue sauce and an appearance on *Candid Camera*, but she had to learn how to cope with disappointment, especially on the audition treadmill. Nancy had also sent her along to try out for *Les Misérables* but she was not chosen. Nancy told Lynne and Jamie that if there was something she thought Britney should audition for then she would get back in touch and ask them to come in. In her book *Raising a Star*, Nancy Carson lists the qualities that successful young performers all possess. The top three qualities are motivation, a winning look and talent. And the most important of these is motivation. Britney would have to *want* to come back.

Nancy did not have long to wait to find out the extent of Britney's motivation. She called Lynne to tell her that Britney should come and audition for an Off Broadway musical melodrama called *Ruthless! The Musical*. The play was based on *The Bad Seed*, a cult film of the fifties, which featured a murderous eight-year-old girl. The demon child has become an accepted offshoot of the horror genre in recent years, with films like *The Exorcist* and *The Omen* receiving popular acclaim. In *The Bad Seed* the girl, Rhoda Penmark, is all sweetness and light on the surface but underneath she is a cold-blooded killer who murders a classmate.

For the new stage version, which was originally called *Seedy*, the writers Joel Paley and Marvin Laird introduced a twist which Britney watchers have always found deeply ironic. The 'heroine',

Tina Denmark, is a child who is desperate to land the lead in her school play. Unfortunately she is cast in the role of a poodle called Puddles. The only way to get the lead is to bump off her school friend. Tina is the original little devil in disguise. Nancy explains, 'It's about a little girl who kind of has no conscience and she will do whatever it takes to get what she wants. It's really kind of a chilling story but as a musical it was very funny and there's a song called "I was Born to Entertain" that kids sing all the time as an audition piece. It's just a great song.'

Britney, however, did not audition for the lead but for a smaller child role. She didn't get it and had to go back to Parklane Academy. Fortune was soon smiling on her because the girl who was successful decided not to stay in the show. The producers contacted Nancy Carson and asked if Britney would come back and audition again. This time she was offered the part but, more significantly, she was also made the understudy for the leading child actress, Laura Bell Bundy. Britney would have to leave her school, her friends and her father and brother and move full time to New York with her mother and baby sister.

From the outside this might appear a huge leap, but Britney, like many child performers, had a sense of destiny. Nancy Carson sees it time and time again among her charges. 'They come to New York and believe that they have finally found a place where they belong. They don't always feel they belong where they are. They know what they want to do in life and it's not something they can achieve in the third grade in Kentwood, Louisiana.'

Fortunately for Britney her third grade teacher Darlene Hughes was completely supportive. She recalls, 'I thought it was awesome. It would have been such a waste not to get to try with the talent she had, especially as her mother was prepared to help her so much. Her mother Lynne and I talked quite frequently and she came in and told me that they were going to New York. She knew I supported what she was trying to do and I helped put together some lesson plans for her. Britney had the best of both worlds because Lynne was a very dedicated mother as well as being a teacher.

'When she went off I sent her a little card and a little spending money which she put towards a doll. She loved her porcelain dolls.'

Britney's new school was the prestigious Professional Performing Arts School (PPAS) on West 48th Street between Eighth and Ninth Avenues. It was a bit like the *Kids from Fame* in that every child was intent on developing a talent and becoming a star. You also had to pass a tough audition just to enrol. The school was only founded in 1990 but quickly became established as an essential cog in the wheel of New York entertainment, offering children like Britney the chance to maintain a professional career at the same time as going to school and learning maths. The difference between PPAS and the average high school was the never-ending sound of music filtering down the corridors.

Before she started in *Ruthless!* Britney embarked on her now famous *Star Search* adventure. She had first auditioned for the show in August 1991 but had to wait eight months for her big chance. *Star Search* was the great American talent show. Rather like *Opportunity Knocks* in the UK, it was a heady mixture of the awesome and the awful. The junior section of *Star Search* was a showcase for precocious and slightly objectionable children seeking fame. Lena Zavaroni famously won the British talent show as an impossibly talented youngster. Imagine a show full of little Lenas and you have a picture of *Star Search*. In the days pre

Pop Idol and *American Idol* there was no Simon Cowell to send cringeworthy youngsters off with a flea in their ear. Instead *Star Search* was hosted by kindly Ed McMahon, best known as Johnny Carson's sidekick on *The Tonight Show*.

The *Star Search* gimmick was that it was a straight contest between two contestants. You were either eliminated by the judges or you lived to fight another day and come back next week. Future stars who aimed for showbiz glory on the show included Beyoncé, Christina Aguilera, LeAnn Rimes, Alanis Morissette, Rosie O'Donnell and Justin Timberlake. They all had one thing in common – they all lost. Britney also lost, but in circumstances that upset her agent.

After she had sailed through the preliminaries, Lynne and Britney flew to Los Angeles to film the finals for broadcast in April 1992. The idea was that if she got through one round she would come back the following week for the grand final. It was an illusion because the whole thing was filmed back to back in a few hectic days and the children all went home having signed on the dotted line not to reveal who was champion. Nancy Carson's kids were always going on the show to showcase their talents. On this occasion she had Britney and a farmer's son from Missouri called Marty Thomas. Nancy encouraged the two of them to get together, and to introduce their mothers to each other so that they were on friendly terms: 'I told them they could still like each other even though they were going to compete because then they'll be happy if the other one wins.' That was the theory.

Britney had to have all her outfits, her songs and her backing tracks prepared in advance to maintain the pretence of coming back the next week if she was successful. She won her first contest singing a number called 'I Don't Care', which was ironic considering just how much Britney did care about the contest. After the 'bout' in which she had beaten another little girl who sang an opera excerpt, she had to cope with some gentle humour from Mr McMahon. He asked her if she had a boyfriend back home and when she said no he asked her if he would do. Britney, perhaps a little embarrassed, said she would have to think about it.

The problem for Britney was that *Star Search* insisted that she perform the Naomi Judd Grammy-award-winning song 'Love Can Build a Bridge' in the final. Country singer Judd was a hugely popular figure at the time as well as being the mother of film star Ashley Judd and fellow country artist Wynonna Judd. 'Love Can Build a Bridge' was her big song, so much so that she used it as the title of her autobiography in 1993.

It was not Britney's big money song. Lynne called Nancy to tell her the producers were not letting Britney change her song for the final. Nancy recalls, 'I don't know if the *Star Search* people thought they knew better but I knew it wasn't the right song. It's very frustrating when you had to go out there and sing what you know is not the best number and it's the final.'

Nancy spoke to the show's producers and did her best to get them to change their minds but they wouldn't budge. By a twist of fate Britney ended up in the final against Marty Thomas. She knew him a little because he was also at the Professional Performing Arts School and the two of them practised a few hoops before the show to calm their nerves. Britney wore a little black dress with a lacy white collar and sported a huge bow in her long curly brown hair. She belted out the song but it was really a power ballad for a mature, grown woman who had been through the mill. Judd herself had received the sympathy of the nation in 1990 when she revealed she had been diagnosed with hepatitis C. Britney did her best but was pipped by Marty by just a quarter of a point. It is a clip shown in every Britney documentary.

In retrospect, the reality is that they were both pretty terrible – but don't say that to Nancy Carson, who is fiercely loyal to her charges. She is still fuming, 'I was very frustrated. I felt bad for Britney. At the same time I was happy for Marty but would have felt happier if the playing field was level. But Marty was a fabulous performer.'

They took it almost as hard in Kentwood. Everybody in town was glued to their television. The last they saw of their little heroine was her graciously accepting defeat. They didn't see her backstage, collapsed sobbing on a couch. She really wanted to win, and although Nancy Carson observes that getting a silver medal was still a big deal, it was no consolation to Britney, who wanted to win and expected to win. Jamie Lynn summed it all up succinctly when she later commented, 'It wasn't fair.'

Poor Marty Thomas has had to live with the sobriquet of being the kid who beat Britney Spears in a talent show for the whole of his professional career to date. Nobody recalls, or in fact cares, that he was the one crowned 1992 Junior Vocalist Champion on *Star Search*. He has managed, however, to put it behind him and progress his own career. In 2005 he has been back on Broadway, appearing in the musical *Wicked*.

Ruthless! opened on 6 May 1992 at the Players Theatre, a small Off Broadway venue. Laura Bell Bundy's performance as the murdering little girl made everyone sit up and take notice. She was an effervescent child actress who appeared to be going places and was nominated for both an Outer Critics Circle Award and a Drama Desk Award. Laura's experiences strangely mirror what happened in Britney's life. She moved with her mother to New York from Kentucky when she was nine. They left her father behind and he would fly into the city when he could, although she has since acknowledged that her career took its toll on her parents' relationship. Like Britney, she went to PPAS but missed home. Eventually she went back to Kentucky when she was fourteen and attended a regular high school, but her parents' marriage did not survive.

Laura is the same age as Britney and, although she has not achieved the same superstardom, she has a successful career, slightly away from the mainstream. Her latest one-woman show is called *Shameless! The Life and Times of Laura Bell Bundy*. She describes it as a spin-off from *Ruthless!*, playing a variety of characters including Julie Andrews, Judy Garland, Marilyn Monroe and, tongue in cheek perhaps, Britney Spears as a symbol of teenage rebellion.

Britney had to wait patiently for her chance to go on in the lead role. She was still taking dancing and singing classes, as well as going to the school and doing auditions. Money was very tight – Off Broadway barely paid enough to cover rent – and she and her mother stayed in a one-bedroom apartment with Marty Thomas and his mother at the Strand building on 43rd and 10th. Nancy had helped Marty land a role in a Broadway production of *Secret Garden* and she had found them the apartment.

Marty told the VH1 documentary *Driven*, 'We were just living off our bootstrings. We lived in the littlest apartment. Britney didn't play after school, she went to class. Sometimes she didn't get along with other kids who didn't have the same drive.'

Although New York could have been on a different planet from Kentwood, Britney's own world was a surprisingly small neighbourhood. She lived, practised, went to school and classes and went on stage within an area of a few blocks. When she and Lynne had some spare time they would drop in to see Nancy – Lynne still struggling out of the elevator with Jamie Lynn in a stroller.

Nancy recalls, 'They had got into the habit of coming in that first summer. Then she would want to go over material for auditions with me. I had to make sure she wasn't sounding too Southern! Later we just enjoyed each other's company. She would tell me about Kentwood and sometimes if they'd been home she would bring me back something. I remember her telling me about the family crawfish place. Britney was mature in her performance but in her personal self, the Britney who came into my office and hung out, she was just a nice, polite and normal kid. She wasn't pushy or out there or hey look at me, and she wasn't one of those kids that ran in and kissed me and hugged me inappropriately. She was a good kid.'

Nancy's pet hate is mothers who tell their child, 'Go kiss Nancy. Go kiss Nancy.' Lynne was not one of those mothers. 'I think it might have been hard for Lynne at times and she probably missed home a bit, but she was determined to let Britney have this opportunity.'

Her big break came when Laura Bell Bundy was offered a small film part – Britney didn't have to murder her – and had to take two weeks off. Nancy Carson had purposefully not seen the show before because she just wanted to watch Britney play the child monster Tina Denmark. 'I felt like this was a big deal for Britney and she was wonderful – everybody thought so. Britney was a natural actress.' Marty Thomas thought she 'glowed' in her performance. Britney's own view of her performance is very down to earth: 'I kill my best friend in the show. It was funny but in a really sick way. Everybody really seemed to love it.'

After the triumph and relief of being a star for two weeks, it was inevitably a let-down when Laura returned to resume the lead role. Britney was getting very bored of the routine, which more and more seemed like drudgery. Not for the first or last time in her career she was tired and fed up. New York had been fun at first, loud and bright like a giant fun fair, but it was not the place Britney or her mother wanted to spend Christmas 1992. It was Christmas Eve and Laura had gone back to Kentucky for the holiday, leaving Britney to hold the fort. Nancy Carson was in her office when she took a phone call from Lynne: 'She said, "I miss home; Britney misses home and I know this is a great opportunity but it's time for us to go back home. We want to go home for Christmas and can you get us out of the show?"'

Nancy could get them out of the show and she was happy to do it: 'It was time for them to go home; they needed to go home and be in Kentwood again. I don't care where you go, home is still home.' Ten years later, Nancy, in a new office on the twentieth floor, had the satisfaction of hearing Lynne Spears declare on television, 'The best advice I ever got was when Matt Casella told me he knew an agent . . .'

'When she performed it was like you turned a key.'

FOUR

Mouse Dancing

Britney was just eleven years old when she joined some of the older girls in *The Mickey Mouse Club* for a dance routine. Keri Russell, Nikki DeLoach, Ilana Miller and Britney brought the filming to a halt as all heads turned to see these girls dancing up a storm. Why was it so memorable? They were all dressed as Catholic schoolgirls and the notorious video for '. . . Baby, One More Time' was more than four years away.

Britney Spears, fledgling superstar, was taking giant steps forward. Her New York adventure had left her in a formidable position for someone who had just celebrated her eleventh birthday. She had been plying her trade at some of the most respected institutions in the entertainment world and they had transformed a raw talent into something much more accomplished. She had also learnt the discipline of appearing in front of a live audience night after night. Britney Jean Spears, however, was a tiny girl, fed up with gazing upwards at buildings in the sky, tired of throwing herself into a daily grind where she was wound up to become the all-singing, all-dancing child performer. She was a little girl who wanted to see the big Christmas tree in the living room of her Kentwood home and not a spindly shrub in the window of a claustrophobic apartment in Manhattan. She achieved that wish for Christmas 1992 but soon after New Year the professional path of Britney Spears was about to sweep her on again.

Matt Casella was on his nationwide tour of big cities trying to find a fresh batch of kids for *The Mickey Mouse Club*. His job was to find contenders for about half a dozen new spots on the show. As the oldest children left, Disney would bring in younger performers to fill the vacancies. Nationally, more than 20,000 child hopefuls would try to catch the eye of Matt and his team. When he was due to come into New York he phoned Nancy Carson to see if she could recommend anybody. She recalls, 'I just said "What about Britney? She's grown up a whole lot in her performance. She's aged up." He was keen so I called up her parents and I said, "OK, are you ready to do another adventure?" So she came back up for the audition. I knew she was ready and she just went in there and blew their socks off.' Each child had to deliver a song, a dance and a speech. Britney sang 'Running Back to You', which had been a recent top twenty hit for Vanessa Williams, and delivered a monologue called 'The Tooth Fairy'.

She did not hear right away because more Disney people had to see the tapes before a final decision could be made. While she was waiting for news, she was offered a part she had also auditioned for in New York. She was cast opposite a talking pig in a film called *Gordy*, 'the talking pig who made it big', which was overshadowed by the hit movie *Babe* when it was finally released in 1995. Just how there came to be two films about talking pigs at the same time remains one of those unfathomable

Hollywood mysteries. Britney has always been more of a performer than an actress. She decided not to take the role, although the money would have been helpful, and waited patiently for news from *The Mickey Mouse Club*. She was called back for the audition 'camp' in Orlando, a three-day screen test where twenty-three children were in competition for just seven places. Her opposition included Justin Timberlake, Christina Aguilera and Jessica Simpson.

She was back at school in McComb when the phone rang and Nancy was on the line to tell her she was going to be a Mouseketeer. 'It was the cherry on top of the sundae,' observes Nancy. 'So often you have to tell them bad news, I really like to have the chance to tell them something good.' Britney was jumping for joy, bouncing round the house shouting 'I'm so excited. I'm so excited!'

Britney's Orlando audition was appraised by Gary Spatz, the acting coach on *The Mickey Mouse Club*. He gave the hopefuls marks out of ten in six categories. Britney's scores were: vocals 8½, acting 8½, camera persona 8½, dance 8½, personality 8½, and appearance 8. Perhaps it was the fact that Britney was still small for her age that lost her the half point for appearance. Britney's total mark was the highest at the auditions, ahead of both Justin Timberlake and Christina Aguilera, although everyone was outscored by Christina in the singing category, where she was given a 9. Even at this early stage of her Disney career Britney impressed everyone with how focused she was. Jessica Simpson, however, would have to wait for another day, famously losing it and storming out when she had to follow Christina on stage.

Even though Kentwood had grown used to its young resident disappearing to glamorous locations, *The Mickey Mouse Club* success was big news. The local newspapers had covered the story of her appearance on *Star Search* but this time Britney's progress was deemed worthy of several pages. Ironically the Disney Channel in those days was only available on cable so practically nobody in the area had seen the show. That did not stop them declaring Saturday, 24 April 1993 'Britney Spears Day'. Local businesses decorated their windows with good luck messages, the local baseball team presented her with a cake and there was a big party in the Kentwood Lions Club Ballpark where Britney sang Whitney Houston's 'I Will Always Love You'.

The Town Mayor, the Honourable Bobby Gill, even issued a proclamation to mark the day, which concluded:

WHEREAS, this year for the first time, the state of Louisiana has had a participant chosen and she is one of ours; we have watched her grow and her talents mature – and have seen her performances – given with such warmth and noticeable enjoyment and,

WHEREAS, the people of Kentwood and the surrounding area wish to give tribute to this well-deserving young lady as she continues her work in Orlando, Florida,

NOW THEREFORE, I, Bobby Gill, Mayor of the Town of Kentwood, do hereby proclaim, Saturday, April 24, 1993,

BRITNEY SPEARS DAY

And invite everyone to 'applaud her accomplishments and wish her great things as she takes this next exciting step in her promising career.'

Anyone unaware of the Southern emphasis on courtesy and decorum might scoff at such aggrandisement but this send-off for Britney was done with genuine warmth. Her family responded in a similar vein:

Dear Kentwood,

Britney has many memorable moments to remember in her short, little life. But April 24th has to be the most sentimental moment yet. It's so exciting to have these new experiences but what makes it so wonderful is to have so many loved ones you can share them with. Thank you Kentwood for your support and encouragement. We love you.

The Britney Spears Family

Britney was single-handedly responsible for bringing cable television to this part of the Deep South.

Lynne, Jamie Lynn, who had just turned one year old, and Britney set off for Orlando leaving Jamie and Bryan once more to look after themselves. By this time Bryan was sixteen and driving himself to Parklane Academy every day. The grandparents were there to help if Jamie had to go away to work so Lynne was not so worried about leaving her son for a long period of time.

Britney, aged eleven, was the youngest and smallest of the seven New Kids on the Lot. But her audition had revealed that she was probably the most accomplished at this stage. Her Broadway experience, however, was not something she flaunted. Her fellow Mouseketeers and tutors had no idea that she had ever been out of Louisiana before. Instead she was just one of a nervous but excited bunch of children and parents who gathered in a meeting room at the Disney/MGM studios at the end of April, ready to start the six-month 'season'.

Lynne had picked out an apartment among the Disney property at the quaintly named Kissimmee, just outside Orlando, and now it was time to meet the people who would shape her daughter's showbusiness future. The *Mickey Mouse Club* would provide Britney with what Gary Spatz calls a 'million-dollar education'. For these ambitious children, so intent on becoming stars, it would be priceless. It came as a big surprise to discover that the most important person they were going to meet on that first morning was the head tutor. School! His name was Chuck Yerger and it was his job to ensure that *The Mickey Mouse Club* met the very strict legal requirements regarding their young stars' schooling.

Chuck had moved to Florida from Pennsylvania and found a job working for a company called On Line Education, which specializes in teaching child actors and performers while they are working. His first job was to tutor Macaulay Culkin's elder brother Shane, while the *Home Alone* star was filming *My Girl* in and around Orlando. From there Chuck moved on to *The Mickey Mouse Club* where his firm but friendly approach proved just the right blend so that within three years he was the principal of this Disney 'school', responsible for hiring, firing and the all-important timetables. He also taught for Nickelodeon in Orlando where one of his favourite students was Melissa Joan Hart, who would later become famous as Sabrina, the Teenage Witch. 'I taught her for six hours every Sunday,' recalls Chuck. 'She was a marvellous young lady.'

Chuck remembers Britney from that first morning because she was accompanied by a little toddler, Jamie Lynn. 'It was impossible not to notice Britney because she was such a bubbly, fresh-faced, innocent young girl.' Chuck also noticed Justin Timberlake because he was wearing a leather brace on his wrist as a result of a basketball injury. 'I thought to myself "Oh here's a prima donna who's always going to be injured. What did he do – hurt his wrist tap dancing?" I wrongly thought I was going to have someone who was going to be a problem. I had no idea what an athlete he was.'

At that first meeting the executive producer of *The Mickey Mouse Club*, Dennis Steinmetz, told the parents and their fidgeting offspring that all the children had to be in school for a period of three hours a day, a total of fifteen hours a week. They would have to follow a strict curriculum from their home school – in Britney's case Parklane Academy. Disney took their educational obligations very seriously, mindful that the whole *Mickey Mouse Club* would be at risk if inspectors came in and discovered just one child falling short in their schooling requirements. Steinmetz gazed around the room, pointed at Chuck and declared forcefully, 'This man will tell me if you are allowed to perform.'

Chuck, meanwhile, was astonished at what he saw. He knew the producers of *The Mickey Mouse Club* were trying for an older feel to the show and so was expecting some streetwise teenagers: 'I was dumbfounded. These were little kids. They were rugrats – that's a teachers' term for little kids who play on rugs.'

'Britney, Christina Aguilera and Justin were sitting side by side and I swear that Britney's feet didn't even touch the floor yet.'

That first morning there was no sign of the older members of the club. They were busy making an MMC album, a slightly embarrassing Disney stab at rap. Technically the show was called

The All New Mickey Mouse Club, but it was called by a variety of names, including MMC, which was a misguided effort by the producers to join the fashion for letters and initials and give the show a more streetwise edge. The cast preferred to call the show 'Mouse Club'. At this time they were also shooting episodes of *Emerald Cove*, an episodic surfer soap that would run (and run) as part of *The Mickey Mouse Club* show. In their first season Britney and Justin et al. would be learning their trade and would be in effect a 'featured' cast rather than the stars of the club.

The first task for the new Mouseketeers was to rehearse and perform a breaking-the-ice show for all the production staff and the older cast. The idea was to familiarize the new intake with the pressure of having to present new material and to perform in front of the other cast members. These were serious performers, one step away from adult careers, and they were not predisposed to holding the hands of little kids just starting out. This would not be a problem for Britney, who always took work seriously.

The show also gave everyone the chance to see the strengths of the new cast. Christina, it was obvious to everyone, was a great young singer. The strength and power of her voice, at the age of twelve, was almost freakish. Much has been written about the relationship between Christina and Britney. Are they friends or sworn enemies? They were the two smallest and scrawniest girls and, quite naturally, were drawn to each other. They lived in the same apartment complex and their mothers became good friends. The girls, however, were very different characters. While the preteen Britney was reserved, Christina was outspoken and far more outgoing. They did not remain close after the show ended.

Christina had followed a strikingly similar path to Britney to reach this point in her career. She too had sung Whitney Houston songs in talent contests, had auditioned for *The Mickey Mouse Club* when she was eight and been deemed too young and had sung on *Star Search* and been beaten by an older boy. She may not have trodden a path to New York but she had been born there, in the borough of Staten Island. From the age of eight she had lived in Beaver County near Pittsburg and regarded that city as her home town. Christina was much more a city girl than her Kentwood contemporary. She was also brought up well away from Bible Belt country.

The rivalry between Britney and Christina on *The Mickey Mouse Club* was little more than two children chasing the same school prize. It made them try harder but did not mean they were not going to share an ice cream together on the way home. Tony Lucca, who watched the two talents mature, observes, 'I would say that Christina became a better dancer because of Britney and, for her part, Britney aspired to be a better vocalist because of Christina.

'This is the healthy aspect of being surrounded by kids with so much talent. It's beneficial. If one cast member did something cool then you would want to do something as cool yourself. This is only my impression but I remember Christina having a grudge about her when people would sort of marvel over Britney's charm and sweetness. Christina always wanted to be the diva.'

While Britney and Christina hung out together because they were small and female, Justin Timberlake was a 'weenie' – a child in between small and big – who graduated towards the older boys and was, to some extent, accepted by them as an equal. He was, however, quite enamoured of his scrawny co-star and told his grandfather on a visit home that one day he was going to 'marry that girl'.

Britney and Justin certainly enjoyed puppy love while with *The Mickey Mouse Club*. They were too young for it to be anything more, although it was enough to forge a foundation of affection which they could build upon when their paths crossed again. Britney actually was mad about Tony Lucca, her first real crush. Tony prefers to keep this quiet these days but Dale Godboldo confirms, 'She had a huge crush on Tony. So did all the girls. Christina and Britney used to try things older girls would normally do to try and impress him. We all thought it was pretty funny.' Justin was a more practical target and Britney did at least get to kiss him during a knockabout game of truth or dare with her mischievous cast mates.

Britney's public professionalism and private sweetness were never more clearly defined than during *The Mickey Mouse Club* years. Chuck Yerger noticed in those early days that there were two Britneys and would continue to be aware of it as her fame grew: 'The Britney Spears in public just knew how to be gracious and professional. The Britney Spears in private was the most wholesome, huggable little kid that you'd ever want to see. If anybody had walked into my classroom and seen Britney there they would have said, "What is she doing here, she's just a little kid in school."'

Chuck never had the feeling that there was any career master plan with Britney. He was one of those who had no idea she was a long-term showbiz child: 'I had the sense that this was her first experience; there was a kind of a feeling that she was the cutesy girl next door who said, "Let me go and audition down at the mall for Disney" and she made it and it's like "Oh my gosh, I'm here." Everything about the time I spent with Britney was that this is the all-American girl, a perky little soon-to-be-high-school cheerleader type with the all-American family.'

In the school bungalow in her first Disney year Britney studied four subjects – English, History, Social Studies (Geography and Science) and Mathematics. Surprisingly she achieved straight As. That sounds slightly more impressive that it actually was in practice. Her work plans were quite basic and young for her age. And the ratio of tutors to students was so high and the level of personal attention so good that students rarely failed to attain an A before they moved on to the next part of their curriculum. Britney was very competent, if not inspired. Her most interesting area of study was her required reading, *The Old Man and The Sea* by Ernest Hemingway. The novella by the great figure of American literature exposes an old man to the elemental forces of nature. It is a quest for honour in the struggle between a hunter and his prey, in this case a marlin. That struggle or battle of skill and determination is one of the defining characteristics of the Southern male – appreciating the beauty of a creature as you kill it.

Out of the schoolroom, Britney's dancing continued to impress. The bungalow where she would practise her dance routines became her home from home. She was quickly established as the star dancer of the younger cast. Tony Lucca recalls her skill: 'They would get her to dance in an afternoon and tape it that night. She was so capable. I don't know if it was the tutoring mentality she had but she could just get it and sell it. She was good.'

The Disney dance tutor, Myles Thoroughgood, had a difficult

job. It wasn't just enough to show the kids their marks and make sure they hit them. He had to instil in the cast an awareness of how a particular move might look to the camera. Tony Lucca recalls, 'He had one of the toughest jobs. It went beyond teaching some dance steps. He had to show us not just what we were doing but what the camera was actually seeing. He had to take kids of different dance abilities and rhythm, or lack thereof, and put them through the most demanding schedule. He always had everything on an even keel even when the recording was getting pretty insane.'

Britney was particularly malleable, taking direction really well. Myles was a seasoned actor and dancer when he became the Mickey Mouse choreographer, trying to shuffle the pack of twenty-four Mouseketeers every day. 'Britney was the dynamic dancer', he observed. Every week Myles would have to put together three numbers and a music video. Four hours of rehearsal on each number would culminate in four full takes where the cameras would be set to film different angles to maximize the dynamic effect. Sometimes the cast would be at work before daybreak.

This was an unglamorous treadmill. Even a normal day would begin with a wake-up call from Lynne at 7 a.m. to catch the cast van for early morning lessons with Chuck. Sometimes Lynne would drive and park in a space marked 'Reserved for Mouseketeer Parking Only'. Everyone would eat lunch together, a buffet specially prepared by outside caterers which would include enough fish, meat, vegetables and salad to keep Jamie Oliver happy. The television chef would also have approved of the enlightened thinking behind *The Mickey Mouse Club* school dinners. Early on in the life of the show, the powers that be realized that children performed better if they ate well and were able to relax together, especially as the day was a long one. Rehearsals followed lunch, before hair and make-up prepared the cast for filming to start at 3.45 p.m. The cameras stopped after three hours of non-stop filming. It was a twelve-hour day for an eleven-year-old child.

The show always began with the cast running from backstage while the credits and theme tune rang out. They would high five the audience (the 'crowd'), do some splits and jumping jacks before striking a pose, when the music would end. Then three or four of the cast would go and sit down on the steps to introduce the show while the others dashed off for a costume change. Britney took her turn at introducing the show: 'Hi, I'm Britney, welcome to *The Mickey Mouse Club*.' Every Mouseketeer had to deliver that line at some stage. Then they would run through what was in store that day. Monday, for instance, was music day, which featured artists like TLC and Brian McKnight; Tuesday was Guest Day; Wednesday was 'Anything Can Happen Day'; and Thursday was Party Day. The last show of the week was called Hall of Fame Day where ordinary kids performed and were then inducted into the Mickey Mouse Hall of Fame. The strategy behind it all was living room appeal – any one of the Mouseketeers would have been welcome to sit on your sofa and break open a can of cola.

At the end of each show the entire cast would join hands for a large slice of Americana – the Mickey Mouse theme song:

> And now it's time to say goodbye
> To all our company
> M-I-C, see you real soon! K-E-Y
> Why? Because we like you! M-O-U-S-E!

This was followed by some (spontaneous) hugs, high fives and hullabaloo, all carefully rehearsed. Britney soon learned the off-stage alternative goodbye:

M-I-C, see you real soon! K-E-Y
Why? Because we get paid to! M-O-U-S-E

The pay itself was very acceptable to the Spears family, especially as Jamie's own work in Kentwood had dried up and, more and more, he was working away from home. Lynne was given Britney's money every Thursday. The producers had quickly established that it was a bad idea giving one of the children a cheque for $1,500 as they were likely to lose it in their homework.

One of the aspects of *The Mickey Mouse Club* that the public never knew was that fan mail dictated the content of the show. The cast were never shown the laudatory letters but, behind the scenes, they were taken very seriously. The more the public wrote in praising Britney's dancing, the more dance numbers she was given. During the two years she was on the show she probably only sang three or four solos but, conversely, she took part in all but a handful of dance numbers.

The power of fan mail was best exemplified by Ricky Luna, by far the most popular member of *The Mickey Mouse Club* cast. Ricky was the resident Latino, a super cool, extremely good-looking fashion plate who was probably the best dancer the show ever had. Tony Lucca, not far behind in the pin-up stakes, but not a dancer, recalls, 'Chicks went crazy over this guy. But he couldn't carry a tune in a paper bag, nor was he a great actor. But he knew how to perform. Put him in front of a crowd and he'll knock you dead. The fans loved him so they kept finding more and more rap songs for him to perform so that he had a larger role in the show.'

Britney could carry a tune but she was no Christina Aguilera, who some of the cast nicknamed Mariah after the queen diva, Mariah Carey. Britney sang passable versions of 'Born to be Wild' and 'Can't Help Falling In Love' but it was her duet with Justin Timberlake, 'I Feel For You', which made everyone sit up, take notice of her singing for the first time and wonder whether Christina was watching. Britney's vocals did improve during her time in Orlando, thanks in no small measure to working with the club's singing coach, a husky-voiced siren from Texas called Robin Wiley.

Robin is better known for her later work with 'Nsync and Justin Timberlake, who affectionately gave her the nickname Wiley Coyote after the Roadrunner's cartoon adversary. She improved everyone at the Mouse Club, even accomplished singers like Tony Lucca, Christina and Britney. She set up a music room in a mini trailer on the lot where there was just enough room for her keyboard and a few kids to practise their scales and harmonies. She gave the potential pop stars of the future the discipline they needed. The warm-ups and exercises took almost as long as the rehearsal. Tony recalls, 'Robin was the coolest thing in town.'

An essential part of the MMC million-dollar education was selling your professional self to the public. This is not a God-given talent like perfect pitch or natural rhythm. The Disney kids were taught how to conduct themselves in public right down to learning the best way to smile in order to show off their astonishingly white, perfect teeth. This technique, which the girls in particular were encouraged to master, was dropping your lower lip when you smile to reveal the maximum number of gnashers. Chuck Yerger noticed how the younger kids would rapidly become more polished: 'Their smile would be a little more practised; they would know how to toss their heads when they flashed a smile.

'When these kids went out among the public they were representing Disney. They had a certain way about them, they knew how to be public people in the way they prepared, did their hair, shook a hand, signed an autograph or cracked a smile.'

This public perception was a very serious part of the Disney world, so that a Los Angeles company had the PR contract to coach the Mouseketeers in interview technique. They would do mock interviews so the youngsters would never say anything out of place or controversial. Britney was very receptive to this sort of indoctrination, which perhaps explains why so many of her interviews lack spontaneity. Tony Lucca observes, 'I guess you could see it as fascist but it's not uncommon. You see it all the time with sports stars that have been too involved playing ball to learn people skills. It needs to be taught.'

The new intake had to get used to the plethora of fanzine trivia that always follows around celebrity. The first Britney Spears 'fact' sheet of favourite things recorded:

Singer:	Whitney Houston
Actors:	Tom Cruise and Demi Moore
Movie:	*The Hand that Rocks the Cradle*
Best Day of Life:	When I found out I had gotten *The Mickey Mouse Club*

The movie, a thriller about a sinister nanny, is slightly surprising, but the list is distinctly saccharine. Christina Aguilera's favourite colours, according to the fan fodder, were turquoise and purple, while Justin Timberlake loved chocolate chip ice cream. Little titbits like this were trying to give the impression that here was a bunch of ordinary kids. The reality was that the great majority were nice, white, middle-class children. They fitted a Disney profile which is best encompassed in one all-American word: 'wholesome'. Fellow Mouseketeer Dale Godboldo observes that Britney in particular was a Disney poster child in that she encapsulated the image they were seeking: 'She had the right look and the right personality to be the all-American kid. She was the perfect little buddy.'

The Disney polish would stay with *The Mickey Mouse Club* cast for their ongoing professional careers. This coaching was a watershed moment in the career of Britney Spears, not because she was going to embrace a 'wholesome' image but because it was the birth of the idea of the artist as a product. If Disney was the department store and *The Mickey Mouse Club* the cosmetics counter, then Britney and her fellow Mouseketeers were beauty products arranged on the counter. They were all attractively packaged and sweetly scented in such a way that their target consumer would buy them.

Selling the artist is the essence of entertainment and a lesson the Mouseketeers learned much earlier than the average showbiz wannabes. It gave them a head start. As a result Britney was able to sell her teen sexpot image as if it were a second skin – nothing should be allowed to deviate an artist from selling the image and if that meant promoting fiction then it was all part of the game. For superstars like Madonna, Kylie and Robbie Williams the problems arise when the boundaries become blurred. Britney herself would have to face that same merging of her public and private self.

Justin, Christina, Britney and their peers are confident and accomplished when it comes to handling an interview, presenting an award or appearing on *Saturday Night Live*. Every little detail is part of a performance and they make few, if any, mistakes. Even at moments of great stress and self-doubt, the professional mask is always in place. Only occasionally, as she grew older, would Britney's mask slip.

Britney's role model within *The Mickey Mouse Club* was Keri Russell, now an award-winning actress for her TV show *Felicity* and a co-star in the Tom Cruise film *Mission: Impossible 3*, but then a teenage girl on the verge of stardom. Like Britney she came on to the show primarily as a dancer but blossomed within the show's format into a promising actress. Britney and Christina and the other new girl, Nikki DeLoach, would try to copy her clothes. Nikki, eighteen months older than the other two, was a stunning Southern girl, a Georgia peach. After flirting with a singing career she had enjoyed some success as an actress too.

Christina explained, 'We would always look up to Keri because she was like *sixteen*! She had the car. She had the boyfriend. She was more developed.'

Tony Lucca and Keri Russell were the king and queen of Mickey Mouse. They shared an apartment away from the other families. They no longer needed to be chaperoned and their parents had gone home to get on with their own lives. As a consequence, they were likely to be called on if anybody had a baby-sitting crisis – something which happened to Lynne on at least two occasions. Tony had more contact with Britney than he would normally have expected: 'My impression of her was that she was a doe-eyed, very soft spoken, quiet girl. Keri took her under her wing to a degree. Keri's mother certainly befriended Lynne, giving the sort of good advice mums need.

'Sometimes we would keep an eye on Britney, take her to the mall. She was very into shopping but she was just a young girl and she would pick Keri's brain about work or some boyfriend/girlfriend thing.'

Keri was only with the Mouse Club for Britney's first season before Hollywood beckoned and she moved to Los Angeles. 'I used to really idolize Keri', acknowledged Britney. 'I wished I had her beautiful, long curly hair. I'd want so badly to look and be like her.' Britney was suffering the adolescent agonies of the majority of girls – she hated her hair, she hated her nose, which she thought too big, and she hated her teeth. Keri Russell, it seemed, was perfect.

By the end of September Britney had survived six months of an exhausting schedule filming fifty-five shows. Episodes of the show would start airing the following month. By that time she was back at Kentwood but her contemporaries were barely aware there was a star in their midst. Classmate Kelly Burch observes, 'She didn't come back bragging about it so, unless we heard from one of the teachers, we had little idea of what she was up to.'

Nobody had any idea that the next season of *The All New Mickey Mouse Club*, would be the last. Britney's working day was restructured for her second season. The day no longer began with several hours of schooling. Instead every cast member had their own schedule and would fit in lessons whenever they had a break from filming or rehearsal. Having just been foot perfect on a particularly hard dancing number, Britney would be told to hurry over to the school bungalow for double mathematics.

Everyone was growing up fast. The difference in the rugrats was striking, especially in group photographs. Britney was still only twelve but her make-up and organized curls suggested a teenager of fifteen. She was still too young to jump in the cars and go downtown with the older cast where they would drink coffee and listen to jazz. Pleasure Island, a mini Orlando theme park, was the preferred place for the younger set where they could go dancing or record a video of themselves singing karaoke. Otherwise, Britney would go shopping or eat ice cream with Lynne and Jamie Lynn.

The end, when it came, was a total shock. The ratings were still respectable but production costs had been creeping up. The season was finished but the cast of *Emerald Cove* still had another six weeks of shooting to complete. They had just finished a table read of the latest script when the senior producer Lynne Symons, director of original programming for Disney, or 'mother mouse', as she was known, broke the news. Britney was not there that day but everyone had heard by the time of the wrap party the following week. The older cast were already planning for life after Mickey but the younger ones were devastated: 'The kids were all just sad,' recalls Tony Lucca. 'They were crying. It was like the end of friendships that were well underway.'

Britney's Orlando adventure lasted less than two years. It would be entirely wrong to suggest the old cliché that everyone knew she was going to be a star. She lacked the charisma of the young Justin Timberlake, the raw power of Christina Aguilera, the looks of Nikki DeLoach or the comedic acting ability of Ryan Gosling. Watching from the wings, Chuck Yerger explains, 'She'll hate me for saying this but Britney seemed to be good at a lot of things but not excellent at any of them. She was the all-round cutie.'

Being surrounded by such a talented bunch merely reinforced Britney's work ethic. She understood that she had to put twice the effort in just to get noticed.

'It was like going to Fame High School.'

FIVE

Me and Mister Jones

The endless round of practice and classes was getting to fifteen-year-old Britney. She complained to her boyfriend, Reg, who recalls, 'She goes, "I'm tired of doing this, my mom is on my back, I'm tired of it. I just want to live a normal life. I've done all I want to do."'

When Donald Reginald Jones Jr first met Britney Spears she was just the kid sister of a footballing buddy, running round the house in a T-shirt and her underwear. It was Christmas 1992 and Britney was delighted to have escaped the grind of *Ruthless!* in New York. She was excited to be home and paid little attention to Bryan's new friend. 'She acted very young,' recalls Reg, as everybody calls him. 'I never thought I would be dating her in a few years' time.'

Reg is actually a year younger than Bryan but his sporting prowess meant he joined a small group of older boys at Parklane Academy who played basketball and football together. Bryan was not exactly the leader of the pack but he was the one that everybody aspired to be like. Even though Jamie Spears had begun to spend more time working away in Jackson, Mississippi, the recession had not properly hit the family yet. The teenage Bryan drove the nicest car and had the sharpest clothes among his friends. They called him 'Spears' although he himself preferred to be known as Bryan 'the Boss' Spears. The only thing he had in common with Bruce Springsteen, however, was his initials.

While Britney was growing up in *The Mickey Mouse Club*, the Spears house off Highway 51 was becoming like a second home to Reg Jones and his pals. They would take advantage of Jamie working away and Lynne being with her daughter in Orlando to hold some big parties. Reg was accustomed to sleeping on the Spears couch long before he started going out with Britney.

When *The Mickey Mouse Club* finished, Britney settled back into being a full-time schoolgirl at Parklane. She went out with a boy, Mason Statham, who was regularly voted 'Most Handsome' in class. They were both very young but went on a few dates to school dances and the movies. Mason was the first local boy she kissed but it was a very tentative toe dipped in the water. The day after, Britney was distraught because he totally ignored her. 'He didn't say two words to me,' she recalled. 'I started thinking "Did I do something wrong?" I started analysing myself. Of course I got over it but you beat yourself up.' In the foyer of Ruby Tuesday's, across the road from Wal-Mart in McComb, is a picture of Mason and Britney taken at Parklane when they were voted 'Beauty and Beau' in their grade. Britney, 'Beauty', is a slightly awkward-looking brown-haired teenager while Mason, the 'Beau', looks smug.

By coincidence, Reg Jones was at this time dating Stacey Statham, who was Mason's older sister. Reg had yet to give a thought to dating Britney. Nor she him, or so he thought. A short time after he and Stacey had broken up, Reg was in the Block-buster movie store in McComb when Lynne walked in to rent a movie and the pair started talking. 'She asked me who I was dating and I told her I had just broken up with Stacey. And she said, "Well, if you can wait a little bit longer, Britney's got a crush on you and you can ask Britney out."' Reg had no idea, but then he was a teenage boy.

As far as home-town boys go, Reg was as good as it gets for a mother looking for a suitable date for her daughter. He was very eligible. His father, Reggie Sr, was an attorney and judge in the neighbouring town of Liberty. His stepfather Dr William Austin was the leading ear, nose and throat specialist in the area and his mother, Gay, was a prominent Mississippi artist. As a young man he was an excellent sportsman and a young Southern gentleman, a superb shot, who went to church on Sundays and was respectful of adults. To this day he still calls Britney's father 'Mister Jamie' and her mother 'Miss Lynne'. It's the Southern way.

Despite what Lynne had confided about her daughter's crush, Reg was still apprehensive about the age difference. Britney was now fourteen but he was seventeen and into his last year at Parklane. Her brother Bryan had graduated that summer. During football season, life went on the same as always. The big game on a Friday night would be followed by some drinks and some pool. Reg was wide receiver on the team which meant that, combined with good looks and great physique, he was the glory boy with a lazy Southern drawl and, theoretically, a babe magnet. But, as Homecoming drew near, one thing was missing. He had no date for the dance. Dare he ask Britney?

Fortunately, two of his class buddies, Wes Holmes and David

Simmons, had started dating girls in Britney's class. Wes was going out with her cousin Erin Simmons, while David had started seeing Alison Price, one of her best friends. It swayed things for Reg and he waited for the right moment: 'I thought why not me ask Britney? They're all in the same grade and it would be cool for us to be hanging out with our girlfriends who are younger than us. I also heard from my sister that another boy named Joey was fixing to ask her, so I made up my mind that if I was going to do it I had better do it now. The next day I stopped her outside the gym on our way to lunch and we were sitting there talking and I just came out with the question, "Do you think your Dad would mind if I took you to the Homecoming Dance? Would you want to go?" And she said, "Yes I would love to go. Let me ask my Dad."'

The message from Mister Jamie was that Reg needed to go and ask him properly himself: 'I had to go down to Granny's Seafood Deli the next Saturday and help him clean crawfish. We talked about me taking Britney out. I was respectful. I had known him a few years now through Brian so I wasn't scared of him. He just wanted me to understand that this was his baby girl and I had to look after her for him. He told me that if I was going to take her out and she was going to be in my care then I needed to treat her right and keep his baby girl safe. I assured him she would be safe.'

This traditional Southern style of gentlemanly behaviour is not far short of an arranged marriage. Britney and Reg were practically going steady before they had a date: 'I knew after talking to Mister Jamie that we were getting into this for the long haul, you know what I'm saying. I don't know if he would have wanted me to come and talk to him for just a one-date deal. We'd had all served time as unpaid chauffeur, cook and bottle washer. Lynne was made of sterner stuff and is very much her own woman. It was Lynne, however, who hit the phones to try and breathe life into Britney's career. Britney Spears, hard-working, dedicated performer, was about to overtake Britney Jean Spears, schoolgirl of Kentwood.

The Mickey Mouse Club connection provided the initial impetus for them to think in mid 1997 that this was the right time for Britney, who was coming up to sixteen, to leave Parklane and go into a home-schooling programme so that she could pursue her career. She was enrolled in a Christian-based programme run by the University of Nebraska. Home schooling is very popular in the US, particularly among young entertainers. Britney still had to sit an exam to be allowed on to the programme. Tests of this nature were not exactly Britney's forte but she struggled through, although she later admitted, 'It was so hard. Oh my goodness!'

The academic world was never much of a priority and later, when her career was going crazy and she was recording in New York, she would send her papers back home to Reg Jones, who would dutifully complete her work and send it back to her. 'She just had such a busy schedule that she didn't have time to do it,' he says loyally. 'I would complete her classes for her, send it back to her in New York and then she would send it in.' Reg is unsure as to whether Britney copied his work or just sent it straight in. He does remember, however, that he generally scored a B grade as Miss Britney Spears.

That was some months in the future and for a while it looked as if Britney would end up in Orlando rather than in New York. Justin Timberlake's mother Lynn Harless had decided she wanted been building up to it because I knew she had a crush on me. I finally pursued that crush and we just fell right into each other. It was fireworks from the beginning all the way to the end.'

They were already a young couple by the time of the Homecoming Dance in September. The first 'date' saw Reg turning up at Britney's house with a couple of movie videos under his arm. 'Miss Lynne cooked supper, some salmon and some stuffed bell peppers and we would all eat and talk. Afterwards we cooked popcorn, I put in the movie and we all sat round and watched it as a family.'

Bryan met with short shrift from Reg when he told him he wanted to speak to him about dating his younger sister. Reg recalls, 'I said "What are you going to talk to me about man? Me and you are friends. You know I'm going to treat your sister right. Come on." It may have irked him a little but there was nothing he could do, so we just ticked along. I saw no reason for me not asking her out whoever's sister she was.'

Bryan has always looked out for Britney. He used to get exasperated when she would go round the house singing all the time and he would tell her to shut up. Reg observes, 'She's his kid sister so he would give her hell.' He was a Spears man in that he liked a drink and to have a good time. He was good-looking, popular and a quarterback on the football team. He was a quintessential jock. He had a steady girlfriend through high school called Blaize Piggott, who was very attractive and well liked. They were engaged to be married but eventually split.

Bryan had his wild moments. Lindey Hughes Magee recalls that he had a souped-up car with glass pipes out the back. It was so loud you could hear Bryan Spears coming down the road from five miles away. 'I think he was just driving it temporarily because he had wrecked his last car. We were going to a fish fry and there was just a ton of people in the car. I was stuck in the middle on the console. We came off the interstate at the McComb exit and he was just doing a hundred miles an hour down the ramp. He was such a daredevil. It was fun, I guess, after I realized I was still alive.'

The pairing of Reg and Britney quickly became the hot topic of corridor conversation at Parklane. Fate also lent a hand. Before the dance it was traditional for the football team to escort the Homecoming 'maids' onto the field. The names of all the maids were put into a hat and each player would draw one out. In a Hollywood moment, Reg unwrapped his paper to reveal Britney's name.

That evening Britney went over to Erin's house to get ready, while Wes joined Reg at his home in McComb. When they went over to Erin's to pick up their dates, her father told them briskly, 'Right boys, you'll have these girls home by one o'clock.' To which the boys replied, 'Yes sir!'

Britney wore a pretty black evening gown which she didn't quite fill. Reg wore spectacles and a blazer. They danced the night away to a disco of eighties favourites including Michael Jackson, Madonna and Dexy's Midnight Runners. And the boys dropped off their ladies ten minutes early.

For the first few months of their courtship Britney was at the chaperone age. In Southern parts a girl is not supposed to be left alone with a boy until she reaches the age of fifteen. This rule of etiquette meant most of their time was spent in the company of a parent, although sometimes the chaperone was actually Jamie Lynn, when the teenagers were called upon to babysit. Sometimes they would go to the movies and Jamie Lynn would usually go with them.

At this early stage a kiss goodnight would be a little peck on the cheek. The first proper kiss they exchanged was after Britney had failed her driving licence test. This is a permit test teenagers can take when they are fourteen which enables them to drive with an adult who has a full licence. The moment Reg heard she had missed out, he sent round a bunch of roses with the message on the card, 'It's OK Baby, you'll get it next time. I love you, Reg.' Later that evening Alison Price was having a party at her house after the weekly football game. Reg and Britney were strolling next to the pool when Britney suddenly grabbed him and said, 'Babe, I never got to thank you for the roses you sent me.' They stopped by the diving board and Britney stood on tiptoes and gave Reg what he cherished as a 'sweet, sweet kiss'.

'Well, thank you,' said Britney.

'No, thank you,' replied Reg.

The young couple were in danger of becoming an old married couple while still teenagers. 'We were in love,' observes Reg, simply. 'It was right between us. She kept saying I wish we could get married and I agreed but we couldn't. She was still only fifteen.'

They were still expected to observe proprieties by their parents. One day after basketball practice – Reg was now the captain of the team – they went back to his house, where they went up to his room to listen to a CD. 'We were just chilling, kissing a little bit here and there when Mom walked in and said, "What are you doing?" I said "Nothing, why?" and she goes, "Well, this doesn't look good and I don't like it."

'I said, "Mom we're fully dressed!" but she goes, "Just for me, will you all please come out of the room and come and hang out in the games room so you're not locked up in your room." I said, "Yes, ma'am". And that's exactly what we did.'

In the South there is very much a proper way to do things, a code of old-fashioned values which both Reg and Britney followed. The men went shooting and the ladies, they went shopping. Occasionally they would try their hands at the other's 'sport'.

Reg would be called upon to entertain Jamie Lynn when they went on shopping trips with Lynne: 'Jamie Lynn and I played while they shopped. They would shop for anything. We would go to the mall and they would go to the little accessory shops for earrings and what not. And then with clothes she would get me over to give my opinion: "Does this look good on me?" I was all cool with it until it got ridiculous – four hours into the shop!'

Reg had his shopping 'revenge' when he took Britney turkey hunting for the first time. Wild turkey season, which runs from 15 March to 1 May, is the most important time of the year for the Southern gentleman. From an early age Reg had accompanied his father or his stepfather on shoots, mastering the impossible art of calling a wild turkey using just a blade of grass. Reg told her firmly, 'You've got to be real still when you're turkey hunting.' The idea is to stay motionless so that the unsuspecting gobbler comes within range of your rifle.

The problem for Britney was mosquitoes: 'She was getting bit to pieces. She kept swatting them and swatting them. The turkeys were coming towards us but then she started swatting. In the end I said, "Baby, do you want to leave?" and she said, "I love it but

I'm getting bit." We laughed about it afterwards but that was the only time I took her.'

Britney never wanted to try shooting a gun. She did, however, agree to hunt deer with Reg because Jamie Lynn was pestering to go. They went to the Longleaf Estate one afternoon. Longleaf is thousands of acres of prime Mississippi woodland owned by the family of Reg's oldest friend, F.A. Jackson. Reg remembers the afternoon well: 'We ended up killing two deer. Neither of them had been around someone killing a deer. Jamie Lynn went to pet the deer after he died, but she was totally cool with it. She was happy that we had killed the deer – that's what we were there for.' Reg recalls that Britney was also 'cool' with hunting but did not enjoy the experience as much as her little sister, who 'loved every minute'.

When they had finished hunting, darkness fell before they had reached the truck. The woods at night are very spooky and Britney found herself getting jumpy, especially when the coyotes began howling: 'She got upset and started crying. They do have a distinct-sounding howl and that upset her a little bit. She was so scared.'

Britney has never been much of a tomboy. She may have been the apple of her daddy's eye but she was definitely a mother's girl and could on occasions assume the role of a hopeless female. One Sunday Reg had to be dropped off early at his church, the First Baptist in McComb, to help with a breakfast forum for Sunday School. Britney gave him a lift and was going to do some errands before joining him later for the main service. On her way back she braked hard on a red light at the junction near the church and stalled the engine. Reg had already told her that if that happened it was because the truck was low on gas and she just needed to wait a minute before turning the key again. Britney, however, panicked, kept trying it and trying it but the engine would not catch.

After a couple of minutes the cars behind were piling up and honking their horns so Britney jumped out of the truck, leaving the door wide open, and sprinted up the road to the church in her Sunday-best frock to find Reg, shouting, 'It just wouldn't crank. It wouldn't crank.' A red-faced Reg had to run back to where his truck was completely blocking the junction and face the wrath of McComb motorists. Needless to say it just turned first time and he pulled into the church.

Reg was besotted with Britney, perhaps after a while claustrophobically so. He gave up seeing his football buddies and partying, preferring to spend his time at home with Britney. Every morning he would drive over from his house in McComb to take her to school because she hated taking the bus. In the evening he would pick her up and they would either go to his house for supper or to hers. Sometimes Britney would cook but her speciality was waffles for breakfast. 'She tried to cook; she cooked some,' Reg recalls. 'I cooked more than she did. I would cook her a mean steak.'

When Britney was fifteen she accompanied Reg on his senior trip – something every student did in their final year before graduation. It was June 1977 and his mother Gay took them both up to Vail, Colorado, where they stayed in a condominium. It was an idyllic trip and the young couple went rollerblading and white-water rafting. Disaster struck on the third day when Reg ate some bad Chinese food and had to spend the rest of the holiday groaning in bed: 'I was deadly ill and, you know, Britney didn't leave the condo the whole time other than to pop out and buy me a cool, cool shirt and some boxer shorts. Then she'd come back up and lay on the bed with me, just helping me hold the garbage can while I was throwing up; that just made me feel good.'

For a while Reg and Britney enjoyed the perfect teenage romance. They were soppy about one another and it was very cosy: 'We were saying "I love you" and we meant it because we were in love. She was my girlfriend and my best friend and we had each other's hearts.' He bought her a ring and a pretty necklace while she picked out his clothes. He always paid for everything. He explains, 'I treated her, which any gentleman should do.' He took her to see the Oscar-winning movie *Titanic* at the cinema in Hammond. Britney cried her way through a whole box of tissues: 'It's a very emotional movie you know and it just seemed to fit perfectly into our relationship.'

Britney has always loved dogs. The family dog was a Rott-weiler called Cain but she pestered Reg to buy her a dog of her own. She had set her heart on a Shih Tzu. Eventually he found one for sale in Baton Rouge, fifty miles away, and they set off on a cold winter day with ice freezing up the antennae of the car. They had to drive at 50 mph the whole way and met the lady selling the dog in the car park of McDonald's. Britney was thrilled. The little dog, which would have made a nice snack for Cain, was treated with the same care and affection as if it were one of her dolls. Some months later someone came by the house and stole the dog. Britney was inconsolable.

On Friday nights Britney would always be in the stands watching Reg play football: 'She would sit at the fifty-yard line. Whenever I came running up the field in either direction I could look up and she'd be there. It was so cold the night of our final game that my mom had to go home and bring back a fur coat for her. She was the only girl on the terrace wearing a fur coat!'

Reg also gave Britney his 'letterman' jacket. This is an American boy/girl tradition. A teenage boy would give it to a girl in recognition of her status as his girlfriend. The jacket, which was blue with red piping, had patches sewn on revealing his sporting prowess. Reg, for instance, was an All-Star state basketball player, and that badge was sewn on the right sleeve.

The most romantic evenings Britney and Reg ever had together were when they spent time out by the lake on the Longleaf Estate. A small wooden pier jutted out into the water and they strolled out to look at the night sky. Reg recalls, 'We lay down with her head on my chest and I would show her the constellations in the sky. And we'd watch meteor showers. It was perfect.'

In such a romantic setting, Reg may not have been aware of the restlessness that was gripping Britney. At least once a week he would drive her the hundred miles to New Orleans for a dance class. While Britney was enjoying being a normal teenager, there was another side to her in which ambition still burned brightly. The observation that Nancy Carson made that certain inspired, talented children might feel they did not belong in their home town is a telling one in Britney's case. Her mother, in their joint book *Heart to Heart*, confirms that Britney's heart was not in Kentwood. She describes it as being a 'comedown' for her daughter and unchallenging for someone already used to fighting her corner in an adult world. Many of her contemporaries would probably never leave their home town. Yet, by the age of nine,

Britney had been in New York – even Reg, from a well-to-do local family, had never been there.

He was at Southwest Mississippi Community College in the nearby town of Summit when the first signs of what might happen in the future became apparent. He was no longer able to see Britney all the time and, sure enough, word reached her that he had been seen with another girl. He explains, 'I would take a girl from class and drop her off at the next class and someone would call Britney and tell her, "Reg had a girl in his truck." I was just dropping the girl off and there was no harm at all but Britney would get very angry at just little stuff, especially with girls in my vehicle.'

It was, by no means, one-way traffic. Reg admits he didn't like it one bit when boys in Kentwood whom he did not know that well were hanging around – Jason Alexander whom she would later controversially marry was one: 'She was hanging out with them and it ticked me off.' Reg still has a plaintive note from Britney, a poignant example of teenage love. It reads, 'I'm sorry for whatever I did. I hope you're not mad at me! I hope you have a good day! Good luck in your game.' The note is decorated with little drawings of a smiley face, a daisy and a love heart.

The worst time for Reg while Britney was still at home in Kentwood was when she had what he describes as a 'fling' with a local boy called Corey Butler who was in the same grade as her at Parklane Academy. He recalls, 'It seemed like she just did it out of spite because I had some girls in my truck, going with him and doing whatever with him. She was just playing.'

It was nothing serious and just a hiccup for Reg and Britney. Britney, however, was to try this tactic to get her own back on a boyfriend in the future with much more serious consequences. Tragically, Corey Butler died early in 2005 from a drugs-related problem. He suffered a cardiac arrest in his dorm room at college. Another school friend of Britney's, Myra Lee Reeves, was questioned by police for supplying him with methadone. Britney did not go to the funeral.

It was a stark reminder that even in this Southern backwater drugs are a major problem among young people. The special irony about the drugs problem in McComb is that Parklane Academy had an initiative in the eighth grade called the Big Redd Club. The entire year was part of their drugs awareness programme, which aimed to target the children as they began their adolescent teenage years. The affirmed sole purpose of the programme was to 'Refuse and Eradicate Dangerous Drugs' and make Britney and her classmates aware of their dangers.

'I was really head over heels in love.'

SIX

Driving the Train

Reg's mother put Britney's demo on the cassette player for her dinner guests from the local Arts Council Board to hear. She told them that Britney had an agent in New York and was going to hit it big one day. Next to Reg on the sofa Britney was cringing with embarrassment: 'I can't believe you did that,' she wailed.

Reg Jones may have thought everything was cosy in his relationship with Britney. But, behind the scenes, her mother was not that happy. Admittedly, many local girls would have considered him catch of the day. His mother and stepfather had moved into a mansion in a secluded hamlet north of McComb, which was so big they even had an elevator installed between floors. Britney, who lived in a single-storey house, loved to ride the elevator. Her mother, however, did not want her daughter to waste her talents drifting, as she had done, into marriage and motherhood too young. In a candid moment she admitted that the only arguments they ever had were over her steady boyfriend (Reg) spending too much time in the house, watching TV with his feet up on the couch. Lynne thought she was too young to devote so much of her time to just one person.

This was not strictly true about mother/daughter arguments. Lynne Spears was not at all happy about Britney smoking as a teenager. She was relaxed about her having an occasional glass of wine at home – she and Reg would have more than the occasional glass if they were out together – but smoking was another matter. For one thing it was not the best habit for a singer with serious aspirations. Nor for a singer whose mother had serious aspirations for her. Lynne did not appreciate being called out to Parklane when Britney and some pals were caught smoking in the girls' bathroom. She did not trust Britney about this.

One day she went off in the morning as usual to teach at the local elementary school where she was working. As usual, Britney waited for Reg to arrive to take her to Parklane. She settled down to enjoy an early morning cigarette when Lynne whizzed back and caught her red-handed. 'She had a fit,' says Reg. He also recalls the time Britney was driving along Highway 51 on the stretch between the centre of Kentwood and their house. Lynne was in the passenger seat when she announced that she could smell smoke and demanded to sniff Britney's hands. 'She grabbed Britney's hand off the wheel and when she did it made them spin and they spun out of control and were wrecked down in a ditch from her mum smelling her hands. And she told me she had not been smoking, so that was a big ordeal.' Fortunately, neither of them was hurt.

Most of the time mother and daughter survived the teenage years better than many families. Britney was quite adept at wrapping the men in her life round her finger. Jamie, Bryan and Reg

Britney always took centre stage as a child. Wearing her favourite pink, she holds hands with cousin Laura Lynne and future husband Jason Alexander.

The Mouseketeers. Justin Timberlake has his arm around Britney, who is already displaying a bare midriff. An ethereal Christina Aguilera is seated in front of them.

The last shot of *The Mickey Mouse Club* cast before the show was cancelled. Justin is holding the card, Christina, wearing a blue-denim jacket, is on his left, and Britney, already looking much more grown-up, is by her side in a black top.

Below left The real Age of Innocence. *Below right* Britney was voted 'Most Beautiful' in Junior High. Her companion, Mason Statham, was voted 'Most Handsome'. The picture hangs in the foyer of Ruby Tuesday's in McComb.

Happy times with her first boyfriend, Reg Jones. Britney looks stunning by his side at a friend's pool party, and on the porch of his father's house.

A million-dollar smile, for Reg.

Jamie Spears was right behind Britney when fathers escorted their daughters to a school dance.

When Britney was set to join the girl-band Innosense, in 1997, they posed with boy-band heart-throbs 'N Sync. In the end the girls supported Britney on tour.

Above left Shaping up to be a star: Britney first showcased the schoolgirl look on a mall tour in the summer of 1998, before she unveiled it on the video for '...Baby One More Time'.

Above right Revealing the 'growth spurt' at the Teen Choice Awards in 1999, which led to speculation that she had undergone a breast enlargement

Right Britney always puts 110 per cent into shooting her videos but she tried a little too hard performing the dance moves for 'Sometimes' on Malibu pier. She injured her knee and had to rest up for three months.

Above left The look of love: Britney gazes adoringly at Justin during a Super Bowl fundraiser at Planet Hollywood in New York, February 2002. Just one month later she was denying they had split. *Above right* Britney and Justin shared a love of basketball, although she never grew tall enough to be more than a half-sized player.

Below left There's no mistaking the family resemblance. Britney with her mother Lynne and brother Bryan for a night out at Planet Hollywood. *Below right* Two devoted sisters, Britney and Jamie Lynn, aged twelve, backstage at the Nickelodeon Kids' Choice Awards in April 2003. Now they are both young mums.

Above left Britney has so far won more than 160 awards. She collected four at the 1999 MTV Europe Music Awards in Dublin, for Best Female, Best Pop Act, Best Breakthrough Act and Best Song. *Above right* The ultimate Britney Spears picture – beautiful with a touch of off-the-shoulder innocence.

Britney demonstrates her snake-charming abilities while singing 'I'm A Slave 4 U' at the 2001 MTV Video Music Awards in New York.

Madonna supervises her virgin brides, Britney and Christina Aguilera, during their controversial performance at the 2003 MTV Video Music Awards in New York.

Britney and Madonna snog horror! 'No one slipped anyone the tongue,' said Britney.

to start up the American answer to the Spice Girls, who had made a huge impact in the US in January when 'Wannabe' reached number one in the *Billboard* charts.

She was encouraged by the start her son had made in his new career, as a member of the boy band 'N Sync. They had just completed a hugely successful first American tour – the 'I Want You Back' tour – and were excited about their first American release. Another Mouse Club stalwart, JC Chasez, was also in the band, which had originated in Orlando under the larger-than-life patronage of millionaire entrepreneur Lou Pearlman, the man behind Backstreet Boys. Lou encouraged Lynn Harless to strike out in management on her own.

She thought the time was right to start a female 'N Sync, an attractive, all-white group of all-American girls. She already had the name, Innosense, and the first member was right on her doorstep. Ex-Mouseketeer Nikki DeLoach was still living in Orlando and, as the girlfriend of JC Chasez, she already saw plenty of Justin and Lynn. She had grown into a stunning young woman and perfectly represented the sort of girl Lynn was looking to recruit.

Britney was a natural choice when Nikki and Justin's mother sat down to think of possible members for the group. They had heard on the Mouseketeer grapevine that she was looking for an opportunity. The two mothers, Lynn and Lynne, spoke on the phone and, as a result, Britney flew up to Justin's home near Memphis to talk through the deal. It all seemed very exciting, especially as Lou Pearlman was going to bankroll the project.

Everything seemed promising as Britney posed for band pictures with Nikki and the other girls, Danay Ferrer, Mandy

Ashford and Amanda Latona. They looked fantastic, their big hair and cropped tops creating a look eerily similar to the one that Girls Aloud manufactured six years later. They even posed for pictures with 'N Sync, in which Justin sported his new bleached-blond haircut, an alliance which would have given them a flying start.

Britney went back home to Kentwood for a couple of weeks while the formal management papers were drawn up. She had begun to realize just how bored she was but, at last, something was happening. Obviously it was good to meet up with Justin again but he had just started seeing another girl, Veronica Finn, while Britney was still with Reg. And this was business. Britney was about to make the key decision of her professional life. If she had joined Innosense she would almost certainly have sunk without trace. Timing is everything in the music business and the real gap in the market was not for America's answer to the Spice Girls but for a female soloist, a Madonna for a new generation. Intriguingly, among four other stunning girls, Britney failed to stand out.

Britney never signed up as a member of Innosense. Veronica Finn, who would eventually take the place earmarked for Britney, recalls, 'To the best of my knowledge they had this meeting up in Millington, took some pictures and declared to the world, "This is Innosense". Britney flew back home. The day before she was supposed to fly back into town and sign the actual management agreement, they called Lynn Harless and said, "Britney's dad doesn't want her to do this. They think she would be better off as a solo artist so we don't want her to be part of the group." That's when I came in.'

Lou Pearlman, always shrewd about business, recognized

Britney as the one that got away: 'I've missed a few pitches that were thrown right down the middle. I've often wondered what would have happened if I had been paying more attention.' Britney may have had a lucky escape. In 2008, Lou Pearlman was sentenced to twenty-five years in jail for financial offences.

Exactly how much of the decision to go solo was down to Jamie is a moot point. The most important person in the decision-making process was not even a member of the family. He was Larry Rudolph, a New York entertainment lawyer with big ideas and the connections to make things happen. He was the sort of man, still in his thirties, who would grab an opportunity on the conveyor belt as it went by rather than wait for it to come round again. He also was very forthright in his opinion.

Larry Rudolph was the first of a series of new faces in Britney's life who would shape her destiny over the next few years. He had begun a firm called Rudolph and Beer in 1993 with fellow lawyer Steven Beer. Their speciality was to spot talent early, although they did have supermodel Linda Evangelista on their books. Larry Rudolph was a man people might call a 'real New Yorker' and mean it as a compliment.

Larry had first met Britney when she was thirteen, soon after setting up the business. The Spears family were trying to work out what to do after *The Mickey Mouse Club* disappointment. The whole family including Jamie Lynn turned up at his office. He told the *Hollywood Reporter*, 'They were all dressed up. Britney didn't say two words. When she was younger, she was very, very quiet, almost introverted. I would ask her a question and she wouldn't look me in the eye. She would just look around and say, "Yes, sir" or "No, sir". That would be the extent of our conversation.'

Despite Britney's unflinching respect for adults, Rudolph had a feeling that there was something about the girl. He was encouraging but could not identify any opportunities for someone of that age. A couple of years later and it was a different story. It was his turn to emulate Nancy Carson and be impressed by a package in the post from the Spears family. He suggested to Lynne that she send him a demo of Britney singing with some up-to-date photographs. Britney was looking her best at the time because of the publicity shots for Innosense so that was no problem. There was no money in the Spears piggy bank for a proper demo so Britney just sang, karaoke fashion, into a tape recorder and they sent that off.

Larry Rudolph was impressed. He knew, however, that such an amateur effort, however promising, was not suitable for sending off to any record company. He decided to back his judgement and obtain some favours to allow Britney to produce a demo of professional quality. He wanted her to sing something new and fresh, not the same old tired version of a Madonna song. A producer-friend volunteered a song that Toni Braxton had recorded for her new album. It had not made the final press because it was thought too poppy for her soulful style. It was perfect for Britney so Larry sent her two versions of the song – one with the Braxton vocal and one without. The first was to help Britney learn the track and the second for her to record over. When she felt she could do a passable imitation of La Braxton, she went into a studio in New Orleans and recorded the track for Larry. All they could do in Kentwood was wait.

They did not have to wait long. Larry Rudolph sent the track out to Jeff Fenster, a Vice President of Jive Records, where he was responsible for A&R. He had no idea she was singing over a track originally prepared for Toni Braxton, but was intrigued enough to want to hear more. 'It wasn't even in her key,' he recalled. 'But I heard something from the voice on this one single – the delivery on this one song. Then I got the pictures from her lawyer.'

The world of pop is a very small one. Fenster, a former music lawyer, had taken Backstreet Boys to Jive after they had been developed by Lou Pearlman, back in Orlando.

Jive Records – and its parent company Zomba – were the personal baby of multimillionaire record mogul Clive Calder, the Howard Hughes of popular music. As in the case of many very private, hugely wealthy men, a whole squadron of unconfirmed urban legends has grown up around Calder, who is never seen in public or photographed in private. He has never given a single interview to the media, allowing free rein to stories of eccentricity which range from taking board meetings wearing a surgical mask because of allergies to only speaking to his dogs by telephone because of concern over germs.

Some or, more likely, none of the stories may be true, but Calder is arguably the most successful tycoon in the history of pop, combining a necessarily ruthless head for business with an uncanny instinct for the next big thing. From relatively unprom-ising beginnings as a bass guitarist in his native South Africa in the late sixties he was officially named, at the age of fifty-four, as the richest man in pop in 2004, with a personal fortune in excess of £1,235 million.

He started producing local acts in his native Johannesburg before moving to London in the mid seventies because of an increasing disenchantment with apartheid. It was also becoming more dangerous to be associated with the black music he so admired. He formed Zomba Music Publishing and Jive Records with friend and fellow South African Ralph Simon, whom he later bought out. Zomba was the former capital of Malawi while the name Jive was taken from a type of South African music and dance he liked called 'township jive'.

His first notable success was with West Indian-born singer Billy Ocean, who had a UK number one with 'When the Going Gets Tough, the Tough Get Going' as well as, more significantly for Jive, three US number ones. Ocean was well into his thirties when Calder took him on and his career dwindled when he hit forty. Calder also signed former page three girl Samantha Fox in the mid eighties. All the busty blonde's 'classic' tracks, including 'Touch Me (I Want Your Body)' and 'Do Ya Do Ya (Wanna Please Me)', were released on Jive. Calder's mantra from the very beginning was 'whatever it takes to sell a record'. Samantha Fox became a huge worldwide artist and had three top ten hits in the States.

Jive enjoyed more noteworthy success with the burgeoning pop career of actor Will Smith, who, as part of rap combo DJ Jazzy Jeff and the Fresh Prince, had a UK number one with the club favourite 'Boom Shake the Room' in 1993. Calder's biggest commercial breakthrough came when he tapped into teenage talent. He was also a great admirer of Berry Gordy, the founder of Motown, and sought to emulate that company's blueprint for success – discovering and nurturing new talent using a strong inner core of company songwriters, musicians, A&R men, producers and managers. It became a production line. He was able therefore to build one career on the foundations of another. Hence the same faces keep cropping up in the stories of Backstreet Boys, 'N Sync and Britney Spears.

Jive was just one of six appointments which Larry Rudolph fixed up for Britney. He rang to tell Britney the good news. The one drawback was that they did not want to see her for a cosy chat. Instead they expected her to sing three tracks on the spot. Larry booked her a plane ticket and, one sweltering summer day, Britney flew alone up to New York to confront her destiny. In her luggage was a backing tape to the three songs she and Larry had decided she should sing, 'Jesus Loves Me', 'I Have Nothing' and 'Open Arms'. The first two were by her singing role model Whitney Houston. They were excellent choices – as long as the record company executives thought a teenage white girl from Louisiana could successfully sing covers of one of the all-time-great black vocalists. 'Open Arms' had been a top ten UK hit for the Queen Diva of the nineties, Mariah Carey.

At each appointment Britney sang one song to a backing track and the others a cappella. She was, surprisingly for a seasoned professional, very nervous. It had been a couple of years since she has sung seriously on *The Mickey Mouse Club*, and a friend's wedding in Kentwood did not really count. She was most nervous, however, because she wanted to succeed so badly.

She described the day's performances as the 'most nerve-racking I have ever done'. She told the *Hollywood Reporter*, 'It's so different performing in front of thousands of people, when you're pumped and they're screaming and that gets your energy going. But when there's just three people sitting there staring at you, it's so different.' At least she had Larry by her side, trying to encourage her.

The initial reaction was underwhelming. Two of the labels said no, one said maybe and the fourth, Jive Records, was slow in responding. Jeff Fenster, a very influential figure, had liked what he heard and saw: 'She had no material. She didn't write. She was fifteen. But her vocal ability and commercial appeal caught me right away so I signed her.'

The music business is not one, however, that particularly takes chances. No one at Jive could know for sure whether the possibilities they saw in their office conference room would be translated to the studio. They decided to offer her a contract with a ninety-day get-out clause if they did not think she was shaping up. If everything went well it would lead to Britney recording her first album. It was, in effect, a development deal.

The offer was met with jubilation back in Kentwood. Britney stage two was up and running after a hiatus that had lasted nearly three years. The realization that once again Britney would have to leave her home presented Jamie and Lynne with a thorny problem. This time around Lynne would not be able to go with her. Jamie Lynn was now five and had started school so Lynne needed to stay behind to look after her younger daughter. Britney was still only fifteen so there was no question of sending her off by herself, even though she had already lived in New York. It is not something that Jamie, in particular, always mindful of his daughter's welfare, would have considered for a moment. Following discussions with Larry Rudolph and Jive, it was decided that a travelling companion would need to be found. The right woman would be a mixture of chaperone and confidante – as close to a substitute for Lynne as they could find.

The first person Lynne thought of was Felicia Culotta, a Southern woman she had known for some years who had been working as a nanny in New York. She combined a familiarity with the big city with an appreciation of what it was like to have grown up in the Deep South. Felicia first met Lynne when she was working as a children's dental hygienist in a practice near Kentwood. The two women hit it off and Lynne proceeded to tell Felicia all about her talented daughter. She also invited her to hear Britney perform at a local arts and craft fair. That afternoon Felicia had her first insight into the two Britneys. She saw first-hand the mature little girl with a mass of brown curls stride onto stage and belt out a song. And then she witnessed the same little girl come off stage, grab her hand and suggest they go and look at the dolls.

Felicia moved to New York but kept in touch with Lynne and followed Britney's career on *The Mickey Mouse Club*. Fortuitously she had left her latest job the day before Lynne contracted her. They agreed that Felicia should take on the mantle of personal assistant for three months during the initial trial with Jive. They would just see how it went. The job was a little ambiguous. Despite her professionalism, Britney's confidence could be brittle. Lynne impressed on Felicia, or Fe, as they called her, that she had to be Britney's cheerleader. At thirty-two, Felicia was considerably older than her charge but still young enough to enjoy a girls' night out. She and Britney met for a private dinner in New Orleans before they were due to fly out and instantly hit it off. They both wore white tops and blue jeans, which helped break the ice.

Fe Culotta proved an inspired choice, better than even Lynne could have hoped. In effect, she became Britney's big sister over the next few years, by her side when she needed her and a step behind when she didn't. On the thank-you list for her first album, Britney wrote: 'Last, but not least, my Fe Fe – sister's still got it.' Lynne paid an even better tribute in *Heart to Heart*: 'You always pray that your child has an angel watching over her: we were lucky that our angel happened to be looking for a new job.'

One other helpful quality that Fe Culotta possessed was an obsession with taking photographs. As a result there is an unrivalled picture history of Britney from the moment she arrived on the scene. Fe was ready with the camera when Lynne came to the airport to hug her daughter goodbye. The pictorial record became a book in 2000 entitled *Britney: Every Step of the Way*, part of the ongoing marketing of Britney as product. There are thirty-two pictures of Britney and Fe smiling for the camera, although she doesn't disclose who was behind the lens when she was in front of it.

Britney's inexperience in the recording industry did allow Jive one luxury – they could shape and mould their new signing in the way they wanted. Jeff Fenster describes it as a classic A&R job, where his team went out and found the producers and songs that would be best for Britney. They decided on a two-venue recording strategy. First of all they would hook Britney up with New Jersey-based songwriter and producer Eric Foster White and then, if that went well, fly her over to Stockholm to what was at the time the acknowledged international hit capital of the world. If they were not happy with what they heard from Foster Wright they could opt out of Sweden and send Britney back to Kentwood.

Foster White was a multi-talented musician from Detroit who had been part of the flourishing Miami music scene in the late eighties before moving to New York, where he wrote 'My Name is Not Susan' for Whitney Houston and 'Every Time I Close My Eyes' for Backstreet Boys. Whitney Houston is one of Britney's musical heroes so she was thrilled to be sent to work with him.

Foster White was a producer who could probably play all the instruments better than any band recording with him.

His easygoing and relaxed approach was perfect for such an inexperienced artist. He taught her how to wind down between sessions by playing darts or learning some chords on the guitar. He also had some catchy pop tunes up his sleeve for her, including 'From the Bottom of my Broken Heart', which he wrote in one hour, and 'Soda Pop'. Jive had put Britney up in a roomy penthouse on the Upper East Side, where the views of the New York skyline were spectacular. Although not especially homely to begin with, it was a life-changing step up from the poky apartments of her *Ruthless!* days. At this stage, Reg Jones was still very much part of Britney's life. In November he flew up to New York to be with Britney for Thanksgiving, the traditional American holiday. Together they went to the Macy's Thanksgiving Day parade and went ice skating at the Rockefeller Centre, a first for both of them. He stayed in the apartment and remembers how well he was treated on this visit and what a happy time it was.

Reg joined Britney when she went over to Foster White's studios and would sit in the booth with the producer while Britney sang in the studio next door. Foster White would tell Reg what Britney needed to do and Reg would pass the instructions on for the next run-through as if he were the real producer. 'He was a great guy,' says Reg. 'If she messed up, he would tell me what to tell her. I was the man on the mike saying, "Britney, you need to hit this tone." It was fun. Britney was unbelievable. She'd walk in with blue jeans on and a T-shirt, loosen up her vocal chords and then the deal was on.'

Foster White deserves a great deal of praise for steering Britney in an unashamedly pop direction. The original demos in which she sang Whitney and Mariah were not the way for a sixteen-year-old, fresh-faced teenager to go. When Clive Calder, his right-hand man Barry Weiss and the other movers and shakers at Jive Records heard the results they agreed. The ninety-day get-out clause was ignored and Britney was booked on a flight to the European capital of pop.

'She would sing her butt off.'

SEVEN

. . . Baby, One More Time

A demo tape of a song arrived in the post at Kentwood. It was Swedish pop producer Max Martin singing one of his songs. After everybody had listened to it, Jamie Spears turned to his daughter and declared, 'That's it. That's the one that's going to make it for you.' The song was '. . . Baby, One More Time'.

Before she left to fly to Stockholm, Britney wrote Reg Jones a letter from the apartment in New York.

> Well, I'm getting ready to go to Sweden and I'm really excited. I just wish you could come with me. That would be great. I'm sorry about the trip to Singapore. I really wanted you to go with me. I'll think about you when I'm there. I hope you do the same. I know it gets hard when we are apart (at least it does for me) but I just think about the future and know I have something great to look forward to that keeps me going!
>
> Tell your family I miss them very much and I can't wait to see them again. Be careful and *please* don't get hurt when

I'm gone. I think I would seriously die. Please don't forget about me.

I love you so much and miss you terribly.

Love Brit.

P.S. Be *good*!

The note reveals not only her excitement about the trip but also the chronic insecurity of a young girl being apart from her boyfriend. She may not have realized it at the time but Reg was suffering the same insecurity about her launching a new chapter in her life. It would be the first prolonged absence from each other they had faced. While Reg continued at college, the seat next to Britney on a horrendously turbulent transatlantic flight was occupied by Felicia Culotta. The buffeting was so bad that Britney was reduced to tears when she tried to get back to her seat from a visit to the toilet.

Britney's Swedish destination was Cheiron Studios which, for a short period of time in the 1990s, was a tried and trusted route for launching international pop stars. Jive Records tapped into that source of hits. The success of the sound was principally due to two men, Max Martin and Denniz PoP, an unlikely duo who, as both Abba and Stock, Aitken and Waterman had previously done, captured the mood of the moment for catchy pop tunes.

Max Martin was still relatively new to the art of pop production when he met Britney in late 1997. He was twenty-six, with straggly long blond hair and the sallow complexion of someone who was spending too much of the day indoors, in front of a recording desk. He was, as Britney would discover, immensely dedicated and one of the mystery men of music. He had been born Martin Sandberg and grew up a suburban teenager in

Stockholm, nurturing schoolboy ambitions to be a pop singer. He sang with several bands using the stage name Martin White while still at high school, including a glam rock outfit called It's Alive. They impressed local producer Denniz PoP, who ran the Cheiron label with nightclub owner Tom Talomaa. It's Alive recorded one album and toured Europe in the early nineties but never achieved a breakthrough. Instead Martin White was hired as a house writer and producer at Cheiron Studios and began to learn his trade through PoP's patronage.

PoP, whose real name was the less memorable Dag Volle, had been a much sought-after DJ in the eighties responsible for a string of memorable remixes. His treatment of Donna Summer's 'Love to Love You Baby' and Michael Jackson's 'Billie Jean' brought those classics to the attention of a new generation. He teamed up with five other Stockholm DJs to start Swemix Records, a dance music label. Denniz had ambitions beyond being a DJ and made the breakthrough with a track called 'Hello Afrika' by the Nigerian-born artist Dr Alban. That success led to the dance track 'It's My Life', his first UK hit for the same artist, which reached number two in 1992.

PoP reached a wider international audience when he wrote and produced for a new Swedish band called Ace of Base. The group's first UK single, 'All That She Wants', topped the charts in April 1993, selling more than 600,000 copies. Their debut album, *Happy Nation*, also reached number one and stayed in the charts for thirty-six weeks. Even more significant, however, was their success in the US. The album was retitled *The Sign* and became the first by a Swedish act to top the US album charts. Not even Abba had achieved that feat. *The Sign* sold more than twenty-two million copies worldwide, making it one of the biggest-selling debut albums of all time. Denniz PoP, now affectionately known as the 'Dancemeister', was on the international map.

PoP, meanwhile, had given Martin White a new name, Max Martin, because he thought it sounded 'poppier'. Their first collaboration was for one-hit dance wonders Rednex ('Cotton-Eye Joe') on a song called 'Wish You Were Here' before Martin helped on Ace of Base's second album, *The Bridge*. Much more important was when they were contacted by Jive Records to help record a debut album for a new signing, Backstreet Boys. Their Stockholm recording sessions produced three classic tracks of the boy-band era, which cemented the reputation of PoP and made Martin's: 'Quit Playing Games (With My Heart)', 'As Long as You Love Me' and 'Everybody (Backstreet's Back)'.

Suddenly, or so it seemed, Sweden was at the forefront of popular music. A year after Backstreet Boys, Justin Timberlake and 'N Sync breezed into Stockholm for their first recording sessions and recorded their breakthrough single 'I Want You Back'. Both these chart-topping boy bands shared the same marketing strategy. They made it big in Europe before breaking through in the US by touring malls and schools. They were the pathfinders for Britney Spears and their success made everybody feel a little more confident about taking on an unknown fifteen-year-old girl from Louisiana. But not that much more confident.

By the time Britney arrived in Sweden, Cheiron boasted some of the best writers and producers in the business. As well as Martin and PoP, she could call on the talents of Per Magnusson, Kristian Lundin and Andreas Carlsson. They all shared one common trait – they expected their artists to work. If Britney thought she was going to enjoy a few months of saunas and smorgasbord, she would soon be disillusioned. She sent Reg a postcard which illustrated that this was a work camp and not a play camp: 'I'm missing you lots, but too busy to talk to you as much as I want to'. It was a short note, no more than forty words in total and in stark contrast to the letter she had written while she was packing to leave.

After the first month or so Britney was barely speaking to Reg at all – not because they had fallen out but as a result of his mother discovering that the phone bill for his calls to Europe was $1,500. She put a stop to that immediately. She now admits, 'I'll always feel bad about that. All they did was talk on the phone. I said, "If you and Britney are going to make it long-distance, you're going to make it without talking to her five times a day. She's over there to work and do her thing."'

The block on the phone may not have been such a bad idea because it is never the best method of keeping a relationship going. Reg observes, 'The schedules were weird. She would be calling me at 1.00 in the morning and it would be 6 a.m. over there. She was so tired because she was working her butt off. And just little nitpicky stuff would happen like one of us answering the phone in a different tone of voice. The other one would take offence. Just little things set you off when you're apart and you can't correct it over the phone.'

Reg was becoming very jealous of Britney and not being there with her, especially as Max Martin was clearly making a big impression on her. She was in a situation in which he had no input or control: 'I instigated some fights just because I didn't know what was going on. Sometimes they wouldn't let me talk to her and I felt like I couldn't stay in touch with her.' Reg's mother, Gay Austin, would confide in her son some time later that she never thought they would be able to stay together because they had two incompatible lifestyles. She recognized that Britney had embarked on something that required an immense amount of hard work; Britney would need to be entirely focused if she was to achieve her goal.

Mrs Austin was right. The legendary Britney Spears work ethic had taken over and Reg was becoming a distraction. She spent twelve hours in the recording studio, from 2 p.m. until 2 a.m. with a break for dinner at 7 p.m. It was very organized, very methodical and very Swedish. Per Magnusson, who would later write the huge million sellers 'Evergreen' and 'Anyone of Us', recalled, 'We didn't know much about her. She was a shy little sixteen-year-old. We thought it was just another girl getting some tracks.' The Cheiron team enjoyed working with Britney because she again demonstrated the qualities that had impressed at *The Mickey Mouse Club* – dedication and malleability. 'The fun thing is having someone who hasn't released a single yet. You can adjust them to becoming part of your sound.'

While Britney was in Sweden, Denniz PoP was diagnosed with cancer at the age of thirty-five. He continued to work, helping to launch the career of boy band 5ive. He died in August 1998, after Britney had returned home but before she had released any of the Cheiron material. She graciously acknowledged his contribution on the sleeve notes of the first album, unsurprisingly titled ... *Baby One More Time*: 'To Denniz PoP: Your memory lives on in the beautiful music you wrote for me. Thank you.'

Max Martin, who assumed PoP's mantle as the driving force in pop music, never normally gives interviews but said, 'I have lost my best friend and it feels like the world has lost a genius.'

Britney did a lot of growing up in Sweden. For the first time, her mother was not by her side to wish her happy birthday when she turned sixteen. Stockholm was a lovely city, if very cold, but she was spending most of her time in the Cheiron compound. Felicia provided some female company. There was very little time for sightseeing or partying. Her Swedish adventure was a career-changing one for Britney in two regards. Firstly, Max Martin moulded and shaped the vocal techniques that were to become trademark Britney. She sang in a controlled manner, comfortably within her range, incorporating a blend of Madonna and Europop with a touch of growling thrown in. The image of a little girl on *Star Search* belting out 'Love Can Build a Bridge' like a cruise-ship singer was consigned to the scrapheap. The new Britney could easily have sung the vocal on 'All That She Wants'. Max Martin instinctively seemed to know what sounded best for Britney. He in turn was impressed by her ability to catch the melody of a song and take it to another level by stamping her own personality on it.

Secondly, she came home with one of the greatest ever pop songs in the can. One song is all it takes. The irony is that Max Martin did not write '. . . Baby, One More Time' for Britney. He had the black American girl group TLC in mind but they rejected it because, at the time, they were taking a break. The finished article would have been very different if it had been interpreted by the hard-edged chart act rather than a teenage unknown. The strength of the song is primarily in its multiple use of hooks. To begin with, the three opening piano chords are arguably as recognizable as any in the pop canon. It's a good pub topic to try and think of the opening bars of a song that match it. There's no melody, nor a motif that repeats through the song. It's only three miserable chords and yet it could only ever be one song. Perhaps

'Honky Tonk Women' by the Rolling Stones runs it close but that phrase repeats before the song gets going.

The second hook is 'Oh Baby, Baby', or as Britney sings it, 'Oh Baybee, Baybee'. Her throaty rendition of one of the commonest words in pop song lyrics almost became an instant trademark and one imitated in countless karaoke performances every night. The third hook is the chorus line itself 'Hit me baby one more time', which could scarcely be easier to remember. One ingredient of the Swedish hit factory that should not be underestimated is the simplistic use of English, which may have something to do with the language not being a native tongue. Abba, in particular, exploited this with some pretty nonsensical but highly effective lyrics. How could we forget 'Super Trouper ... Su Pa Pa, Trou Pa Pa'? Britney's debut song only contains one word – 'loneliness' – of more than two syllables. Writing songs is not rocket science. The easier it is to commit a song to memory, the more likely it is to become a hit.

'... Baby One More Time' had everything going for it as a pop song. The leap from being a good song to being a great one, however, was made by Britney one afternoon at a school in California. The song made Britney musically. The video they shot at Venice High School would make her a universal brand.

In total, Britney flew back with six tracks that would form the core basis of her debut album. Jive Records were in no hurry. They were delighted with what they heard and decided to raid the petty cash so that by the time the album was released Britney Spears would be the next big thing in pop. They had a plan for instant world domination and Britney had to be ready.

At this stage Britney was not contemplating a future without

Reg Jones. He was there when Lynne came to meet her at New Orleans airport and he sat beside her on the drive back to Kentwood. It was a flying visit home because she was due to finish recording with Eric Foster White almost immediately. Sweden, while a busy and exciting interlude, had been a lonely one. The first thing she decided when she returned was that she wanted Reg to come to New York. He was just as keen as she was, having hated their time apart.

They told both Lynne and Reggie Sr of their plan but their was no way that Reg, a college student, could afford it. At the last minute his father told Reg that he had found an apartment for him, literally one block away from where Britney would be staying. It belonged to an old friend from McComb who said Reg could use it for a few months. His father also stumped up $800 for the air fare.

Reg's first night in New York was almost a disaster. He could not find the roommate he was supposed to be sharing the apartment with and could not get in. Desperate, he rang the intercom of the building where Britney and Fe were happily ensconced in the penthouse. Felicia, claims Reg, would not let him in. It is easy to speculate with 20/20 hindsight that a decision had already been made at a higher level to ease Reg quietly out of the picture. He maintains, 'Felicia is one reason why Britney and I eventually split. We didn't get along. That first night Felicia told me I could not come up. Britney got mad and started crying. She had to call her mama and get her mama to call Felicia and tell her, "Yes, it's fine for Reg to come up and stay because he doesn't have a place to stay. You're not going to leave him on the street."

'Felicia may just have been abiding by Miss Lynne's laws.

I don't know but I didn't like it – to leave me out on the street like that. She's from my home place and she wasn't even going to be courteous enough to just let me in so that I could get a place to stay. Britney was really upset.

'Everything was cool after that but I could see Felicia talking negatively in Britney's ear about me, just to get me out of the picture I think. She had a big influence with her.'

The portents for Britney and Reg were not at all promising. He was a Southern boy from McComb, Mississippi, lost in the big city. She was cocooned from the outside world in a penthouse apartment. Her days were made up of finishing touches in the studio or rehearsing with dancers for her mall tour and various showcases. She was a girl on a mission with a carefully mapped out schedule. She was being 'handled' and Felicia was always by her side.

First up was a trip to Nashville to perform a showcase of the recorded material for executives from Jive and BMG, then the label's distribution company. She wore a canary-coloured party dress which she had bought for $70 in a popular store. It was the sort of dress any girl might wear on a Friday night out. It was the first time in months that Britney had forsaken her preferred casual T-shirt and jeans look. Then it was back to prepare for a whirlwind tour of malls. This marketing technique had initially proved successful in the late eighties for Tiffany, a teenager from California whose first record 'I Think We're Alone Now' was number one on both sides of the Atlantic. The idea was to reach as many people as possible in the shortest time. Backstreet Boys had done it through a six-month tour of high schools and middle schools sponsored by *Educational Scholastic Magazine*. Britney's target audience was exclusively teenage.

Back in New York, Britney was getting more frustrated with Reg. He recalls, 'She wanted me to find a job and I couldn't. Living in New York was such a culture shock to me; I just didn't know how to handle it. My apartment was on the ground floor and I could step out the back onto my little patio, look up and I could see Britney's apartment. I thought that was kind of neat.' Not everything was bad news for the couple. They still enjoyed some good times. They went and saw the comedy film *There's Something About Mary* together. During the famous scene where Mary (Cameron Diaz) mistakes semen for hair gel, Reg became aware of Britney next to him laughing so hard she was snorting. It remains one of Britney's favourite movies, even if some years later Diaz eventually replaced her in the affections of Justin Timberlake. These sort of fanzine question and answers are always changeable but, when asked, Britney usually nominates this film or *Titanic*, which she also saw with Reg, as her favourite.

Eventually, Reg found a job working in an Italian restaurant, where he was responsible for opening the wine. Britney, meanwhile, was being groomed for million-dollar stardom. During his break in the middle of the day Reg would go and watch Britney rehearse with her dancers. She would soon be going out on tour, but, before that, she had to prepare for her all-important first video.

The album was ready so now it was a case of getting as much air play and promotion as possible. The countdown to the release of '. . . Baby One More Time' on 23 October 1998 had begun. Already word was going round in the small world of music that Jive was investing heavily in a new act. They had kept everything pretty quiet for a year but were now bringing on the heavy artillery. The first big gun they put in place was super manager Johnny

Wright. His appointment as Britney's co-manager was not a signal of a lack of confidence in Larry Rudolph but of the level of commitment to Britney and of a determination that she was going straight to the top. He would become the principle conductor of an orchestra of players in which Britney was the soloist but in which everyone had a key role to play.

Wright was a very respected music industry figure who had started out in the business in the eighties driving a van for New Kids on the Block manager Maurice Starr. He had progressed to becoming their tour manager. New Kids on the Block were the pathfinders for the boy band boom of the nineties and, indirectly, the impetus for acts like Britney Spears and Justin Timberlake. They were the direct inspiration for the management teams of Take That and Backstreet Boys.

In the early nineties Wright moved to Orlando to enjoy the Florida sunshine. He was from Cape Cod but had grown tired of the severe New England winters. He was managing the chart band Snap when Lou Pearlman asked him to take on Backstreet Boys. His initial reaction was to say no, until his wife Donna went to see them perform and told him they could be big. That was a good call as his success with Backstreet Boys led to even bigger things with 'N Sync and Britney. His particular forte was tour organization and he would be responsible for 'N Sync's blockbusting stadium tours. In 2000, nearly one million tickets were sold for their fifty-two date tour generating receipts of more than $40 million.

Wright enjoyed a reputation as a no-nonsense businessman which belies his easy-going, mild-mannered approach. While on tour with 'N Sync, Tony Lucca recalls Wright turning up from time to time: 'He was all business but not bullshit. He would say

"How you doing man?" before attending to business. He did his thing and let others do their thing.'

He would be a formidable man to have in Britney's corner as her launch gained momentum. The big advantage of bringing Wright in was that he could help Jive link Britney with other artists to everyone's mutual benefit. Her first tour would be as the warm-up act for 'N Sync. Subsequently Jordan Knight, the lead singer of New Kids, would be the support act for 'N Sync. In 2004, JC Chasez of 'N Sync was the support for Britney. And so it goes on.

Johnny Wright has the precious gift of engaging people's trust. He is, to coin a cliché, a safe pair of hands. His father was a church organist and he held long-term Christian values. He used to wear a baseball cap bearing the letters WWJD – What Would Jesus Do?

Tony Lucca was living in California at the time and making a name for himself as a singer/songwriter. He well remembers a friend of his calling with news of Britney. The friend worked for BMG distribution in Detroit: 'He called me one day and announced, "Britney is going to blow wide open." I said "Why?" and he said, "We got everything through today, the promo posters, the whole shebang. I can't even begin to fathom what Jive's spending on her marketing campaign but it's going to blow. I blurted out, "Britney! What's it all about?" He said, 'Just a female young pop thing." I was genuinely surprised. I thought the first person we would have heard musically from the Mouse Club would have been Christina.'

This was the beauty of the Jive campaign. Nobody saw Britney coming. Christina Aguilera's debut solo release was still a year away. She had created a ripple when she sang 'Reflection', the theme from the 1998 Disney movie *Mulan*. An unseen voice singing a cartoon theme was a world away from the schoolgirl with her hair in pigtails sashaying down the school corridor singing 'Hit Me Baby, One More Time'. From that moment on Christina was playing catch-up. Britney and Jive landed their punch first and she always led the way.

'Britney. Get to know her on a first-name basis.'

EIGHT

Back to School

When she was in New York, Britney smoked dope for the first time while on a night out at a club with a girlfriend who had brought it with her. She had a big fight with Reg Jones when she excitedly told him about it, not because he was a prude about drugs, but because he feared she was being seduced by a lifestyle far removed from the small-town Southern girl with whom he had fallen in love.

Britney Jean Spears was being turned into a product. With increasing speed and sureness her image was being crafted to create maximum impact with the record-buying audience. Every possible aspect of her 'pop princess' persona would be exploited, leaving no possible stone unturned in the relentless pursuit of the almighty dollar. And, it mattered little how many times she or her entourage played it down, the Britney Spears who exploded into the public consciousness in 1998 was all about sex. The accompanying ingenuousness merely augmented the overpowering perfume of Lolita posturing.

The only saving grace as far as Britney is concerned is the

uncertainty of how calculating she personally was in the creation of her product image. She was a young girl swept along in the excitement of it all, working hard and doing, more or less, as she was told. The conception that it all began when the idea for the video of '... Baby One More Time' popped into her head is taking public gullibility too far. She had already begun wearing a school tie when she embarked on her tour of twenty-six shopping malls, sponsored by *Teen* and *Seventeen* magazines in the summer of 1998. Her whole ensemble was a pair of tartan trousers, a white shirt tied up above her midriff and a bright yellow tie with a big knot. Her hair was in two bunches tied with a little red scrunchie. The blouse was a double for the one that would eventually feature in the notorious schoolgirl video.

By now, the very first Britney Spears single '... Baby One More Time' had been produced and was ready to hit radio stations all over the country. It was essential to get as much air play as possible. The modern way of selling a successful record is to get it played as often as possible before the public can buy it in the shops. Britney hurled herself into the hard sale, although she did draw the line at being asked to ride a steer for a radio promotion.

Back in New York it was time to devise and rehearse the video to accompany the release of the first single. Another member of the Jive 'family', Nigel Dick, was hired to direct it. He already had a peerless reputation in music as one of the foremost video directors with a list of credits including Backstreet Boys and 'N Sync. They are just part of a multi-award-winning résumé which includes more than 270 music videos. By the time he teamed up with Britney he was probably best known in the UK for directing the videos of 'Shout' and 'Everybody Wants to Rule the World' for Tears for Fears and 'Wonderwall' and 'Champagne Supernova' for Oasis.

Nigel flew into New York to meet Britney for the first time and get a feel for what might work. She was in the Alley Cat dance studio working out in her usual sweats, which might explain why the first idea he had was not his best. He admitted, 'It sucked.' The basic plot involved Britney as a superhero, a comic-strip blend of Power Rangers and Warrior Princess. Britney absolutely hated it, believing quite rightly that it would strike no chord with teenagers of her age. For the first time she started to stick up for her own artistic rights. She may be a 'Yes, sir' and 'Yes, ma'am' sort of girl but she knew the importance of this video. She confided in Lynne that she was going to look a fool if they went ahead with Power Brit and her mother urged her to come up with something better. She rang Nigel and suggested a video in which she was stuck in a classroom thinking about boys.

The director immediately saw the possibilities and wrote a treatment based on that single idea. Britney also came up with the look of a St Trinian's nymphet based, consciously or subconsciously, on the old Mickey Mouse dance routine from a few years before. It oozed forbidden sex appeal. She tied her white blouse up to reveal her navel just as she had been doing in the shopping malls – nothing is ever quite as original as it seems. The suits at Jive Records loved the concept. Barry Weiss, the label's president and a great supporter of Britney's, recalled going to the studio to watch the rehearsal and being astounded at how Britney changed from being a demure, Southern girl-next-door to a sex cub the moment the song's famous first three chords kicked in. He said, 'I left the room thinking this was much bigger than I thought.' Weiss and others were soon to realize that the camera totally loved her.

Britney decided that she wanted her boyfriend Reg to play her love interest in the video. He would go over to the studio, hang out with the dancers and watch her rehearse whenever he could get time off from work. Fe was also cast as the spectacle-wearing schoolmarm. Nigel Dick had chosen to shoot the whole thing at Venice High School, which as Ryedell High, had been the location for the film of *Grease*, starring John Travolta and Olivia Newton John. It would mean everybody jetting off to LA for a few days. Just before they were due to leave Reg and Britney had another big argument, an occurrence which was getting far too frequent. Reg had learned that the next phase on the journey to world domination was going to be her first tour, as the supporting act for 'N Sync. Britney had long confided in Reg that she and Justin Timberlake had enjoyed a special connection when they were together on *The Mickey Mouse Club* and he was none too happy at their renewing acquaintance night after night. He was dead right to be worried, but probably achieved nothing more than pushing Britney a little faster into the arms of a potential rival.

She told him, 'If you hadn't have got into a fight with me you would be in my video. Instead of you, I'm getting Chad.'

The Chad in question was a handsome, square-jawed cousin who worked as a model for Abercrombie and Fitch. He ended up being the guy in the video who chucks the basketball. While Britney was in Los Angeles, Reg packed in his job, packed up his suitcase and headed home to McComb. He has never again visited the city. He did not realize at the time but his status quo as

Britney's boyfriend was compromised from that day forward. It did not strike home immediately. When he was back home he would pop over to see Lynne a couple of times a week to watch the progress videos of the shoot. He was still excited for Britney.

The final version is not high art but high energy. It begins with a wistful Britney sitting in a classroom, intensely bored. The bell rings and a now slightly surly Britney can dance down the school hallway. The provocative sequence has become one of the most famous in the history of pop videos. The action switches outside where, now in gymwear, Britney shows off the athletic quality of her dancing. In the gym she sings poutingly from the bleachers while watching a young man (Chad) for whom she is evidently pining moodily. Another group dance to the chorus before the teacher (Fe) breaks the spell of what had been a daydream all along.

In the space of three minutes the video to '. . . Baby One More Time' encapsulated the emotions of being a young teenage girl. Here was a pop singer adolescents could relate to and seek to emulate. The simple cleverness of it was to appeal to both sexes. Girls wanted to be like Britney and boys wanted to be with her. The image of a stereotypical sexpot schoolgirl would also ensure that more controlling influences in the world of media would take immediate notice of Britney Spears.

Britney's world had been moving so fast that everyone had forgotten about the record. Lynne was in the gym when she first heard her daughter declare 'Oh Baby, Baby' on the radio. She burst into tears. Reg Jones was behind the wheel of a tractor, pulling his truck out of a ditch in the middle of the forest. He shouted for his friends to come hear. Britney herself was in the back of Lynne's car on her way out of the parking lot at New

Orleans airport, having just flown in from New York. She screamed. She thought it was kismet, not realizing that Lynne had spent all morning setting it up with the local radio station.

Behind the scenes the financial situation had become desperate. It was no longer just a case of being thrifty. Debts had spiralled out of control with problems over mortgage and car repayments. Jamie and Lynne filed for bankruptcy on 17 July 1998. Records showed that they had earned $21,000 during the year but their debts had spiralled to $190,000. Reg Jones recalls the bankruptcy but also remembers the family not making such a big deal of it. But if anyone ever needed a lottery win, it was the Spears family. They were about to get one.

'. . . Baby One More Time' had a phenomenal initial success but it was greatly assisted by something usually forgotten in the hype that surrounded Britney. *Total Request Live* (*TRL*) was launched by MTV on 14 September 1998 and Britney in her school uniform would be the first star of a show that quickly became the essential showcase in pop music. *TRL*'s blend of video requests and live interviews, hosted by the charismatic Carson Daly, made it the station's top-rated show with a tame teenage audience of a million who could make a career in the time it took to spend their allowance. The only surprise was that Daly, all eyes and teeth, had not begun his career as a Mouseketeer. Many of the biggest stars in pop music, Madonna and Michael Jackson included, owed a great deal to their exposure on MTV, which was up and running in 1981. Immediately prior to the launch of *TRL*, MTV had been in danger of becoming stale. *TRL* breathed fresh life into the brand just as record companies were waking up to the fact that twelve and thirteen year olds were buying more records than ever before.

One month after the debut of *TRL*, Britney's own debut was sitting at number seventeen in the Billboard Hot 100 chart. This was a breathless time. The 'N Sync tour was ready to begin in Orlando on 17 November. Being the opening act is never the long straw but, nevertheless, an essential part of growing up in the music business. 'N Sync had supported Janet Jackson. Now it was their turn to be the headliners. The thousands of screaming girls were not too bothered about the girl in the video on *TRL*. They were there to see Justin, JC, Joey, Chris and Lance, not the girl who couldn't spell Brittany. It could have been a disaster waiting to happen. Britney told *Billboard* magazine, 'There were all these girls in the audience but I was able to win them over in the end. I have guy dancers and believe me, that helps.' Her other ace was the growing popularity of her hit song. There is nothing worse than a support act coming on and showcasing a few songs that nobody knows: 'I was able to look out and see people singing along. It was really cool.'

Britney was nervous but she also had years of training to fall back on. It helped that Lynne, Jamie and Jamie Lynn all flew down from Kentwood. Reg was with them too. They all chatted before the concert, which kept her calm. The Spears family already knew Justin from *The Mickey Mouse Club* days and were pleased to see him. They were certainly more pleased to see him than Reg. He looked on sullenly, an outsider, while Lynne and Jamie talked to the star of the show, looking glamorous in a bright red silk shirt. The performance went well and the four of them sat in a row, with Jamie Lynn perched happily on Reg's lap.

The after-show dinner and drinks was a time of relief and celebration. Jamie Lynn was beside herself with excitement and pride. She put on one of Britney's shirts from the show and went around the restaurant telling all the other diners, 'You see my shirt. This is my sister Britney's shirt. She sang tonight. She's gonna do good. She's gonna be big!' It was just the start for Britney, albeit a good one, and she had to do it all again the following night. It was also the beginning of the end for Reg: 'Mr Jamie introduced me as Britney's boyfriend but Miss Lynne, who had all the control, told me she was going to introduce me as Britney's "friend". She goes, "It's not going to look good for Britney and she's not going to be able to do what she can do if she has a boyfriend." That was the first sign for me of the shape of the future. It was bullshit.'

To be fair to Britney she had never tried to airbrush Reg out of the picture. She had introduced him to everyone in New York, had taken him to dinner with Larry Rudolph at the Golden Corral restaurant on the main strip of McComb. She had even wanted him to be part of her first video. Reg was a somebody in his hometown but a nobody in Britney's new environment. She was not yet a big enough star to carry a Mr Britney. Commentators who thought Reg would be Britney's first and last non-celebrity boyfriend were underestimating her. Inevitably, Britney Spears the 'product' was entering the Faustian pact that all stars make: manipulating and misleading the fans in order to promote an image. Kylie Minogue denied that she and Jason Donovan were boy and girlfriend when they were practically living together in a shack at the bottom of his father's garden. Britney would soon embark on her most blatant lie: that she was not Justin Timberlake's girlfriend when clearly she was.

The perceived wisdom for all teen stars is that they cannot admit to having anyone in their lives because it makes them less available to fans, thereby less attractive and, ultimately, less commercial. It would be easier for Britney to reach the top if no one knew she was dating – whether it was Reg Jones or Justin Timberlake. Reg had a name check on the sleeve of the album *. . . Baby One More Time*, but it was no consolation.

The combination of exposure on the tour and *TRL* saw the single continue to climb relentlessly up the charts. Britney had to get used to life on the road, in a tour bus with her four dancers, her hair and make-up assistant, and Fe for company. 'N Sync were old hands, having been on the road, almost without a break, for three years.

Britney shared the support duties on the first part of the tour with a German group called Sweetbox. After Christmas, their place was taken by the young Irish, all-girl group B*Witched. Ironically, B*Witched would probably have topped the bill if the tour had been in the UK. They were in the middle of a purple patch. Their first four British singles topped the charts – a feat they achieved before Westlife were up and running and something not even the Beatles had managed. They were just starting to try for a breakthrough in the US.

It was a gruelling schedule for Britney of thirty-two dates in two months, with a week off at Christmas. Things could scarcely have gone better except when the show rolled into Nashville, Tennessee on 11 December. Her father Jamie, his younger brother Austin and Reg Jones turned up drunk before the show at the Fox Theatre. They had been working up in Memphis and drove down with a couple of other workmates in a motor home (an RV). Reg recalls, 'On the way there Mister Jamie bought beer. Her uncle Austin got so drunk before the show, he was hollering and yelling at her. He just upset her so bad. She told him never to come back. It was just such a big thing because Austin was being a real ass and made Britney cry before the concert. She was embarrassed that it was a member of her family acting like that in front of all these people. He was being an idiot.'

Britney had warned Reg about going off to work with her father but he had gone anyway, not realizing that the power in the Spears family had shifted from male to female: 'I thought Mister Jamie was looking out for me and I figured that by hanging out with him it would mean I wasn't a secret boyfriend any more.' The reality was that Reg joined a lifestyle of drinking far too much. Britney was less than amused when she could smell it on Reg's breath before the concert.

On the way back to Nashville in the RV things did not get any better: 'Austin was raising hell, out of his mind drunk, so Jamie just snapped and attacked him. He pushed his finger down into his eyeball and one of the other men had a gun so they pushed Austin out of the RV. They told him that if he didn't promise to settle down they would put him out on the side of the road.'

Meanwhile Britney had to go on stage and pretend that nothing was wrong. All this was going on against a backdrop of a carefully nurtured image of a sweet Southern girl who had no idea she was a nubile dream. Unsurprisingly, it was the last time she wanted to see Reg Jones or Austin Spears at one of her concerts. A shoulder to cry on would be close at hand – in the next tour bus.

Britney celebrated her seventeenth birthday on stage in Kalamazoo, Michigan. Justin and the guys made her day when they brought a cake onto her tour bus and then sang a barber shop version of 'Happy Birthday' for her. The day was made even better by the news that '. . . Baby One More Time' had officially sold 500,000 copies. Everything was moving so fast, like a juggernaut heading downhill with no brakes. The album, which she had started recording more than a year ago, was due for release in January and, incredibly, it was already time to schedule the release of her second single. The importance of this first tour should not be underestimated. Despite their relative obscurity in the UK, 'N Sync would end 1998 as one of the biggest grossing live acts in the US. The exposure of hanging onto their coat tails was worth much gold to Britney Spears.

Soon after the New Year the inevitable happened and '. . . Baby One More Time' reached the top of the US charts. It had taken Britney just eighteen months from singing into a tape recorder for Larry Rudolph to reach this pinnacle. The timing was perfect. The album of the same name was released and debuted at number one, giving her the win double that all stars dream of but few achieve.

The cover of the album confirmed suspicions that here was a girl being projected as younger than she was. The seventeen-year-old, doe-eyed and hands clasped in prayer, looked years younger on the cover, a gamine figure who might have passed for fourteen. The charitable view would be that she was being marketed to look the same age as the girls who would be buying the record. The less forgiving opinion would be that she was being projected as an innocent Lolita figure. The full-size picture inside showed a smiling Britney facing the camera while sitting astride a white chair. Britney would later protest that she had only been fifteen when some of the pictures were taken and was not especially happy with their use. The questions remain – did she get it and who was exploiting whom?

Britney's meteoric rise to world domination was cemented by

her British breakthrough, which was even more startling than the one in her home country. The combination of notorious video and classic pop song proved irresistible to British fans and media alike. When the single was released in February 1999 it broke the UK record for a debut act's first week sales with 464,000. '. . . Baby One More Time' went on to rack up nearly 1,500,000 sales, one of the top thirty selling singles of all time in the UK, more than any by Whitney Houston, Mariah Carey or Madonna. She became the youngest female to sell one million copies of a single in the UK.

Not everyone was impressed by the Britney phenomenon. The *NME* memorably described the package as 'kindergarten, cutesie-pie cack'.

'I don't want to be part of someone's Lolita thing.'

NINE

Justin

Britney was so excited she just could not wait to phone home with the news: 'I've just gotten to beat Leonardo Di Caprio at ping pong,' she shrieked.

Britney Spears and Justin Timberlake were made for each other. They were the teen dream couple; the Judy Garland and Mickey Rooney for a celebrity-obsessed generation. If not the king and queen of pop, they were certainly the prince and princess. Without exception, those that knew them as skinny youngsters say that there was always something special between them.

If their romance was a Hollywood script, a variation of *When Harry Met Sally*, then the first show-stopping scene would have been their duet on *The Mickey Mouse Club* when they sang an exhilarating version of 'I Feel For You' to each other. It made the hairs on the back of the neck stand up. Tony Lucca still recalls watching them perform it at the dress rehearsal before taping: 'You knew that these kids were going to be huge stars but you also knew that they were going to be together.'

Singing coach Bob Westbrook remembers the first time he

realized that there was a special connection between them. Neither of them knew he taught the other. He had been Justin's original singing teacher in Memphis but also taught students at his other base in McComb, Mississippi. When she was twelve, Britney would take lessons from him when she was between seasons of *The Mickey Mouse Club*. One day she took a tape out of her bag, declaring that she had something she really wanted him to hear. It was the duet with Justin and, of course, Bob recognized his other pupil at once.

'Oh, that's Justin,' said Bob as Britney's mouth fell open in amazement: 'She whipped round and asked me, "Do you know him?" and I said, "Sure I'm his teacher," and her jaw just dropped. They had both talked about their singing teacher but it had not clicked they were the same person because of the different locations. I could tell she was enamoured of him already. She had a childhood crush on him. Don't kid yourself. I could tell!'

Bob knew that Justin had been booked to perform 'The Star Spangled Banner' before the start of an ice-hockey game involving his local Memphis team. Bob asked Britney, 'Would you like to go up there and sing it with him?' She could not believe her good fortune. 'She was asking, "Could I really do that? Could you work that out for me?" So I just smiled and told her, "All I've got to do is make a phone call."'

Two phone calls later and Britney was on her way to Tennessee to sing in public with Justin Timberlake for the first time. Bob enjoys taking the credit: 'I like to tease people that I was the first one to match that love. I wasn't, but it sounds funny.'

Britney made the first of many happy trips to Shelby Forest, the rural community an hour from Memphis where Justin had been raised. She stayed with his grandparents Sadie and Bill

Bomar and sampled Sadie's legendary cooking and Southern hospitality. It was a comfortable reminder of the backwater where she lived, although Justin's roots were more obviously middle class and not at all beset with the financial problems suffered by Britney's parents.

Superficially, Justin and Britney followed very similar paths to success. A closer look, however, reveals that Justin trod the Yellow Brick Road in much more comfortable shoes. Both were indulged but no leap of imagination could see Justin Timberlake living in a one-bedroom apartment off Broadway coping with the disappointment of failed auditions and the possibility of not spending Christmas with his family and friends. He never had to face the periods of uncertainty and chronic fatigue that beset Britney.

One of the most popular misconceptions about Justin is that he is some hip sort of kid from Memphis, a white man born to a black musical heritage. Shelby Forest was more like being born in a pleasant Home Counties village, a stockbroker belt community, where children could travel up to the big city for special treats. His mother and stepfather lived in an exclusive road in a very comfortable house. It was like a gated community with no gate. The main highway between Memphis and the nearest town of Millington lies more than ten miles away. The area is so private that Tom Cruise rented a house nearby when he was filming *The Firm* here. The arrival in the neighbourhood of a real Hollywood star was the biggest event in the recent history of Shelby Forest. When Justin goes home he is still plain ol' Justin whereas this was Tom! His former headmistress Regina Castleberry observes, 'Tom Cruise was a star. Justin's one of us.'

Ms Castleberry's staff was caught up in the hysteria just as much as the pupils were. They slyly suggested to the crossing guard that she might want to let the children cross when Tom's limousine was about to pass by the school. When she obliged, the teachers of E.E. Jeter Elementary School could be seen scurrying to the gates for a proper look.

All the children in the Shelby Forest area went to Jeter's. It was still basically a white, middle-class community but there was no need for a private school to legally segregate. The black population was concentrated in and around Memphis, a city which forever has the stain of being the place where Martin Luther King was shot dead in 1968. The Ku Klux Klan had been founded in Pulaski, Tennessee, in 1866 although its more notorious deeds were further south in Mississippi.

Both Justin and Britney's mothers were tough and immensely loyal to their children. While Lynne Spears wanted her daughter to have opportunities that she never had in her devout, almost puritanical childhood, Lynn Harless was driven more by the difficulties of becoming a single mother when Justin was still a baby and, as a result, wanting to make sure she did the very best by a son deprived of his father. They both grew up in 'Bible Belt' country but Justin's environment, while Church orientated, somehow lacked the zeal of Kentwood and McComb.

Justin's mother, Lynn Bomar, was seventeen when she married Randy Timberlake who, like Jamie Spears, was in the building trade. Randy was only twenty and they were probably too young to settle down. Lynn was still just twenty when Justin was born and the marriage was over within two years. Both of Justin's parents were fortunate to remarry and find far more suitable relationships while still in their twenties. Randy married a local pharmacist and had two more sons. Lynn, who could not survive on child support, went to work in a bank in Millington and fell in love with the manager, Paul Harless.

Both second families live in Shelby Forest. Justin still regularly sees his father whom he calls 'Daddy' and his stepfather who is 'Dad'. Randy provides a greater musical influence than any of the Spears family. He still looks after the choir at his local church and has a resonant baritone voice. His ex-wife has commented, tongue in cheek, that a beautiful singing voice was the only thing Justin got from his father. Justin may have had some issues with his father – as Britney has had with hers – but these are in the past and the two have a decent relationship these days. Again, like Britney, he is much closer to his mother, a strong, dedicated woman. Justin has always been a momma's boy and Britney has always been a momma's girl.

His stepfather Paul, however, had a profound effect on the way Justin behaves. He set standards. In the notes for his album *Justified*, Justin writes in appreciation: 'More and more each day I understand what being a "man" is all about because of you'. This paternal code was no more evident than in the romantic way that Paul had always treated Justin's mother. Justin's first serious girlfriend, Danielle Ditto, explains, 'Justin is a total romantic because his stepdad is like that. He surprised me one Valentine's Day with a lovely dinner and I realized that was exactly the sort of thing Paul would have done for Lynn.'

Danielle enjoyed the benefits of Justin's romantic nature, as Britney would, but also felt the downside of that too idealistic approach. He put her on an impossible pedestal. Justin's expectations were so high that her perceived failure to live up to them would bring enormous pain to both of them. Britney would eventually suffer that same fate.

Justin and Britney's paths crossed for the first time on *The Mickey Mouse Club* but they could easily have met before. They both cut their show-business teeth singing in church and at local talent shows and were very successful. Britney's mother Lynne entered Britney for just one beauty contest in her life and thought it such a ghastly affair that she vowed her daughter would never be put through that ordeal again. Lynne had very strong views on the matter. As she wrote, feelingly, in *Heart to Heart*: 'When you lose a beauty contest, what can you work harder at? Being more beautiful?'

Justin, however, actually won a beauty contest when he was eleven. He swept the board at the Universal Charm Pageant in Nashville winning Best Model, Best Dressed, Best Sportswear, Most Handsome and Supreme Winner, picking up $15,000 for his triumph. It takes a degree of cocksure precociousness to be the only boy in a traditionally girls' domain. That Midas touch deserted him for once when he too lost at *Star Search*. Like Britney, he sang a number that barely suited him. He dressed up like a miniature Kenny Rogers to sing the country classic 'Two of a Kind', a famous Garth Brooks song. It was the first and last time he sang a country song in public.

Both Britney and Justin were recovering from that disappointment when they auditioned for Disney and met for the first time at the Mickey Mouse 'camp' in Orlando. They were both part of the successful seven and sat next to each other round the big table on their first afternoon as Mouseketeers. They were both too excited to bother too much with each other. Justin was more concerned about how he was going to be billed on the show. He had entered *Star Search* as Justin Randall – his second name – but he was not especially happy with that. The choice was an important one because it was this name that would stick with him for the rest of his professional life. Lynn Harless left it up to him and he chose Justin Timberlake because it was the name on his locker at school and he was used to it.

At *The Mickey Mouse Club*, Justin matured quickly through mixing with the older boys. His great asset was his intelligence and his ability to grasp concepts and ideas. He also had a great deal of charisma for one so young. He still spent time with Britney, however, buying ice creams at Jungle Jims on International Drive in Orlando or hanging out at Pleasure Island with the kids from the rival Nickelodeon shows. Dale Godboldo describes the blossoming relationship: 'Everybody could see Britney Spears and Justin Timberlake coming a mile away.'

One of the reasons why Justin and Britney were able to build such a bond is that *The Mickey Mouse Club* was the length and breadth of their world. It was a high school in miniature. Dale confirms that Disney were not keen on the Mouseketeers making friends with the public for fear of altering the carefully cultivated wholesome image of the cast. This proximity is one of the reasons why so many of the cast are such good friends today.

When the Mouse Club abruptly ended, both Justin and Britney went home to resume a normal life and embarked on their first proper relationships at the age of fourteen. One of the intriguing aspects of both young stars is that they have never particularly played the field. They were going steady at fourteen, Britney with Reg Jones and Justin with Danielle Ditto, and have been, more or less, continually in relationships since then. Justin is now on his fourth lengthy relationship and Britney is on her third.

Justin was just fourteen when he and Danielle, a petite and

very pretty blonde, made love for the first time. They had planned it carefully, even going together to buy condoms. It was, she says, 'romantic and sweet'. Justin told her, 'If nothing else, we'll always have this.' Justin was already displaying his romantic nature, even buying Danielle a 'promise' ring, which he gave to her on one knee as if it were a proposal. By this time, Justin had moved back to Orlando as part of 'N Sync and was beginning to struggle with the same problems of absence and mistrust that would infect Britney's relationship with Reg. They were eerily similar. While they were apart they relied on speaking to each other every day on the phone until Danielle's grandmother discovered her bill was $600 and promptly put a block on the phone – just as Reg's mother had done.

Worse was to come when Justin heard rumours that Danielle had enjoyed a fling with a fellow high-school student. It was not true but Justin was devastated. He rushed over to the school and confronted Danielle in the courtyard. 'He came up to me and he was crying,' she recalls. 'He said, "I can't believe you'd do this to me."' That confrontation was the beginning of the end for the couple. They dragged things out painfully for a few months before calling it a day. The very last words Danielle said to Justin were 'You're a prick', before slamming down the phone and hurling the 'promise' ring against the nearest wall.

Justin's romantic nature was up and running again when he met another girl who had grown up in Memphis. When Justin woos, he woos hard. He had never even kissed Veronica Finn when he had to fly to Europe for promotional work with 'N Sync. They had been introduced by his best friend Trace Ayala and enjoyed a laugh together but nothing more. Despite the obvious opportunities for a teenage boy-band member on tour in Europe,

Justin spent his evenings on the phone to Veronica, a girl he had met only once. 'He called me a lot,' she laughs.

They started to date when Justin returned but nothing very serious until Veronica was pencilled in to fill Britney's place in Innosense and moved to Orlando. She recalls, 'I was his girl and he treated me very respectfully. I think Justin does like being in love, most definitely. I think he can get engulfed in that.' Justin and Veronica became lovers and she praises him for being very gentle and caring, an unusual quality in a boy of his age. She laughs, 'Oh yeah, I've dated since then!'

Once more, different schedules and long absences did not make the heart grow fonder. Innosense were trying to follow the same path as 'N Sync so that it seemed when Justin was in Europe, Veronica was in Orlando, and vice versa. Long-distance phone calls became fraught, with unspoken jealousies taking the gloss off their romance. It all ended in late 1998 when Veronica left a message on Justin's answer phone telling him not to call back.

The question of when exactly Justin and Britney became an item is a grey area. Britney went on tour with 'N Sync in November 1998. Both Veronica and Reg Jones are not certain what happened. Veronica, who still sees Justin as a friend, maintains, 'We could have been seeing other people. But I wasn't and, I don't know, even to this day . . . he *says* he wasn't.'

Reg is convinced that Justin started pursuing Britney right from the beginning – even on the first night of the tour in Orlando: 'He was cool to me but I knew . . .' Intriguingly, Danielle Ditto had a boyfriend when Justin decided she was the girl for him and put his rival out of the picture. By the time of the Orlando leg of the Back II None tour Justin had morphed into a very glamorous young pop star. Britney too had been transformed from a scrawny kid into a very hot-looking teenager. For one thing, she was much blonder. Her hair colour seemed to get progressively lighter as her image became more sexual.

Britney almost certainly had cooled inexorably where Reg was concerned after the drunken debacle of the Nashville concert. He had not seen it that way and assumed they had not yet broken up for several months of 1999.

The rumours about Justin and Britney had started well before that. One early report suggested he had bought her a gold ring for her seventeenth birthday. She was still coming home every few weeks but she and Reg were getting along progressively less well. Reg puts the blame squarely on Justin's shoulders: 'I knew where she was on tour but I didn't know what she was doing. I knew who she was with and I know he was definitely trying to persuade her or do whatever it took to get her to be with him instead of me. I feel that one hundred per cent.'

One afternoon in early spring 1999, when she was at home, Reg popped into her house to get a jacket he had left there. Britney was sitting on the sofa talking to Justin on the telephone. Reg went through to Bryan's bedroom to retrieve his coat and then came back and demanded to know who she was talking to: 'She said "It's none of your business." I said, "You're nothing but a fucking bitch" and slammed the door. And that was that.'

It was a horrible way to end things and Reg has regretted it ever since: 'I hated it the way it ended because she was my best friend as well as my girlfriend. I could talk to her about anything and the same held true for her with me. We would talk and we would sing to the radio going down the road and it was a fine time in my life, hanging with her.'

A short time later Britney told a journalist that the problem with Reg was that he had become insecure and that she had just woken up one day and the magic had gone. She also admitted that she had been head over heels in love and said, 'I don't think I'll ever love somebody like that again.' The break-up was still very fresh in her mind and Reg Jones had been her first love. She had been fourteen when they started dating and was eighteen when they finally called it a day. He receives a mention in the acknowledgements of her first album before being consigned to history.

Reg is looking for a closure with Britney that he will probably now never attain. The only time he has kissed her since that awful afternoon was a courtesy greeting on the cheek when she and Justin returned to Kentwood in December 2001 for the funeral of her great grandmother Lexie. He even chatted politely to Justin.

He can never put Britney to the back of his mind. Not a week goes by without her staring back at him from the cover of a magazine. He hears her voice every time he turns on the radio of his truck. She is featured on the news or in her weekly reality television series, *Chaotic*. He goes to Ruby Tuesday's restaurant in McComb and her picture hangs in the lobby. He goes to Nyla's in Osyka and a whole room is a shrine to Britney. There is no escape.

Reg still wishes he had been able to show more trust and that they had hung on for another six months, at least until she had finished touring with Justin. His mother, however, is probably right and they were doomed when she left Kentwood to pursue the dream of Britney Spears, superstar.

Despite his eligibility, Reg has not had a serious girlfriend since Britney, although, in a slightly spooky twist, his first dates after they split were with a girl called Brittney. He tried his hand at a career in the US Navy but found it was not for him and has returned to McComb where he at his happiest, working in insurance and hunting in the forest like he always has. He still visits the lake where he and Britney lay on their backs and gazed at the stars, but the old pier is dilapidated and broken.

Justin has revealed that the first time he and Britney had a real date was when they went out to dinner in Los Angeles. A glimpse at the tour schedule reveals that they were in California in early January 1999. They were both quizzed by *MTV News* later in the month about the rumours that they were dating. Britney said, 'It's not true. They ['N Sync] are just like big brothers to me. I guess they assume that, because we were on *Mickey Mouse Club* together.' Justin treated it like a joke: 'I am actually dating Britney. We've been together for seven years. I'm dating her and two of her dancers.'

The world of celebrity rumour is a peculiarly contrary one. If a bit of gossip is met with an outright denial then it is probably true. If the reaction is more coy, a 'maybe', to keep the story bubbling along, then it is probably false. The cynical use of this tactic, when stars have new records coming out or new films to promote, is a tried and tested one. The Justin/Britney rumours began several months too late for that. They were both sitting at the top of the charts and had little to gain. It was far better at this stage to let the public believe nothing was going on and that they were both available for a million and more fantasies around the world.

'They just had the biggest crushes on each other that you ever saw.'

TEN

Virginity or Bust

Darlene Hughes had no idea if success had changed her old student when she went to see her in concert in New Orleans. She said hello backstage and then watched as Britney went over to a teenage girl in a wheelchair, squatted down beside her and spent several minutes making a fuss of her. 'It just warmed my heart,' said Darlene.

The reality of Britney's relationship with Justin Timberlake is that they did not live their lives in each other's pocket. In 1999, in particular, Britney's life was a total whirl of promotion and performance that left little time for affairs of the heart. She did move to Orlando where Justin was living, ostensibly so that she could be close to Johnny Wright, who based himself in the city and who was busy setting up Britney's first solo tour. In February, both the album and the single '. . . Baby One More Time' were certified platinum, signifying sales in excess of one million. She had no need to hang on to the coat-tails of 'N Sync.

It seems ridiculous now but Jive had tried to bolster Britney's album by giving a 'sneak' preview of the new Backstreet Boys release. After her own music had ended with Track 12, a version of the 1967 Sonny and Cher hit 'And The Beat Goes On', Britney enthusiastically declares, in her best Southern voice, that she has 'something very special' for everyone. It was ten seconds of three songs from *Millennium*, the new Backstreet Boys album. The whole thing left a cheesy taste in the mouth, especially when Britney declared that she thought the song 'I'll Be the One' was going to be 'number one'. She also managed to squeeze in a quick plug for her live shows. The strategy may well have worked. By the end of the year the respective albums were the two biggest sellers in the US.

Britney's debut album would make it to number one in fifteen countries. The impact in the UK was huge. The now notorious schoolgirl video received just as much attention in Britain as it had across the Atlantic. It was overkill on the music channels. Britney would become the youngest million-selling female singer in the history of the UK singles chart. '. . . Baby One More Time' remained in the singles chart for six months while the album of the same name, released in March, stayed in the album charts for more than eighteen months.

The promotional schedule was a punishing one. She appeared on the *Donny and Marie* (Osmond) television show and was booked to appear on the *Tonight Show* with Jay Leno, a good indication of 'arrival'. Disaster struck, however, when she was rehearsing the dance moves for the video to accompany her second single, 'Sometimes', another Max Martin song. The single was not due to be released until June but Britney's life was planned to the minute months in advance. She performed a high kick as one of the dance moves and felt her left knee go pop. Britney was an experienced and accomplished dancer and she instantly knew that something was wrong. She was crying and hysterical while her fellow dancers tried to calm her and helpfully suggested she put ice on it and rest up.

Her injured knee failed to respond to either ice or rest and, a few days later, she was advised that she would need surgery. Britney was little more than three months into her career as a star and the nearest she had come to an operation until then was dental work. She was seventeen and could be forgiven for seeing her ruined career flash before her eyes. The operation itself, which was performed by Dr Tim Finney, chief doctor of the New Orleans Saints American Football team, is a relatively common and simple one. She had a one-inch chip of cartilage floating about in the knee and this was removed. Modern arthroscopic techniques are so advanced that scarring was practically invisible.

Dr Finney advised Britney that she needed to rest for a month and it was decided that she should go home to Kentwood, where Lynne could look after her. She did find the energy to appear on a live MTV event hosted by Carson Daly, where she received the sympathy of a TV nation as she arrived in a wheelchair and then spent the show wrapped in blankets. Afterwards, she went home to endure daily physiotherapy to get her back on her feet.

The case of the twisted knee is long forgotten but her enforced absence from public scrutiny produced one of the great unsolved mysteries of the life of Britney Spears. She emerged from Kentwood with much larger breasts. They were, she said, just the result of a 'growth spurt'. Reg Jones, however, thinks differently. When he knew Britney, she simply felt that she did not have a big enough bust: 'We were still dating and she brought up the possibility of a boob job in discussion. I disagreed at the time and told her to wait until she was eighteen and I said that her dad was against it anyway. But she said her mom had had one and she wanted one. It would make her look better on stage if she had bigger breasts.'

'I wasn't in the theatre when she had it but in my opinion she did it.'

Justin Timberlake, when he was asked about Britney's apparently larger breasts, neatly deflected the question: 'I don't know about her breasts . . . I was too busy staring at her butt.' This was probably quite truthful because Justin's former girlfriends confirm that a big 'booty' was definitely something he favoured.

Very few stars ever admit to a boob job preferring blatant denial, hoping the cock never crows three times. The principal drawback to admitting any enhancement, at least as far as Britney is concerned, is that it makes her image appear transparently calculating. Innocence is more appealing if it is more natural and less faked. The controversy was quite helpful in terms of keeping her in the public eye at a critical time. Internet sites sprang up showing before and after pictures and inviting users to vote on whether they thought Britney had undergone a boob job. At first, the official line from Britney's camp was that it was a personal matter.

The speculation reached a crescendo with the publication in April 1999 of Britney's first in-depth interview with *Rolling Stone* magazine, the bible of the music business. There was no concealing the overt sexuality of the piece, nor the accompanying pictures which fuelled the boob-job rumours and endorsed the Lolita image that had originated with the schoolgirl sexpot video for '. . . Baby One More Time.' By any standards, it was a deliberately provocative image. Britney, in a black push-up bra and skimpy briefs, posed on purple satin sheets with a Teletubby in one hand and a pink telephone in the other. Her lips, coated in a frosted-pink lip gloss were parted in an obviously suggestive manner. Inside the magazine, another picture showed Britney slurping an ice cream while bending over to reveal the word 'Baby' painted on her pert derrière. A girl's bicycle stood next to her. The photographer David LaChapelle had conducted the shoot at Britney's home. She posed in bra and hot pants in her own bedroom surrounded by her doll collection.

In terms of 'the' Britney, these images were inspired. They created controversy, generated a goldmine's worth of publicity and created a million and more lustful new fans. The writer Steven Daly did his bit by introducing his piece by describing Britney extending a 'honeyed thigh' across her sofa and referring to her 'ample chest'. He also posed the very relevant question: 'Is Spears jailbait, jaded crossover diva or malleable Stepford teen?'

The question remains unanswered, at least directly. Daly, however, did perhaps unintentionally reveal part of the answer by spending most of the article describing Britney at home as a very ordinary, family-orientated, Southern girl. Lynne spent the interview folding laundry and fixing Britney her favourite grilled cheese sandwich. In effect, the pictures were of 'the Britney'; Britney Spears, the newest teen sensation. The text, however, was about the girl Britney. It was blindingly obvious that the pictures were an artificial creation, projecting an image to make sure that Britney was going to be a name in the spotlight for years to come, not just for one record.

Intriguingly, Jive was not totally convinced that Britney would last, despite their financial commitment. One record company insider, who obviously cannot risk being named, explains, 'They were a little bit worried that she was going to do just one or maybe two albums. The fact that she went so big has a lot to do with her personal drive.'

Britney admitted to *TV Guide* that the *Rolling Stone* 'thing' was not really her. 'It was like dress-up, to see myself in a different way.' She also vigorously denied having breast implants, claiming that she had put on twenty-five pounds in weight since she first signed to Jive two years earlier.

The *Rolling Stone* controversy refused to go away. The influential and very straight-laced American Family Organization (based in Tupelo, Mississippi, birthplace of Elvis Presley) denounced Britney publicly, spokesman Tim Wildmon declaring that she displayed a 'disturbing mix of childhood innocence and adult sexuality'. He also called on all 'God-loving Americans to boycott stores selling Britney albums'. Commercially, such a high-profile pronouncement on a star so early in her career was fantastic news. There is nothing better for street credibility than the sound of outraged conservatism getting on its high horse. In the UK it was as good as being savaged by Mary Whitehouse. No wonder the single '. . . Baby One More Time' sold more than 8.5 million copies around the world. For good measure, the offending issue of the magazine sold out.

Another Church organization, the Church of Scotland's Board of Responsibility, joined in on the side of disapproval, stating that it was important that famous people behave responsibly: 'The message they send out should be constructive rather than destructive of a positive lifestyle.'

The question that the *Rolling Stone* article did not raise was: *How aware was Britney of what was going on?* Did she just go along with everything because of her inherent childlike trust, or had years of hard work and preparation for stardom given her the hard edge to make the right decisions for herself and her professional future? The same record company insider is in no doubt, 'She was always going to do it her way and she got her way right from the start. But she can make a stupid decision.'

It would be very surprising if Britney's people were not given the opportunity to 'sign off' on the cover and picture content before publication. Picture approval is a staple ingredient of any media contract. Later in the year Britney said in an online interview that she thought the pictures came out really well and that the whole shoot had been very laid back. Journalist Hettie Judah, writing in the *Guardian*, caught the mood. 'For her age Britney is a highly astute marketing woman, and knows exactly who she is selling to. Fifteen-year-old girls may buy her singles, but it is hard to imagine that she doesn't know who else will enjoy watching the video to ". . . Baby One More Time".'

A year later and Britney is more straightforward in discussing her image with *Rolling Stone*. 'That's not me. It was about being in a magazine and playing a part for that magazine. It's like on TV, if you see Jennifer Love Hewitt or Sarah Michelle Gellar kill someone, do you think that means they go out and do that? Of course not.'

Britney did finally concede that being a sex object for men old enough to be her father was not something she wanted to think about. 'It freaks me out,' she declared.

The overt Madonnaesque controversy did seem to conflict with Britney's more wholesome Christian beliefs. Her stock answer on such occasions is to claim that it is perfectly all right as long as she personally is comfortable with what she has done. Her quotes about it all being laid-back would appear to confirm that. She would always question why it was such a big deal and point out that she had really strong morals.

The next controversial topic in Britney's life was either a guilty reaction to that religious conflict or a realization that playing the private virgin off against the public slut was a stroke of PR genius. Other teen stars like Tiffany and Debbie Gibson never seemed to progress in the public persona. Britney's role model, however, was Madonna, always changing and never predictable. Britney progressed into being the most famous virgin in the US.

Friends of Reg Jones remain convinced that he and Britney slept together. Reg has never admitted this, which has won him many admirers. Schoolfriend Lindey Hughes Magee observes, 'He said nothing but nice things about her. Good for him. It would have been easy for him to be a jerk.' Reg received thanks from an unexpected source for his discretion where Britney was concerned. Her father Jamie rang him and thanked him: 'He said "I just want to thank you for saying what you said in the proper manner."'

Britney told a German magazine that she was a virgin and intended to remain so until she was married. It was a statement which reaffirmed her Christian values in the eyes of the public. She admitted that she wanted sex like any normal girl but wanted to wait until it was in a committed marriage. Perhaps Britney was really saying that she wanted to marry Justin Timberlake. Statements regarding chastity are always met with a healthy dollop of scepticism by the British public, if not by the moral majority of the Deep South. The virginity question became quite comical when Justin Timberlake found himself entangled in it and had to be a virgin as well. His grandmother, Sadie Bomar, was quoted in *heat* magazine reportedly claiming that both Justin and Britney were virgins and that Justin did not believe in sex before marriage because 'Justin has high moral values and has not slept with anyone'.

The remarks were well meaning and well intentioned from a loving grandmother reflecting her own high moral standards but Justin's sexual history makes a mockery of them. His first girl-friend Danielle Ditto has revealed that they were keen to have as much sex as possible when Justin was fourteen. He subsequently also enjoyed an intimate relationship with his second serious girlfriend, Veronica Finn. Both girls were nice about his prowess as a lover. At the time nobody knew about this so it was perfectly reasonable, if a little unbelievable, for Justin to declare, 'I'm probably the only guy my age that I know who's a virgin. And that's OK with me.'

Now, in hindsight, we are expected to believe that he was prepared to cease all sexual activity when he started dating Britney Spears.

Unsurprisingly, an anonymous businessman contacted Jive and offered the sum of $10 million, give or take a million, for the pleasure of relieving Britney of her virginity. Britney failed to find it funny. 'It's a disgusting offer. He should go and have a cold shower and leave me alone.' Exactly how such an offer was made public remains a mystery, but it was obviously a cheapskate bid. Britney the brand was worth a great deal more than that.

The real question of Britney's virginity is not *if* but *when*. She was evasive about even dating Justin for so long that there was little prospect of her admitting that they were lovers. The nearest she got was in May 2000 when she admitted, 'I adore him.' But, even then, she declined to confirm that they were boyfriend and girlfriend. The same old coy angle could be trotted out again, claiming that they just hung out and mainly talked when they met. She also screamed that her manager was going to kill her when she confided that she had kissed Justin.

It was the worst-kept secret. Whenever there was a need to promote something new then the 'are they/aren't they' saga dragged on. In September 2001 she was moved to declare, 'I'm not ashamed to say that I love him from the bottom of my heart.' That was just as well because, by that time, they were living together in Los Angeles and friends who went to visit them described them as an 'old, married couple'.

When Britney was with Justin – the real Britney not the product Britney – she would be unrecognizable to the fans who desperately wanted more information. She was quiet, modest and thoughtful. Tony Lucca recalls one visit: 'He was wiped out and she was very tired. We were just hanging out and catching up and she didn't have much to say. I definitely got the sense that she had been through a great deal.' Dale Godboldo observes, 'They were like old souls. I think 80 per cent of what they had together was shared experience but that can and does lead to love.'

Away from the spotlight, they were a couple who very rarely let the public into their true lives. The tenderness between the two of them, however, could not be concealed for ever. Justin was quite soppy about Britney. They were photographed draped all over each other at her eighteenth birthday party in December 1999. For her nineteenth birthday in 2000, when their love affair was at its most romantic, he ordered twenty-six dozen roses to be placed in her suite at the La Quinta hotel in Palm Springs. He didn't stop there. He arranged for the petals of another ten dozen roses to be scattered on the carpet and on the bed. It was like something out of the romance novels Britney liked to read. The roses were for Pinky, Justin's pet name for Britney and the one he used for her on the 'N Sync album *Celebrity* when he said he could not breathe without her.

On the evening of her nineteenth birthday she appeared on stage at an 'N Sync concert in San Diego wearing a wig and glasses, which fooled no one. Justin and the boys tried to get the crowd to sing 'Happy Birthday Britney' but were met with a degree of good-natured booing from the female fans who were there for Timberlake. The following month they were at the Rock in Rio festival where they reportedly shared a suite for three days and nights, eating Britney's favourite fried chicken and chips and drinking cans of cola. Not long afterwards she declared she was having difficulty keeping her pledge of chastity.

When Britney went with Justin to his home in Shelby Forest, she proved to be very popular. The local preacher, Brother Barney Austin, and his wife Pat were visiting Justin's grandparents when the young couple popped in. 'She had a peaches and cream skin,' recalls Pat. 'She didn't wear much make-up. He came over and gave us a big hug. She was very nice.' An old school friend of Justin's saw them together several times at concerts in Nashville and Chattanooga: 'She's beautiful – a girl who would turn a head when she walked down the street, but also when she walked into a room you wanted to be around her because she has one of those vibrant personalities. She and Justin seemed to have a lot in common. I most noticed what good friends they were. They were comfortable with each other – you could tell that by the way they kept criticizing one another.'

Britney clearly felt right at home in Tennessee. She would go shopping with Justin's mother at Wal-Mart in the nearby town of Millington. One Christmas it was announced on the local radio that Britney was shopping at the giant chain store. Within minutes it was complete chaos, with cars flooding the approach road trying to get into the car park just to get a glimpse of her.

The couple were not as widely seen in Britney's home patch. For one thing the family home was not as secure, being quite near the highway, and they were fed up with gawping fans and souvenir hunters who would even try to make off with dirt from the backyard. When Serenity was built, it was much more secluded and offered little chance for photographers or fans to spot their prey unless they decided to leave.

Justin did join Britney for the funeral of great-grandmother Lexie in 2001. The Granny of Granny's Seafood was the rock of the Spears clan and had followed her great-granddaughter's career with all the enthusiasm of a teenage fan.

Britney's time with Justin was happy and comfortable. Besides the shared experiences, they both loved basketball and could laugh at the same things. He called her Pinky and she called him Stinky. They were also both expert in pulling goofy faces, the very antithesis of the polished smiles they had spent so long perfecting.

Justin also likes to shop, especially for clothes and jewellery, which is the fastest way to Miss Spears's heart. He gave her a ring which cost $100,000. She once spent that in an afternoon in Beverley Hills, buying him an array of expensive Christmas presents. American gossip journalist Janet Charlton says she hit the boutiques of Rodeo Drive and came away with leather jackets, leather coats, leather trousers, cashmere sweaters and jewellery. She bought him a $30,000 diamond-encrusted watch engraved with the words, 'To my Justin, love you always'. Britney is extremely generous when she is in love.

Justin has a sure touch when it comes to spoiling the woman in his life. For her nineteenth birthday he gave her, among other presents, a day at her favourite health spa. On her twentieth he bought her a dozen presents including some silver candelabras, Baccarat crystal glasses and a teddy bear in her favourite colour of baby blue.

They also treated each other to fantastic holidays. Britney whisked Justin off to the Caribbean for a week where he described their romantic idyll as being straight out of the *Blue Lagoon*. He took her to a log cabin in the mountains of Vail, Colorado, for New Year.

During their time together, Britney was far more famous than Justin Timberlake in the UK. She was justifiably placed at the top of the tree of young female stars. Justin was a member of a boy band which was not in the same league as Take That or Backstreet Boys. Justin was Mr Spears. In the US it was an entirely different story. 'N Sync were arguably the biggest American band. Their 2000 album *No Strings Attached* was the fastest-selling album of all time, selling 2.4 million copies in the first week. The accompanying 52-date tour generated ticket receipts of $40 million. When Justin finally went solo it was the equivalent of Paul McCartney starting off on his own.

For a while they were the number one fairy-tale couple in the world – their popularity far more widespread than Posh and Becks or Brad and Jen. Only the ill-starred Charles and Diana generated a greater fascination. Could any relationship stand such intense scrutiny? The low point came when hackers placed a hoax announcement on the Internet that Britney and Justin had been killed in a car crash. It was apparently a joke but that did not stop the rumours spreading like wildfire that their car had been in collision with a pretzel truck. The source of the story turned out to be two disc jockeys. A spokesman had to officially deny that it was true. In the aftermath of the very real death of Princess Diana in a Paris car crash, it was not exactly a funny spoof.

A few months later Justin and Britney were staying at a mansion in Destin, Florida, when thieves broke in and stole video equipment and clothes belonging to the couple. A story quickly went round that they also made off with a video tape allegedly containing footage of Justin and Britney making out. Police arrested a gang of teenagers before they had the chance to post the film on the Internet or try and blackmail them. The exact nature of the content remains a secret. It all added spice to the interest in the exact nature of their sex life.

Britney spent the majority of her relationship with Justin Timberlake either denying they were a couple or maintaining she was a virgin. Just when everybody was getting bored, they split up. Ironically, as soon as they were no longer a couple they seemed to be sharing far too much information about their physical relationship.

'There's something about Britney that is somewhat calculated and entirely intentional.'

ELEVEN

Do It Again

After a successful concert in Virginia Beach, Florida, the girls from Innosense, the support act on Britney's first solo tour, headed up the coast to the beautiful Heather Beach for some sun, surf and relaxation. Britney declined the chance to go with them. She stayed behind to do a sound check.

Touring can be an exhausting and tedious part of the music business. Justin would try and drop by if he could but he had his own schedule so Britney had to cope by herself staying in anonymous hotels and motels, travelling between gigs in her tour bus and trying to remember what town she was in when she thanked the fans for turning up. At least she had Felicia and Big Rob with her.

Big Rob was a massive minder called Rob Feggins who had been hired after Felicia and Britney had a security scare in New York when fans mobbed them after an appearance at the MTV studios. Rob was from Virginia and reputedly could bench press 350 pounds. Britney, who is a petite girl, not much more than an inch taller than Kylie Minogue, came up to his knee. Big Rob could have hidden Britney up his sweat shirt and nobody would have noticed. On tour he was the life and soul. Veronica Finn, who was in Innosense, recalls, 'He was really, really big. He was big enough to intimidate and he could play that part well. He had that sternness that good bodyguards have. Our bus would usually follow Britney's and when we got to a rest area he would be outside telling jokes with everybody but, at the same time, very alert and doing his job.' Having a bodyguard around twenty-four hours a day was a sure sign that you had arrived as a bona fide star. The girls from Innosense had to make do with a large bus driver.

Having Innosense on tour was a welcome bonus for Britney. She had known Nikki DeLoach from her first day on *The Mickey Mouse Club*. Nikki, from Georgia, was yet another link in the Southern chain. While not exactly a Southern mafia, it was reassuring for Britney at her young age to be surrounded by familiar and friendly accents. She hit it off in particular with Jenny Morris, a new member of Innosense, who has since become one of her closest friends. Jenny perfectly illustrated the incestuous world of Orlando pop. Jenny was dating Justin Timberlake's best friend from home, Trace Ayala, so, when Amanda Latona left the group, she was the obvious choice to fill her place. Trace had also been the original matchmaker between Veronica and Justin.

Veronica Finn had long since forgotten about any awkwardness over Justin. She had a new boyfriend, a singer called Jive Jones, so she and Britney 'were fine'. The chance for Innosense to support Britney had come about because Lynn Harless, Justin's mother, had contacted Johnny Wright and suggested it. Wright would come and watch the show from time to time. He always impressed Veronica: 'I'd first met him when I was hanging with

'N Sync. He's very hands-on a lot of the time. When he was around he was very business, very professional, always thinking ahead. Just a great manager I always thought.'

Lynne would travel from Kentwood when she could but Felicia was ever present. The pair had bonded from the very beginning in New York and Stockholm. 'Felicia was always by her side,' recalls Veronica. 'I know it was her job but, on a personal level, I'm sure she really liked Britney.' Britney called Felicia 'Fe' and in return Felicia called Britney 'Boo'. It was a casual indication that the two ladies, who spoke in matching accents, were easy in each other's presence. Felicia also made a mean cup of coffee, de rigueur for a personal assistant.

Felicia and Britney also had a special signal for when things were getting too much for her young charge and she needed space. Britney would say, 'Fe, it's stormy outside,' whereupon Felicia would clear the room of all the hangers-on. Felicia was Britney's friend but she also had to perform the difficult balancing act of being the baddie, the figure of authority who was putting into practice what Lynne expected.

Surrounded by so many friendly faces – as well as her Yorkshire terriers, Mitzi and Bitzi – allowed Britney the luxury of being herself on tour with no discernable diva-like behaviour whatsoever. Veronica observes, 'She seemed surprisingly humble and just a regular girl. When you talked to her it would be like "I love your shoes!" sort of conversation – just girls talking. It was just normal things that girls would talk about, not at all business-orientated. There was no "What producers are you using?" or anything like that. She didn't seem fake.' Bitzi aka Baby was originally intended as a gift for Jamie Lynn but Britney fell in love with her. Both her little dogs were very pampered.

Britney still found it all very exciting. She enjoyed getting ready before a gig, having something cool and different done with her hair or make-up. She was still a teenager. Providing Big Rob was with her, she was her old Mouseketeer self if a fan approached for an autograph, signing with a practised 'How you doin'' greeting before resuming whatever she was doing. She did not seem to find it that bothersome.

Her reputation for drinking and partying was some way in the future during the first couple of years. When she went out with Veronica and the girls to a nightclub in New York she had a good time but was not the last to leave. Britney's happiest times with Justin Timberlake coincided with the golden age of her first incarnation as Britney Spears. She was ecstatic when he would turn up and stay over with her. The feeling seemed to be entirely mutual. 'He was very proud of her,' says Veronica.

1999 was a brilliant year for a fledgling career. Britney won fifteen awards worldwide. The trouble with such undreamt of success at the very beginning was that you had to do it all again without delay or else critics would question your longevity. In November 1999, Britney went back to Cheiron Studios to record the bulk of her follow-up album with Max Martin. The only discernable difference from her first trip two years earlier was that Martin had rejected his seventies roadie look in favour of a short spiky haircut. The Swedish pop master, with his sidekick Rami, wrote and produced seven tracks for *Oops! I Did it Again* including the title track which began the album with the same instant hook appeal of '. . . Baby One More Time'. The *NME* thought it 'easily as good as her breakthrough single'. Other critics thought her vocal sounded as if she was singing down a telephone line. The song was named twenty-fifth in a list of 100 greatest pop songs by MTV and *Rolling Stone*. It also contained the phrase 'Not that Innocent' which almost became a millstone round Britney's neck.

Most of the album had the Swedish recipe of easy hooks and disco rhythm. 'Lucky' was another song of teenage angst which was chosen as the second single from the album. Of more interest were the non-Cheiron songs. The producer Rodney Jerkins put together a version of the famous Jagger/Richards song 'Satisfaction', a curious choice for Britney. The Rolling Stones in the sixties had a bad boy image that could not be more diametrically opposed to that of Britney Spears. Where Britney was marketed as naughty but nice, the Stones were naughty but nasty. The *NME* considered it ill-advised. When she left Stockholm, Britney travelled to Switzerland where she worked with Mutt Lange, husband of Shania Twain, on the catchy ballad 'Don't Let Me Be the Last to Know'. It could have been a Shania record. Perhaps most significantly, Britney earned her first songwriting credit on the unassuming, sugary ballad, 'Dear Diary', which closed the album. Britney may well have written the lyrics in her journal: 'Dear Diary, today I saw a boy . . .'

The new video to accompany the 'Oops! I Did it Again' single was keenly anticipated, especially after the hilarious controversy that surrounded the clip that was shot for 'From the Bottom of My Broken Heart', the fourth American release from the first album. The song was a fairly predictable teenage lament and director Gregory Dark produced an innocuous, plaintive video. That was all fine until the media realized that Gregory Dark aka Gregory Hippolyte was the director of some of the most popular porn films of the last twenty years. His oeuvre included *Black Throat* starring porn queen Traci Lords, *The Devil in Miss Jones*,

Parts 3 and 4, and *Between the Cheeks*, Parts 1 and 2. Bizarrely, he might have been the perfect choice to direct some of Britney's raunchier videos, but the one he was responsible for is quite demure. Britney, however, chose not to use him again.

The 'Oops! . . . I Did it Again' video was not demure. Nigel Dick, responsible for the almost iconic first schoolgirl video, was brought back to direct. As befitting her new status as the number one young female artist in the world, the budget for the three-day shoot had tripled since then to just shy of $1 million. Britney phoned Nigel who recalled, 'She wanted to do a dance video on Mars with a cute guy.' The now famous result opens with an astronaut finding a picture of Britney in the sand. She then turns up in the flesh wearing a spray-on shiny red catsuit, which she found unbearably hot.

Not everything went smoothly at the shoot. The front end of the camera, the 'matte box', fell on Britney's head. It became a near-death experience in the newspapers but Britney was a 'trouper' according to Nigel. She rested, calmed down, had a few stitches in a small wound and was back dancing before the end of the day. Nigel explains, 'She was not rushed to hospital, there wasn't blood gushing everywhere and it didn't happen in the middle of the night.'

Nigel Dick is in a good position to judge the change in Britney from the very first video when she was just a 'cute unknown who could sing and dance' to superstar. Writing online, he observed that Britney was no longer the kid he first met, but was now a young woman. He thought it scary how the world around Britney had changed. When they shot the first video in Venice High School, Britney could walk around the campus unnoticed. That was no longer the case. Nigel's abiding memory of the shoot was of Britney coming on set with a squadron of cameramen walking backwards in front of her, pushing their lenses into her face. Britney had to go straight from that into the first shout of 'action' with barely a moment to draw breath.

Nigel's observation may be unsettling, but at least Britney was working. She was being Britney Spears, *the* Britney. The truly scary thing is how many paparazzi follow her around every minute of the day when she is just being a civilian. Imagine queuing to use the toilet and having fifteen people taking your picture.

The video helped launch 'Oops! . . . I Did it Again' as an instant hit. The album, which was released in May, was the fastest-selling by a female artist in history, shifting more than 1,300,000 in the first week. 'Oops!' also went straight to number one in the UK, selling not far short of a million copies. It was her third British number one but, surprisingly, she would have to wait four years for a fourth.

The *Oops* tour was considerably larger than her first headlining shows. One concert in Denver even had to be cancelled because the venue was too small to hold the new extravagant stage show. A convoy of a dozen buses and trucks now transported the Britney roadshow across the highways of America. Britney's own bus was the height of luxury with its own tanning suite, living room and a star's bedroom at the back full of candles, lace and lavender. Britney the brand was expanding with a range of endorsements from Clairol hair products to McDonald's, milk, Polaroid cameras and, most famously, Pepsi. Britney always gave good professional value to any client. For Clairol she recorded a song entitled 'I've Got the Urge to Herbal' for use in their advertising campaign. For Polaroid she would stop her shows to take a picture of the audience with her 'new' camera.

As befits a new star of her magnitude she had to deal with the problems of over-eager fans – not eleven-year-old girls but older guys. At one concert Britney was suddenly confronted by a man running across the stage taking his shirt off. For the first time there was a hint that it was not quite so much fun as it had previously been.

To alleviate the boredom of life on the road, Britney and Felicia would play a game in which Britney would pretend to be a famous person. Her favourite impersonation was of sex-crazed rocker Lenny Kravitz whom she had met when he called by to visit his friend, the photographer Mark Seliger who was shooting the cover picture of Britney for *Oops! I Did it Again*.

Not everything was a smooth path to unlimited success. Britney was nominated for two Grammy awards – Best New Artist and Best Female Pop Vocal Performance – for the first time. She was still a relative novice in the music business and had to perform in front of a group of her peers including Whitney Houston and Mariah Carey. She sang 'From the Bottom of my Broken Heart' and '. . . Baby One More Time'. When the time came to announce the winner of Best New Artist, it was widely thought she was a certainty. But the winner was Christina Aguilera. Of all people! Afterwards Britney said she felt bad for Lynne, who had wanted her to win so badly. She was also nominated for two Brit awards but failed to win either of those. Somehow, picking up the Kids Choice Award for Favourite Female Singer did not have the same ring to it. Britney has so far failed to win any Brit award, which is a shame for headline writers. She would have to wait until 2005 to collect her first Grammy: Best Dance Recording for 'Toxic'.

Another hiccup was a lawsuit filed against Britney, her parents and Jive Records by a man called William Kahn who claimed it was he who launched Britney's career. Kahn filed a complaint that Britney had approached him shortly after the collapse of *The Mickey Mouse Club* and that, for a brief period, he was her 'exclusive personal manager'. He was demanding a sum of $75,000 as his standard 15 per cent commission for this period. The suit was settled out of court. Britney commented, 'Everything's going so well, then there's, like, a stomper.'

Kahn would feature briefly in Britney's life again a couple of years later when a pair of songwriters claimed he had asked them to write a song for Britney. The result, they claimed, was 'What You See Is What You Get', which appeared on the second album as 'What U See Is What You Get'. A subsequent court case found in favour of Britney and Jive. Kahn, it transpired, had settled with Britney and then subsequently been employed by Jive.

During the Oops tour, the thorny question of lip-synching was aired for the first time. An enormous video screen projected the image of Britney performing and quite clearly her mouth was out of synch with the music. Britney maintained there was a delay on the screen and she was singing as hard as she could but, sometimes, she would need a little help if she was out of breath during an energetic dance routine. Then the sound desk would step in.

For some reason, lip-synching has become a major issue in music. Elton John even drew attention to it in 2004 when he attacked Madonna for lip-synching. It entirely depends on what you expect from a concert. It would have been shocking to go to a concert by Frank Sinatra and discover he was lip-synching. He was a fabulous singer, pure and simple. But Madonna, Britney, all the boy bands, Spice Girls, Girls Aloud, S Club 7 and co are/ were all putting on a show revolving around dancing and carefully choreographed moves. It is physically demanding and it would be almost an impossibility to sing at the same time. Britney concerts tend to be very loud so it is impossible to tell when she is and is not singing live. The best general rule of thumb is that if an artist is wearing a headset that looks as if they are Lt Uhura from *Star Trek*, they are not singing live. The classic con is then to turn the microphone on at the end of the song so that the performer can declare 'Thank you, *Top of the Pops*' or 'Thank you, Wembley'. Nobody is fooled but they still do it.

More and more, concerts are becoming all-round entertainments like circuses or Disney rides. Most fans are just happy to see their heroes in the flesh. Now, if it were revealed that Britney in concert was really a hologram, all hell would break lose.

The concert itself consisted of thirteen songs and lasted about eighty minutes, which was hardly going to give Bruce Springsteen or the Rolling Stones sleepless nights. Britney did change costume six times, however, because she felt it important to dress the mood of each song. As a result of having to change so often, she kept on leaving the stage, which some found irritating. Fireworks, ticker tape, a floating spaceship and Britney disappearing in a burst of fire took everybody's mind off any thoughts of lip-synching.

During the summer, Britney reportedly gave her family $1 million to pay off all their debts and be in good shape for the future. Charity did not just begin at home. She also set up the Britney Spears Foundation with the sole intention of helping children in need. Almost all millionaire entertainers set up charitable funds on advice from their tax consultants. Britney's, however, is a genuinely interesting one. Her philosophy, admittedly a little cheesy, is that music and entertainment has a healing quality that can truly benefit underprivileged children.

The key component of the charity is an annual summer camp for the performing arts in which children aged eleven to fifteen can participate, free of charge, in classes designed to help them make the most of their talents. The comparison with Britney's own 'summer camp' in a one-room apartment in New York is a poignant one. The foundation affirms, 'Kids learn about life here in an empowering, enchanting and exciting environment.'

Tour commitments prevented Britney from visiting the first camp in the Berkshire Mountains of West Virginia, but eighty-five children were chosen to attend from more than 200 applicants. The plan was for the camp to be an annual event and the following year more than 140 children went to Cape Cod in New England. This time Britney was able to schedule a visit.

Britney gave her first British concert at Wembley Arena in October 2000 as part of a short European tour which also included a trip to Stockholm. It gave the British press the chance to evaluate Britney's progress from the schoolroom of '. . . Baby One More Time'. Elizabeth Wurtzel in the *Guardian* believed Britney's entire appeal lay in denying her entire appeal, a neat phrase but one which had the ring of truth about it. Britney Spears had progressed into an image that was all about sex on the one hand and denying anything sexual on the other. In the playground she would have been labelled a prick-tease.

The saga of Prince William and Britney Spears is priceless. Whoever dreamed it up deserves a gold medal for sheer advertising balls. The idea that the Queen's grandson and the most famous teenage pop star of the time were infatuated with one another occupied page upon page of press coverage. Amid all the speculation that she might one day be Queen Britney it was conveniently forgotten that she was very happy with Justin. Nobody was meant to know about that.

Two alternative dictionary definitions of the word 'image' encapsulate the celebrity game. The first is that an image is 'the opinion or concept of someone or something that is held by the public'. The second is that an image is 'a mental picture of something not real or present'. In practice it did not matter how an image was achieved as long as it reinforced the brand. It could be, and invariably was, built on baloney. Prince William and Princess Brit was masterful baloney. It would have been more believable if Prince Philip, a man with an appreciative eye for a pretty blonde, had shown an interest.

The rumours first surfaced towards the end of 1999 when it was revealed that William had a crush on Britney. He may well have fancied her. He was seventeen and she was a teenage sexpot fancied by millions. She apparently sent him a signed copy of her album and a selection of some photographs – a classic marketing ploy.

The beauty of the Prince William plotline is that it could be trotted out whenever a suitable opportunity could be found. It was, for instance, announced that Britney was buying a $2-million house called Battledown Manor, about twenty minutes from William's family home of Highgrove in Gloucestershire. Then sources close to Britney allegedly reported that she broke down in tears when she found out the Prince was dating a more socially acceptable girl called Isabella Anstruther-Gough-Calthorpe.

Her tears were far more likely to have been caused by the

accident while she was filming the video for the single release of 'Oops! I Did It Again'. In a British context, speculation on whether Britney and Justin Timberlake were an item was not that interesting at this time. He had not broken through as a solo artist or as a sex symbol. Prince William, however, was the most eligible male in the land and anything involving him was news and absolutely guaranteed to make the front page. Being linked to William was certain to stimulate interest in Britney if she had a single or a tour to promote.

The pair of potential lovebirds were apparently supposed to meet up when Britney was in London but it had to be cancelled when the press heard about it. The flames of the Prince William story were fanned by the publication of *Heart to Heart*, a ghostwritten book in which Britney and her mother Lynne gave their own perspectives of her life so far. The book was genuinely fascinating even if its relentlessly feelgood atmosphere was for fans only. Celebrities have woken up to the way in which books can be exploited to help build the brand. On the Prince William front, Lynne revealed that he was 'a big fan of Brit's' and that they were supposed to go to Buckingham Palace but William called it off because he was foxhunting. A girl from the Deep South would understand that nothing comes between a man and his hunting.

Britney was also quoted in the press as saying, 'Marry Prince William? I would love that – who would not want to be a princess.' Buckingham Palace were not exactly thrilled at this one-sided romance. Prince William's only reported comment on it was contained in a press statement on his eighteenth birthday: 'I don't like being exploited in this way but as I get older it's increasingly hard to prevent.'

Whether Prince William ever sent an email or letter to Britney Spears is open to considerable doubt. It is, however, a completely irrelevant question. Much more interesting is the way it was a topic that refused to go away. More than two years later Britney was still answering questions on it. She appeared in a cringe-making interview on the *Frank Skinner Show*. Skinner asked her if she and William had become 'quite friendly'. She replied, 'We exchanged emails for a little bit and he was supposed to come and see me somewhere but it didn't work out – so that was it, so, and then everyone was like "oh, she met him" and nothing ever happened.'

Skinner added, 'You were blown out by Prince William?' Britney said, 'Yeah.'

And that was it – nothing ever happened. The Britney interview was considered a major coup for the *Frank Skinner Show*. She was promoting her single 'Overprotected' and was reportedly paid £100,000 for her appearance. She earned every penny by having to sing a duet with Skinner of the Sonny and Cher hit 'I Got You Babe'.

She clearly had little idea who Frank Skinner was and later referred to him as 'that old guy, right'. Of all the questions that Britney Spears could have been asked, rehashing the Prince William story again revealed the whole thing to be PR genius. Justin Timberlake has never commented on all the stories. He probably found them funny.

'This is a little crazy.'

TWELVE

Crossroads

Britney's first morning as a film star began in glamorous fashion on the set of *Crossroads*. She was sprayed from head to toe with insect repellent to try and keep the mosquitoes, who had always taken a fancy to her, at bay.

The discount shelves of video stores are littered with the failed attempts of female pop stars to move their celebrity up a notch with a box-office smash. Mostly there are two kinds of star movie vehicle – one requires a degree of acting where the singer has to shed their own brand a little in return for making a half-decent picture. The second is where they just play an extension of an already-established public image. In effect they are just playing themselves, as the Spice Girls did in *Spice World*.

Lady Sings the Blues, the film debut of Diana Ross, is a fine example of a pop star stretching herself to the limits of her capabilities. Ross was unlucky not to secure the Best Actress Oscar in 1972 – she was pipped by Liza Minnelli in *Cabaret* – for her portrayal of the tragic life of blues legend Billie Holiday. Whitney Houston also made a decent start in the movies with

The Bodyguard in 1993 although this had more to do with the charisma of Kevin Costner than her own role as a superstar singer.

The most successful actress/pop singer of modern times – not including Streisand – is Cher, who has made a string of excellent films, including *Moonstruck*, for which she won a Best Actress Oscar. She was also Oscar-nominated for *Silkwood* and won plaudits for *Mask*, *Mermaids* and the *Witches of Eastwick*. Unusually, she is arguably a better actress than singer. Jennifer Lopez is a more recent example of an actress/singer, although she has made a number of mediocre films including *Gigli* and *Shall We Dance* in the last few years, which suggests she should stick to music. She does, however, have three new movies at various stages of production.

Britney's career model Madonna is the most interesting of modern singers who have tried to become movie stars. For some unfathomable reason, it just has not happened for her. She is by no means the worst actress in the world and some of her films, like *Desperately Seeking Susan*, are bordering on the classic. She has made twenty films in twenty years, an impressive number for someone who does not enjoy movie star status. Perhaps the problem for Madonna is that she can never shake off enough of her music image. Her last starring role in her husband Guy Ritchie's *Swept Away* was savaged by critics and public alike. Madonna is always Madonna and seems to have little credibility left as a movie actress.

The all-time turkey for a singer-turned-actress belongs to Mariah Carey for her 2001 release *Glitter* in which she played a young singer aiming to be a big star. Mariah 'won' the Razzie for worst actress and the film was nominated as worst musical of the last twenty-five years. The Razzies are a popular antidote to the ersatz congratulations of traditional awards shows, celebrating everything that has been awful in the previous year's cinema.

Faced with this motley collection of triumph and disaster what would Britney do? She chose to make a film called *Crossroads*, a candy-floss flick about a young Southern girl (Britney) growing up on a road trip from the South to California. She may not have been playing a girl whose character name was Britney, but she might just as well have been. *Crossroads* was all about reinforcing Britney Spears the brand. In the first two minutes of the film, she had stripped down to some pink underwear and was singing Madonna's 'Open Your Heart' into a spoon while bouncing around on her bed. Instantly she was reeling in the two important sections of her fanbase – the pre-teen girls who could relate to hairbrush-style singalong and forty- and fifty-something men who could dribble silently into their ice cream.

Britney, or more precisely her management, would get a continuous stream of scripts for her to consider, but for her movie debut she needed something purpose-built. This was a point when Britney was about to leave her teens behind. In terms of public image there is a huge difference between being a teenager and a twenty something. Britney needed a script which would help the brand move on to the next age without alienating any of the fanbase. Larry Rudolph brought in a screenwriter called Shonda Rhimes, who had earned praise for her script for the 1999 made-for-TV movie *Introducing Dorothy Dandridge*, which starred Halle Berry. Shonda, a young woman of thirty, met Britney in Los Angeles and having spent a few afternoons hanging out with her, went away to write a movie based on the impressions she had of the star.

The film is not in any way autobiographical but it does project a very real sense of Britney Spears the brand. The only concession to Britney's actual life is that the heroine hails from the South, which was chosen so that she would not have to take time-consuming lessons to lose her Southern accent. That would have meant Nancy Carson's advice about losing her Southern drawl coming back to haunt her.

Britney's character is Lucy, an eighteen-year-old virgin from Georgia who graduates top of her year and has to give the valedictory speech. She has a stern father who wants her to be a doctor but she would rather pursue a career in music. Her best male friend is her lab partner, a school nerd with whom she considers losing her virginity in the second scene in which she is stripped to her underwear. It's a film so even the nerd has an enviable six pack.

Lucy also has two girlfriends, Mimi (Taryn Manning) and Kit (Zoë Saldana), with whom she made a childhood pact at the age of ten, burying a box of keepsakes which they would reopen on graduation. A now-pregnant Mimi persuades the other two to accompany her to California. Ben, a Ben Affleck lookalike played by Anson Mount, agrees to drive them and they embark on their rites of passage on the road. The inevitable happens – Britney sings a karaoke version of 'I Love Rock and Roll'. She also gets laid by the modest, unassuming, yet hard-as-nails hunk Ben. Anson Mount was reluctant to take on the role at first because he thought the movie a little cheesy. At the time he was filming the thriller *City by the Sea* with Robert De Niro, who happens to be a closet fan of Britney Spears. He encouraged Mount to take the part and then helped further by reading with him. The great movie actor read Britney's lines.

Moviegoers hoping to see some hot action from Britney Spears in *Crossroads* are disappointed – this is soft corn not soft porn. Reports afterwards did suggest there were scenes involving a topless Britney, but these did not make the final cut. They have also, surprisingly, not found their way on to the Internet. The film also acts as a showcase for 'I'm Not a Girl, Not Yet a Woman'. The song, written by Max Martin, Rami and, of all people, Dido, is what the *San Francisco Chronicle* called 'the worst kind of bad song – bad and catchy'. The climax of the film sees Britney singing the song at a talent contest. Jive Records' President Barry Weiss predicted that the track would become a classic in the same league as Whitney Houston's 'I Will Always Love You' or Celine Dion's 'My Heart Will Go On', which was a little fanciful.

Crossroads is a far more interesting film than at first appears. The obsessive coverage of Britney tended to obscure the issues at least touched on if not fully explored. Everything is a bit 'filming by numbers' but, in no particular order, it introduces teenage rape, teenage pregnancy, maternal rejection, oppressive parents and cheating boyfriends. The list reads like a problem page from a magazine for the teenage girl. The script also illuminates the ongoing Britney Spears paradox; giggling girlishly with her girl-friends and then grinding her navel with a microphone in her hand. But whatever she's doing, she's wearing pink! *Crossroads* is a very pink film.

Cynics afterwards spotted that the corporate duty was being done with the three friends seeming to have an ongoing thirst which could only be quenched by swigging from a Pepsi bottle. Metaphorically speaking, every last drop was being squeezed from this movie because every last drop is a dollar. That included the book of the movie, which was called *Britney Spears' Crossroads Diary* by Britney and Felicia Culotta. It was more picture book than diary and was strictly for young fans. The overriding impression from its fifty pages was that Britney spent most of the movie feeling very tired.

Much of *Crossroads* was shot in and around Louisiana with just the interiors back in Los Angeles. Britney had the opportunity to see friends and stay at home in Kentwood. Her mother Lynne as well as Jamie Lynn and Bryan were all present. Jamie Lynn had a small role playing Lucy as a young girl. She looked so much like Britney they could have been twins. Her father Jamie did not get a mention. The Britney entourage included Felicia, a videographer keeping a video diary for MTV and an acting coach. The most exacting piece of acting that Britney had to do was crying convincingly. In real life Britney cries easily. *Titanic* was a three-hankie film for her. To cry on cue, however, was totally different. The cameras were rolling and no matter how hard she tried, the tears would not come. She recalled, 'It's the end of the day, and you're just like, "Man I can't get sad. What's with me?"' In the end Britney cried well.

By modern standards, *Crossroads*, bankrolled by Clive Calder, was made on a shoestring budget, estimated at $12 million. It premiered in the US in February. The takings for the opening week were $17 million which more than recouped the costs – a resounding success. The critical reaction was far more lukewarm than that of Britney fans. *Rolling Stone* described it as 'one long chick-flick slog'. The consensus was that this was film as an investment protection and not as creativity. The reviewer, Pam Grady, thought Britney 'pleasant enough' on screen without having her acting abilities tested in any way. She added, 'Spears is herself at something of a crossroads. Her fan base is getting older and most will soon be moving on to other interests.' David Levine, at www.filmcritic.com, was scathing: 'Crossroads does nothing to enhance what precious little acting talent Spears has, turning into a shameless promotion of her music and her image.' Levine added that he would be very surprised to see Britney turn up in another lead role.

She fared a little better in the UK where Jane Crowther on BBC Online found Britney 'natural, endearing and extremely likeable'. She added that in terms of pop-star vehicles Crossroads was 'positively superior'. Empire, the film magazine, thought the film a good deal better than Glitter but said that it suffered from a lack of tension. This was true. A lot of the action seemed to take place off camera. The audience never see the emotional confrontation between Lucy and her mother (Kim Cattrall). Instead her mother says gravely that they have to talk and then we cut to Britney in tears. Perhaps the problem lies in the pop-video generation, which is used to having everything served up in four-minute slices.

One of the more interesting pieces of criticism came from Justin Timberlake: 'I told Britney I thought she did a good job, but someone over there didn't spend a lot of time thinking about the material. If she had a clue, she wouldn't have made that movie.' Timberlake has taken a very different course for his own movie debut. Edison is not a star vehicle for him but an opportunity to be a co-star to two of the finest actors of the day, Morgan Freeman and Kevin Spacey. Justin only gets third billing. He has completed two other movies, Alpha Shot and Black Shot Moon, as well as voicing the part of Artie (young King Arthur) in

Shrek 3. Timberlake never does anything half-heartedly and this would appear to be a real bid for movie stardom.

The suspicion remains that *Crossroads* was not a serious bid to launch a film career for Britney but to tick another box on the brand balance sheet to go alongside books, records, videos and every possible piece of merchandise and endorsement. *Crossroads* was big business and not just at the box office.

When she finished filming *Crossroads* in May 2001 Britney set about putting the finishing touches to the album which would accompany the film. In the movie she only sings three proper songs so the album was never intended to be a soundtrack. Instead, the aim was to move Britney's music forward in much the same way as *Celebrity*, the third album from 'N Sync (ignoring their dire Christmas CD), progressed the career of Justin Timberlake. At the time, Justin and Britney were living happily together and sharing the same manager, Johnny Wright. Naturally they gravitated towards using the same producers and writers. Justin's input was far greater in *Celebrity* than in previous albums, which were almost exclusively produced by the Swedish hit factory.

For some reason, the new album was unimaginatively entitled *Britney*, which seemed better suited to a debut album than a third. Perhaps the idea was to signal that this was a more personal album and that Britney's true personality was coming through. By far the biggest change was in the songwriting credits. The name of Britney Spears featured on seven of the fifteen tracks as a co-writer. The publishing aspect of the music business is extremely lucrative and every artist will eventually take a percentage of this, even if all they have done is to insert the full stop at the end of the song. The extent of Britney's contribution is unknown, but it is true that she always wrote song lyrics during leisure time even as a teenager. Invariably, when friends came to the house with Bryan and asked him what Britney was up to, he would reply that she was in her bedroom writing lyrics in a journal that she had. Part of the plot of *Crossroads* had her character writing poetry and showing something she had composed to her hunky new man. Ironically this was 'I'm Not a Girl, Not Yet a Woman', one of the non-Britney lyrics on the album.

An indication that Britney was moving her music forward came in the very first track. Both her debut and second albums had begun with Max Martin classics – '. . . Baby One More Time' and 'Oops! I Did It Again'. The third album began with an altogether edgier dance track, 'I'm a Slave 4 U', written and produced by the Neptunes, who were fast becoming the hottest producers currently working in music. Justin had become a great friend and admirer of their work since they collaborated on the track 'Girlfriend' on *Celebrity*, probably the best 'N Sync song and one which became a showstopper on Justin's first solo tour.

The Neptunes, Pharrell Williams and Chad 'Hip Hop' Hugo, were high-school friends from Virginia who founded their own Star Trak record label promoting R'n'B talent before moving on to more mainstream artists including No Doubt, Nelly and Justin and Britney, the Prince and Princess of pop. Pharrell Williams, in particular, was a great fan of Michael Jackson and much of the material he wrote for Justin Timberlake could equally have been recorded by the controversial singer. Williams even had a radio conversation with Jackson in which he bizarrely called him 'Sir' throughout. He also shared Jackson's belief that music is a gift from God, a sentiment echoed by both Britney and Justin.

Michael Jackson had a great deal of influence on the musical careers of both Justin and Britney. When Britney was on location shooting *Crossroads* she sent Jackson a bunch of orchids by way of apology for missing his induction into the Rock 'n' Roll Hall of Fame. Her accompanying card was particularly gushing, telling the creepy one that he would be in her prayers.

'I'm a Slave 4 U' served notice on her adoring public that Britney meant business on this album. The *NME* called it 'lusty electro funk', offering the mantra that it was better to be a slave to the rhythm than a slave to any man. The accompanying video, however, was not as clear on that issue. It showed Britney at her most sexual wearing a very small cut-off white top and impossibly tight low-slung blue jeans revealing a bejewelled belly button. All her male dancers, and Britney herself, glistened with sweat as they gyrated to the rhythm. It was difficult to know, however, who was the slave.

The track received even more attention when Britney sang it at the 2001 annual MTV Video Music Awards in New York. She had been nominated for 'Stronger' from her second album but took the opportunity to perform what would be her new single. She appeared on stage at the Metropolitan Opera House wearing a burlesque outfit which would have made a chorus girl at a *Playboy* revue blush. A green strapless silk bra top was complemented by bejewelled pants and brown boots. A few scarves hung from her waist to give a vaguely eastern, jungle feel to it all. The outfit was eye-catching enough but it was the accessory which captured all the headlines – a seven-foot-long live albino python. Britney draped the beautiful but deadly snake around her neck in such a carefree way, revealing yet again her complete professionalism or the possibility that nobody told her pythons, while not poisonous, could squeeze you to death. The whole ensemble was either erotic or sleazy depending on the personal taste of the observer.

The idea behind all such stunts is to be the person that everybody is talking about the next day. Britney achieved that perfectly as she fielded a host of questions about the snake: 'It kept turning its face, looking at me and pointing its tongue out. I got so scared I broke out in hives everywhere,' she informed concerned naturalists. Other observers were of the opinion that Britney was portraying herself as Eve after she had taken a great bite of the apple and was now dancing the night away with the Devil disguised as the serpent. The stunt was showbusiness gold but was conceived solely to sell copies of 'I'm a Slave 4U'.

The rather dark opening track did not herald a new dawn. The rest of the album presented a much safer platform which would not intimidate existing fans. Max Martin and his long-term collaborator Rami took over on the second track, 'Overprotected', an unmistakeable slice of Swedish studio pop which also featured in *Crossroads*. Martin and Rami wrote three tracks as well as collaborating with Dido on 'I'm Not a Girl, Not Yet a Woman'. Dido was pushing thirty at the time. Ostensibly this was the key track on the album, dovetailing neatly with the movie to hammer home the message that Britney Spears was growing up – just a little. The *NME* noted, 'That it takes Dido – a woman staring into the harsh glare of her thirties – to sum up the projected mood of a young woman bidding farewell to the comfort of her teens is ironic.'

Britney sings the ballad nicely but the suspicion remains that she was unwilling to push her voice to the max. The little girl who sang on *Star Search* would have given it a much more powerful treatment.

One of the more intriguing revelations in Britney's *Crossroads Diary* is that she had to talk to Clive Calder about the Martin/Rami song 'Bombastic Love'. Britney gives the distinct impression she did not care for the song, expressing herself 'satisfied' that it was not going to be used as a single release from the new album. Her reluctance may have had something to do with a tortuous lyric of 'Super Trouper' standard which rhymed bombastic with fantastic.

The Neptunes did contribute one other track, 'Boys', which comes across as 'I'm a Slave 4 U' part two with a similarly grinding, sexual rhythm as opposed to the more commercially poppy beat of the Swedish tracks. The one cover on the album, 'I Love Rock 'n' Roll', is the big number from *Crossroads* with Britney delivering a passable version of the old Joan Jett and the Blackhearts 1982 hit. The producer Rodney Jerkins had also been responsible for Britney's cover version of 'Satisfaction' on the second album. Of the two, this was more successful, although it did require an acceptance of Britney as a grungy rock chick. That looked to be the image she was cultivating on the cover of the new album.

Two further collaborations helped to move Britney away from just being a carbon copy of the first two albums. 'Before the Goodbye' was the piquantly titled collaboration with BT, aka Brian Transeau, the fashionable California-based producer who had worked with Justin on the 'N Sync hit 'Pop'. BT was the producer responsible for encouraging one of Justin's trademarks – the human beatbox. Britney utters the plea 'Forgive Me' in the song, which, ironically, are the two words Justin claimed she was unable to say when they hit troubled waters.

Of more interest, if for nothing more than curiosity, was the track 'What's It like To Be Me' written by Justin Timberlake and his great buddy of the time, Wade Robson, who was better known as the choreographer on 'Slave'. Justin's backing vocals worked particularly well though the track is nothing special.

The reviews for 'Britney' were quite good. The popular press may have been ready to turn on Britney Spears but the music critics discerned some grit among the froth. All Music Guide (www.allmusic.com) noted, 'Rhythmically and melodically the whole album is sharper and tougher than what came before.' *Britney* was praised as being her best album so far.

After the publicity generated by Britney's python dance, everything seemed in perfect shape for a massive hit, both for single and album, leading neatly into a blockbuster release for *Crossroads*. Britney had boarded a plane for Australia on the morning that Jive were releasing details for her upcoming tour. Then two passenger planes crashed into the World Trade Center in New York rendering the schedule of Britney Spears irrelevant. Britney had no idea of the tragedy that had unfolded until she touched down on the other side of the world. She immediately telephoned her mother to make sure that her brother Bryan was safe. He was now living in her New York loft apartment. Britney was distraught and reportedly inconsolable. She reflected the shock that her whole nation felt – terrorism was something that happened on someone else's doorstep. Britney was from a region where the majority of her contemporaries would never even leave the state let alone the country.

Britney, with advice from the Jive executives travelling with her, cancelled her first press conference, saying it would be 'inappropriate', but honoured the rest of her promotional commitments. One small disaster occurred when she was photographed carrying a bottle of Coca Cola, which went down badly with her principle sponsors Pepsi and led to a frank exchange of views between herself and Larry Rudolph. This untypical lapse by Britney was no small deal, jeopardizing a contract worth an estimated $2 million.

Having honoured the rest of her Australian commitments, Britney cancelled further promotions in South America and Europe and flew home. One of the first things she did was arrange to give one dollar from every ticket sold on her tour to young children who had lost family in the Twin Towers tragedy. The gesture raised more than $2 million.

'I'm a Slave 4 U' hardly captured the mood of the nation but began to move steadily up the *Billboard* charts, although the sales were not earth-shattering. The album *Britney*, however, went to number one in its first week of release, selling a very healthy 745,000 and knocking Michael Jackson's *Invincible* off the top spot. It also topped the Internet album chart. *Britney* has been put up as an example of Britney's popularity on the wane. Sales of four million were a big drop from the fourteen million of . . . *Baby One More Time* and the ten million of *Oops! . . . I Did It Again*. The drop in sales did not prevent the album becoming her third to debut at number one. Success is always relative and *Britney* also enjoyed the third highest first-week sale by a female artist with sales of 750,000. *Oops!* with more than 1.3 million is at number one on this list.

Similarly, somewhere along the line, *Crossroads* has become perceived as some sort of turkey. The gross at the US box office was $37 million, an impressive profit of three times cost in just ten weeks, more than enough to support another project if Britney chose to do one. By comparison, *Glitter* cost $22 million and grossed less than $2.5 million in its first weekend and never looked remotely like making a profit. Britney was crying all the way to the bank. Britney also looked stunning – in pink – at the Los Angeles premier of the film. Justin Timberlake was on her arm.

Three years on and *Crossroads* is more remembered for what happened to Britney at the various premieres around the world than for the film itself. Her private life was about to fall apart in spectacular fashion. Real life would have made a much better script than the one dished up for movie audiences.

'What do you do when your life becomes an entertainment?'

THIRTEEN

The Split (1)

Britney's interview with talk-show host Diane Sawyer took an unexpected twist when she was asked what it felt like to lose Justin. She began to weep, sniffling, 'It was pretty rough. It was kind of weird. Hello. Um, oh my goodness.' Her whole face was contorted with surprise and anguish and she had to ask Sawyer to stop the interview while she regained her composure.

One of the funniest episodes of Britney's favourite comedy series *Friends* is 'The One Where Ross and Rachel Take a Break'. Rachel suggests they take a break because of Ross's insistent jealous questioning over her friendship with Mark. Overnight she has second thoughts and goes round to his apartment the next morning to admit she was wrong. Unfortunately, Ross has already had a one-night stand with a girl from the copy department. When Rachel finds out about this all hell breaks loose. Ross maintains that they were on 'a break'. Rachel takes the view that he is a cheat and tells him that it has changed everything forever.

    Ross and Rachel had different interpretations of what

constituted a break. At one point Rachel says to Ross, 'You think you are going to get out of this on a technicality.'

Just before she burst into tears on the Diane Sawyer interview, Britney refused to confirm that she had been unfaithful, as Justin had implied: 'I'm not technically saying he's wrong, but I'm not technically saying he's right either.'

A friend in Los Angeles reveals, however, 'They were on a break.'

Justin Timberlake's view of their break-up was more black and white. In a now-famous account of betrayals, he claimed all his first three girlfriends had cheated on him: 'Britney was the third: it was the same with her as with the first girl who broke my heart and the second. They've all gone down the same way. All of them. Three strikes I'm out.'

Justin's version of events differs considerably from the recollections of his first two girlfriends, Danielle Ditto and Veronica Finn, who both strongly refute the implication that they cheated on Justin. Britney's behaviour is clearly more of a grey area. In each case, however, the problem was not so much what any of the girls may or may not have done, but what Justin believed they had done. In Britney's case he explained, 'She has a beautiful heart, but if I've lost my trust in someone, I don't think it's right for me to be with them.'

Just a few months earlier, nothing, it seemed, could prevent the smooth progression of Britney Spears to becoming Mrs Justin Timberlake. She had hinted at that scenario on more than one occasion and told the audience of the Saturday morning TV show *CD: UK* in October 2002 that the marriage would happen 'some time in the future'.

She had assumed, perhaps naively, that she would be with

Justin for the rest of her life. She maintained that she had sex with Justin because of her honest belief in that vision of her future.

They were living the life of an old married couple at Britney's new home in the Hollywood Hills. They had originally planned to buy the house together but in the end Britney bought it herself. During the best times of their relationship they had come together, delighted to see each other, after they had both been jetting off to all parts of the world. Living together for weeks at a time was not the same. A friend observes, 'There were a lot of similarities in their lives but they were actually entirely different kinds of people. It could have been just a natural separation over a period of time.'

Everybody's a grade A student in the fanzine version of celebrity history. Justin genuinely was. He remains an insightful and thoughtful man, bright enough to be an Apex student at school, which signified that he was a gifted student able to move faster with broader academic skills than the average boy or girl. Like many stars, Britney is smart about her own persona and her place in the showbusiness spectrum, but she is not a deep thinker. She could happily spend an afternoon in Wal-Mart before retiring to the veranda for a cigarette and a browse through the latest Danielle Steele novel. This is not the style of Justin Timberlake. He was always too bright for Britney, however much that issue was clouded by the glamorous trappings of their success.

Exactly what triggered the break in the first place is a mystery. The most likely scenario is that it was the usual celebrity curse – the long-distance telephone call. They had a deal, Britney revealed, never to go more than three weeks without seeing one another. For globetrotting superstars, that is a tall order. In November

2001, Britney said she could not ask for a 'kinder' and 'lovelier' boyfriend. She maintained that they just worked out any problems. In December, Justin, presumably tongue in cheek, told a magazine that certain things about Britney drove him up the wall. In February 2002, Britney told Oprah Winfrey about the first time she had kissed Justin while they were on *The Mickey Mouse Club*. One month later she had to deny rumours that they had split.

Throughout the month Britney struggled to deny that their relationship was on the rocks while embarking on the promotional tour for her first film *Crossroads*. She flew into London at the end of March for a press conference at which journalists were banned from asking questions about three important world issues: the 9/11 tragedy, her virginity and her relationship with Justin.

Justin's mother Lynn Harless, however, added flesh to the rumours when she told *People* magazine – a more reliable source than many publications for Britney stories – that they had 'hit a rough spot'. She added, 'They are just having problems right now. They are two kids who have intense feelings for each other.'

Britney herself admitted that for the past few months they had only communicated on the phone, which was clearly not part of the agreement to see each other regularly. To make matters worse Justin was seen in the company of a woman described as a 'busty brunette'. She turned out to be Jenna Dewan, a stunning dancer with 'N Sync, who is now making a career as an actress. She did date Justin a few times after he had split from Britney, but it was nothing serious.

At first it was generally assumed that Justin, being a typical man, had been the partner who strayed, but it soon became apparent that was the not the case, as Justin was quick to intimate. The realization that Britney, the essential virgin, might have been the erring partner let loose furious speculation about her alleged lover's identity. One fanciful idea was that it was Ben Affleck, whom Britney had once admitted having a crush on. The favourite, however, was choreographer Wade Robson. They had first met in 1998 when she was searching for a choreographer for her first tour and one of her dancers introduced her to Wade. She was incredulous that at sixteen, nine months younger than she was, he could be such a talented dancer. 'He's just a baby,' she said. The spiky-blond-haired Robson had a considerable input into the changing image of Britney from Catholic schoolgirl to sexy siren in a catsuit. He was nominated for an MTV video award for his choreography on 'I'm a Slave 4 U' and was the inspiration behind the notorious python dance.

The rumours surfaced again that his was the shoulder Britney chose to cry on when she and Justin were on the 'break'. Neither Robson nor Britney have ever made any comment on the gossip. The only clue is in the way he suddenly seemed to disappear from Justin Timberlake's life when they had been the best of buddies, riding scooters and going skydiving together. There had been a lot of male bonding going on. He and Justin wrote four songs together for the 'N Sync album *Celebrity*, the second fastest-selling album of all time on its release in July 2001. Justin could not have been more enthusiastic about Wade on the sleeve: 'Wade – never in my life have I clicked with someone creatively like I do with you.' On Justin's first solo album, *Justified*, which he started recording in May 2003, there is a big fat zero where Wade is concerned. Coincidentally Justin does not receive any mention on

Robson's Internet biography. It merely says that Robson co-wrote and produced four tracks on *Celebrity* and one on *Britney*, without naming his collaborator.

Robson has achieved even greater notoriety in recent times by being revealed as one of the young acolytes of Michael Jackson. He admitted sharing a bed with the singer when he was ten but said nothing untoward happened. Jackson called Robson 'the little one'. Robson said he had shared Jackson's bed on many occasions: 'He slept on one side. I slept on the other.' The Jackson connection certainly gave Wade a good start in his career. He was a brilliant dancer as a kid, just like Britney, and had appeared in the videos for 'Black and White' and 'Heal the World' by the time he was nine. Britney's close friendship with Robson was an early indication that she had a special affinity with fellow dancers.

Britney was crying buckets over her split from Justin and needed a shoulder. Over a period of twenty months she went spectacularly off the rails in her personal life while trying to keep her professional career in one piece. Justin, however, seemed able to channel his very real upset into a great surge of creative energy. He recorded *Justified* in a blistering six weeks. He was telling his friend, the R'n'B singer Brian McKnight, about how he felt about the split with Britney. McKnight, a very accomplished pianist and composer, started playing with a simple melody on the piano and Justin, almost without knowing he was doing it, began improvising a few lyrics. In a short space of time they had composed a whole song together, the moving soul number 'Never Again'. The track, which is the thirteenth on the album, showed off the emotional element of Justin's voice, moving McKnight to comment, 'The best songs are the ones that you don't have to labour over.' The lyric is poetic and heartfelt and includes the sentiment that the unnamed girl (Britney) did not say sorry when all she had to do was apologize.

The most notorious burst of creativity came with 'Cry Me a River' and, more specifically, the explosive video that accompanied it. The tone of the record was a similar one to 'Never Again', although it had a much darker feel thanks to the Timbaland production. It would have been just another album track about a broken relationship without the video, which seemed specifically designed to hurt and humiliate his now ex-girlfriend. A quite obvious Britney lookalike was cast in the role of a cheating girlfriend. Justin played himself, the wronged man. 'Britney' was played by model Lauren Hastings wearing a newsboy cap and a pair of tinted pink sunglasses, two of the real thing's favourite accessories. Justin is seen spying on his supposed ex getting into a car with another man. His revenge is to break into her house, make a film of himself with another woman on the Britney lookalike's bed and leave the tape running on her TV for her to watch on her return. When she saw it, Britney made the memorable comment, 'I was shocked to s**t.'

Justin was dealing with the break-up in the way that worked for him. Britney was just not dealing with it in any way. She could not believe it when he went on the Barbara Walters TV show and talked about their sex life, which she claimed 'sold her out'. He didn't, in fact, have much to say on the subject. When Walters asked him if they had stayed true to Britney's values he answered with a sarcastic sounding 'Sure'. He had much more to say on a radio show when he admitted on air to giving Britney oral sex. 'I am dirty, man,' he shouted, entering into the spirit of some studio banter. He later claimed it was a joke – and it might have been, but Britney did not find it at all funny.

Her behaviour, especially within the public gaze, bore all the hallmarks of a woman on the verge. Britney had grown up with a code of behaviour stamped on her forehead. She was a Mouseketeer where you learnt to smile and sign autographs in a way that maintained the corporate image at all times.

2002 is the watershed year in Britney's life. This was the year when it all started to go wrong. She lost control of her personal life to such an extent that it threatened the hitherto good health of *the* Britney. Her professional life, her brand, the Britney product, the corporate image were all being threatened by her personal unhappiness. Up until now she had managed to keep them separate. She was the little girl who, while shy offstage, would transform when the lights came on into the consummate young professional described by her fellow Mouseketeer Dale Godboldo as a 'poster child for Disney'. She was the modest and likeable teenager loafing about in sweats and shopping at Wal-Mart who would become sex on a stick when the first few bars of '. . . Baby One More Time' started up.

The Britney Spears brand had been skilfully built up over the preceding five years. The sincerity of the brand is a matter for debate, but Britney herself would frequently declare that 'it wasn't really her'. Under the guise of being Britney Spears it was perfectly acceptable to be an unenhanced virgin in love with the prince of pop.

Now she was growing up, had finally admitted to being sexually active and was no longer one half of a fairy-tale romance.

The first sign that all was not well came in Paris when Britney abruptly cancelled a promotional concert due to take place after the French premier of *Crossroads*. Before the film had ended she had left her seat and been whisked away in a limousine, leaving 3,000 disappointed fans behind. Instead, she flew home to Kentwood to talk things over with her mother, a break in her schedule she had originally planned to spend with Justin.

British fans had their first indication that all was not well at the end of March when Britney flew into London for the premiere of *Crossroads* at the Odeon cinema in Leicester Square. More than 4,000 fans waited patiently outside for her to arrive for the screening. They had started gathering early – some waited seven hours – to try and get a good position. Just a few weeks before, Tom Cruise had treated everyone to his popular Leicester Square walkabouts before the premiere of *Vanilla Sky*. Cruise has perfected the art of working the crowd at these evenings, seemingly able to speak to everyone, shake every hand and say 'Hi Mom' into any number of outstretched mobile phones. He is a pro, but then so is Britney, so the expectation was high especially among young fans that they would be able to meet their idol.

Expectations were still high when Britney was more than an hour late, but they were finally dashed when she showed up, got out of her limousine and, with a cursory wave, walked straight inside the cinema. One teenage fan told reporters, sniffing an anti-Britney story, 'All I saw was a flash of sequin and that was it. It wasn't worth my time.' Later, when Britney appeared on the cinema balcony to wave to everyone, she was greeted by some hearty booing and jeering. The next day the media put the boot in to Britney, quoting disappointed parents. One Essex mother, who had brought her eleven-year-old daughter, said, 'She's crying her eyes out because she couldn't see a thing.'

After a four-year love affair with Britney, the backlash had begun. Her behaviour was interpreted as Grade A diva. The day after, Britney's people blamed security fears for her failure to meet the fans. The film grossed more than £5 million in the UK which, while not a total disaster, was less than half the gross attained by *Spice World*. *Crossroads*, was not helped by sharing its name with a long-running television soap about a Midlands motel.

'I was completely heartbroken.'

FOURTEEN

The Split (2)

Reporters staking out Kentwood decided to follow Britney's father Jamie in his white truck. He drove to a field where there was a bonfire party and joined his friends eating and drinking beer. At the end of the evening a group of men picked him up and threw him in the back of the truck and drove him home. 'He was legless,' said an eye-witness.

Just when it seemed that life could not get any worse, Britney's mother and father were getting divorced. Britney was in Las Vegas about to resume her *Dream Within a Dream* tour when she received the news in a phone call from her mother. Unnamed friends were quoted as saying she was crying her eyes out and begging them to reconsider. Britney was a great deal more philosophical when she said, 'It was always in my head that it might happen, but it never did.' She also trotted out the same comments she had first used talking about her split from Reg Jones when she observed that one minute you can be so in love with someone and then it's gone, just like that.

She may have been upset by the finality of it but the news was hardly a surprise. Her parents had been leading largely separate lives for many years. The newspapers had a field day blaming Britney's success for the split and speculating that Lynne thrived on her daughter's stardom while Jamie preferred the quieter life. It was the last thing Britney needed but it was hardly a surprise. The divorce had very little to do with Britney and much more to do with three classic ingredients of a marriage heading for the rocks: financial worries, time spent apart and alcohol.

The money worries had been ever-present in the Spears household long before Britney's success brought them to an end. When work dried up in and around Kentwood, Jamie was forced to spend his weeks in Memphis, only coming home at weekends. Lynne spent months away at a time with Britney, either during her New York adventure or in Orlando while she was with *The Mickey Mouse Club*. They suffered the same problems that Britney struggled with, first with Reg Jones and subsequently with Justin Timberlake. Absence does not make the heart grow fonder; it makes it weaker and prone to jealousy. On one occasion when Lynne went out line-dancing with some of the other Disney mothers, Jamie was unhappy when he could not get hold of her and thundered straight down to Orlando. Britney had to be farmed out to babysitters while Mr and Mrs Spears sorted things out. That happened again at a later date when Lynne had to return abruptly to Kentwood to deal with another problem at home.

Britney, according to Reg Jones, blamed her dad's drinking and his working away for the marriage problems: 'She didn't blame herself. She blamed her dad, being gone working and drinking – that was her blame.

'Miss Lynne frowned on it and I could see her reason for that but most of the time he was off working and living with a bunch of men. He was just a guy being drunk. He'd grown up drinking beer and he just liked to do it. He would overdo it sometimes.

'When he was away he would call home and Miss Lynne could tell if he'd been drinking that night which started up an argument and it would go from there. She would keep it in check so we didn't hear them busting and fighting.

'Britney's smart and she knew because she had grown up with the way the family worked. They didn't get to see each other much. Miss Lynne would go off with Britney and Mister Jamie would stay at home and, when they were home, he would still be off working.'

Seeing what had happened to her father, Britney was fiercely against Reg going to work with him in Memphis, a situation exacerbated by her smelling beer on his breath. It also goes a long way to explaining why she was so upset when Jamie and Reg turned up in Nashville with her very drunk Uncle Austin.

Despite his own problems, Jamie Spears has always done his best for his daughter. She is the apple of his eye and she could, say friends, twist him round her little finger. He would always be prepared to drop everything to drive his daughter fifty miles to a class. He did appear to be progressively more of an outsider in Britney's life, unlike her mother and Felicia, who were always at her side. Lynne was the driving force behind the book *Heart to Heart*, where mother and daughter swapped recollections and anecdotes. Jamie only features in one photograph, a group family shot with Britney, Lynne, Bryan and Jamie Lynn. Felicia is in six and Britney's cousin Laura Lynne in twelve. Even Larry Rudolph makes it into two shots. Another clue to the state of affairs in 2000, when the book was published, is when Britney mentions the house she is building in Kentwood. She describes it as a house 'for my mama'.

The house, Serenity, is set in seven acres and is considerably grander than the old family home. It is safe and secure although fans can take pictures through the railings. Lynne has decorated it to her own taste, including one room which is a shrine to her daughter's success with wall-to-wall gold and platinum records. She also commissioned Reg Jones's mother Gay to paint a picture of something in London because she so enjoyed her visit to the city when Britney was on tour. Gay had never been to London but painted the Tower of London from photographs and this now proudly hangs on a Serenity wall.

Reports suggest that Jamie could not settle in the new home, but he never really moved in. It was the best time for a break. After the divorce he became more of a loose canon. He moved to New York ostensibly to remodel Britney's $3.5-million loft apartment. He spent time helping to oversee Nyla's, her ill-fated restaurant in Manhattan, but the press were more interested in lurid stories surrounding a friendship with a 'coke-addled' cigar club hostess. The lady in question allegedly told a *National Enquirer* reporter that she and Britney's father had been dancing on the table at an Italian restaurant, as well as a selection of much crazier things.

The *Enquirer*'s hit squad didn't appear to have anything better to do than trail Britney's dad around some New York nightspots. Under the banner 'Britney Cocaine Tragedy' they gleefully reported that Jamie's new friend snorted cocaine in the toilet of a piano bar and another of his party snorted cocaine as they left the club. They suggested that Jamie was 'partying wildly in a world of seedy cocaine sniffers and dangerous mobsters'. It was all good knock-about fun, but perhaps the most disturbing aspect was that Britney's father was becoming the story. He did not have a carefully assembled product image to hide behind. He did not have a fantasy life to fall back on.

Britney merely shrugged when she was questioned about it and said that good-looking men like her father would always be a target for women.

Worse was to come, however, when four teenage girl fans drove up outside the old Kentwood family home where Jamie still lived. Their car was surrounded by three intimidating German shepherd dogs and a rottweiler before Jamie appeared brandishing a large silver revolver. One of the fans told a reporter, 'I thought we'd kind of be welcomed if we showed up. I certainly didn't expect Britney's father to pull a gun on us.' Britney's publicist Lisa Kasteler explained that Jamie had fetched the revolver as a precaution and before he realized they were just teenagers. He later told journalists that he often saw off sightseers in this fashion. He said, 'With the death threats we get and the thousands of people who come here, that's what I do.'

If Britney Spears had not become one of the most famous women in the world, then the spotlight would almost certainly have never fallen on Jamie Spears. He was just an ordinary Southern man who liked sport, drank beer and kept guns. He never gives interviews or appears on television. After the failure of his business and subsequent bankruptcy, he was looking for something to do with the rest of his life. Britney was genuinely upset by her parents' divorce. It may have been inevitable and it may have been brewing for years, but marriage and a proper family life remained one of the principal ambitions of her life. She had talked about marriage with Reg and had clearly expected to become Mrs Justin Timberlake. It was very important to her.

She loved her daddy and wanted him to be happy, but she was going through the worst year of her life and could not even help herself. Things were going to get a lot worse before they both came out the other side.

The demise of Britney's New York restaurant Nyla is a classic example of how nothing was going right for Britney in 2002. She might have guessed the project was doomed when the opening night in June was a washout, thanks to a torrential thunderstorm. Guests arriving at the restaurant, on East 41st Street right by Grand Central Station, were left looking like drowned rats as they hurried past waiting photographers. A-list invitations must have been lost in the post because the best known of those who took a turn on the red carpet were magician David Copperfield, eighties teenage pop star Debbie Gibson and Nikki Hilton. Unfortunately, Copperfield was unable to make the food disappear.

Britney herself, true to her 2002 form, kept drenched fans waiting for an hour before posing briefly for pictures and disappearing inside to the sound of boos.

Restaurants are always a popular sideline for celebrities. Both Justin Timberlake and Ashton Kutcher have been involved in very successful ventures in Los Angeles. Robert De Niro's Tribeca Grill is a New York City institution. Nyla, however, was getting off to the worst possible start, with the opening party being dubbed the worst of the year in the media.

When she had stopped to talk to reporters on that first night, Britney had said that the restaurant was going to be her 'hangout place' from now on. Sometimes the idea that a celebrity may be at the next table can rescue a place, but in Nyla's case Britney was the invisible woman.

Jodi Wasserman, who dealt with front desk phones and bookings, recalls, 'She rarely came in. I think I only saw her twice. I don't think she had much to do with it to be honest with you. I mean most of the people calling all day would be like little girls calling to ask to speak to her and old men as well. The little girls would go, "Hi, is Britney there?" and the old guys would be "Hey, I'd like to speak to Britney." It was weird – little girls and older men.

'After a while I'd be like "I'm Britney" and they'd be like "No, you're not" and I'm just like "Yes, I am!" If all these people had been customers, maybe we would have made it.'

Britney's involvement in Nyla may have been cursory, but the naked hostility of the media to the project meant it faced an uphill struggle from the outset. The restaurant was large and colourful, set on two floors and staffed by waitresses chosen for a fleeting resemblance to Britney Spears. The decor was not the problem. The food, admits Jodie, was not good. It began as a Southern restaurant serving catfish and other Cajun favourites. It was serving meals you might get in a diner in Louisiana but charging fancy New York prices. The critics did not help, nor stories of food poisoning and a stabbing outside. If ever a restaurant was a candidate for *Ramsay's Kitchen Nightmares* then this was it, although even Gordon Ramsay might have struggled to tempt anyone into Nyla's. Jodie remembers evenings when there were no more than ten people spread across two floors. It was a disaster.

In the end, Britney's involvement with the restaurant business did not see out the year. In December she 'terminated her relationship' with Nyla after its financial problems became public. It was reportedly $350,000 over budget on opening night and was facing bankruptcy when Britney jumped ship.

A curious aspect of the Nyla affair was the name. Nyla allegedly stood for New York–Louisiana (La is the state's abbreviation). When it was revealed that Nyla's was also the name of Britney's favourite burger place near Kentwood, the press took it as an example of Britney misleading them.

The Nyla experiment was a rare example of a Britney brand mistake. She certainly did not appear to approach it with her usual professionalism. She may have intended it to be a project for her father to take his mind off the divorce. 'Her father used to come in a lot,' recalls Jodie Wasserman. 'He seemed like a nice, regular down-to-earth guy with no airs about him.'

Throughout the first half of this annus horribilis, Britney had been continuing to promote the 'Britney' album on a Pepsi-sponsored *Dream Within a Dream* world tour. The final leg in Mexico was a nightmare and proved irrefutably that she had had enough. She was leaving Toluca airport, some forty miles from Mexico City, when she apparently gave the finger to the waiting crowds in the universally acknowledged way. The whole Mexican nation seemed to take it as an insult to their country.

Afterwards, Britney had to engage in yet another exercise in damage limitation, claiming that she was actually giving the finger to the paparazzi who were causing a danger to the vehicle in which she was travelling. This may have been true but Britney's actions were petulant at best, whatever the reason. Imagine Britney the Mouseketeer giving the finger to the waiting queue outside *Pirates of the Caribbean* – her feet would not have touched the ground as she was ejected from the show. 'I'm human,' said Britney. 'I get mad like everyone else.'

Her Mexican fans seemed to have forgiven her when more than 50,000 poured into the Foro Sol baseball stadium in Mexico City to see her last show. The weather that day had been wretched, with thunderstorms raging all over the city. Britney came on, performed four songs and then during 'Stronger' just stopped. She paused before saying into the microphone, 'I'm sorry, Mexico, I love you. Bye,' and walked off the stage. The crowd, stunned at first, went mad when the house lights went on. They booed and hissed – the not-so-happy sound effects that seemed to be following Britney around in 2002 – and threw things at the stage. Yet again Britney fought a rearguard action, claiming weather conditions meant it was not safe to continue.

London, Paris, Mexico . . . Britney needed to stop giving everyone an excuse to have a go at her. Throughout Britney's career there had been signs every so often that being Britney Spears was all getting too much and she was tired of it all.

Wisely, it was announced she would be taking six months off.

'I thank God every day for my parents.'

FIFTEEN

Under-protected

Everyone was excited when Britney appeared on her hotel balcony with the handsome black dancer. What would they do? Would they have a drink, smoke a cigarette or share a kiss? Laughing, they proceeded to make paper planes and launch them into the Rome sky.

The most ironic event of Britney's wretched year came in June, when the prestigious *Forbes* magazine named her the 'world's most powerful celebrity'. She was twenty-one years old. This was not a lad's mag where she was up against Abi Titmuss, Rachel Stevens, Jordan and other assorted cover girls. She was number one on a list where those placed behind her included Tiger Woods, Steven Spielberg, Madonna, U2, Oprah Winfrey, Michael Jordan and, perhaps most pleasingly, 'N Sync.

One of the first things Britney did after splitting with Justin was to remove from her finger the $100,000 ring he had given her. He had never officially proposed but the gift was one she had previously treasured. Now it would be an unwelcome burden for a young woman intent on spreading her wings and getting back on the dating carousel. Britney had never properly played the dating field. Justin had finally revealed that they were together for three and a half years, which put the time they started going out as late 1998, when she had first opened on the 'N Sync tour. Before Justin she had been with Reg Jones for three years, which meant that from the age of fourteen until twenty she had been spoken for, give or take an alleged indiscretion or two.

The next thing she did after her tour ended so ignominiously in Mexico City was to go out partying every night. The press lapped up any suggestion that she might be smoking, drinking, binge-eating, engaging in bad behaviour or having sex. 'Who cares if I have sex?' she announced. 'If I mess up, I'm human. If I have a drink or I'm with someone, I'm human.' That all sounded very level-headed, but at one stage her mother Lynne was so concerned about Britney's behaviour that she called Justin to see if he could help. Justin was on tour at the time and, reluctantly, had to tell Lynne that there was nothing he could do.

Even Larry Rudolph was sucked in to commenting, 'She is not having a breakdown. This is a girl who has been on the most unimaginably wild rollercoaster ride for the last five years without a break. She is going to stop being the public Britney Spears and start being the private Britney Spears.'

All very commendable, but the private Britney Spears managed to get herself involved with Fred Durst, the lead singer with the group Limp Bizkit. He was literally the last person anyone would have nominated as a likely suitor. The idea of a 'balding, pot-bellied, goateed nu-metaller' romancing Britney was bizarre, a sort of American nightmare meets the American dream. Durst, originally from North Carolina, had a grungy, bad-boy reputation to live up to. A former skate-boarder and tattoo artist, he had been married at twenty and had a daughter but spent a month in jail after an assault on the man with whom he claimed his wife had been cheating. His appraisal of himself would gladden any mother's heart: 'I've sinned so many ways, it's unbelievable. I've robbed stores. I've had plenty of sex. I've lied terribly. I've cheated. I've been greedy. I've lusted. Everything. I've done it all.'

Limp Bizkit were formed in 1994 and fused rock and rap into a fashionable package. They were flavour of the month when rumours surfaced that Durst and Britney were dating and had been seen getting smoochy in Los Angeles nightclubs. He was also spotted leaving her Hollywood Hills home after breakfast.

Durst, unusually, chose the band's own website to bring his friendship with Britney out into the open. Just after the New Year, he posted a message declaring that Britney was a 'sweet, amazing girl and I'm happy to know her right now'. Two days later he wrote, 'Anybody out there who has a serious problem with my feelings for Britney should just chill and worry about their own feelings for a minute.' By the time of his third message he was positively ranting: 'Who really gives a shit if I wanna be with Britney Spears. The only person that should give a shit is Britney.' He also claimed his feelings for Britney were 'simple, honest and pure' and blamed the media for making up some 'unbelievable things'.

Nothing, however, could have prepared an astonished public for Durst's appearance on the Howard Stern radio show in February 2003, when he maintained that their friendship had begun on a professional basis with him writing some material for her. It moved up a gear, however, when he wrote Britney a love letter as they collaborated in the studio one day. He told Stern she went home but returned a few hours later wearing a see-through shirt and no bra. She had an entourage with her and they all went back to Britney's house. The implication was that Durst and Britney had shared an intimate night. It was also suggested that oral sex was involved and that Britney enjoyed 'dirty talk'.

Durst maintained that Britney was not the sweet, innocent girl she seemed to be: 'She definitely parties too much. She drinks and smokes so much. I think it's something she picked up. She's got a crazy life.' He did pay her the compliment of saying that Britney had a better body than his former girlfriend Carmen Electra. Carmen was more toned but Durst said he preferred Britney's because 'I like a woman to have a little bit of curve and softness'. He was interviewed by Dani Behr for British television, but the discussion was apparently so graphic that the exchange was never aired. He was also reported as saying that Britney was 'forward and aggressive' in bed.

Britney steadfastly denied any relationship with Durst. She told the audience of *Total Request Live*: 'I don't really know him that well. He's really sweet but he's not my type.' Her spokesman, for once, captured the mood: 'The situation feels very junior high school.'

Her remarks reveal the incongruity of the match. Durst, the wild ex-punkrocker, was the gentleman suitor writing love letters and becoming generally smitten, while sweet little Britney was the love 'em and leave 'em maneater. Durst later admitted, 'I play up the pimp thing on purpose. I'm not the stereotypical rock star. I'm a hopeless romantic.'

Intriguingly, Durst had an eighteen-month-old son, Dallas, by Playboy Playmate Jennifer Rovero. Britney appears to be attracted to young, recent fathers – something for the amateur Freud to ponder. He also wrote a song called 'Just Drop Dead', which many thought to be a none-too-subtle dig at Britney. The irony of Britney's very brief association with Durst is that it probably did more harm to his credibility than to hers.

The whole Fred Durst thing blew up and blew over in a few weeks. He just stopped talking about her, which may or may not have been following pressure from Britney's people. Britney, with her new reputation as a party girl, was soon being linked with the actor Colin Farrell, another celebrity with a bad boy reputation. Farrell had made a name for himself as a twinkly Irish actor in the television series *Ballykissangel*, a cosy Sunday evening drama with a touch of the blarney. He made a surprising breakthrough in Hollywood in the 2000 film *Tigerland* about a group of raw recruits taken to the backwoods of Louisiana to prepare them for combat in Vietnam. Since then he has been in a string of mainly action hits including *Minority Report* (with Tom Cruise) and *Phone Booth*.

Britney was seen enjoying a steamy snog with Farrell during the premiere party at the trendy Chateau Marmont in LA for his film *The Recruit*. They were later said to have been on a couple of dates, including one where she visited the set for *SWAT*, the new movie he was shooting. Farrell, who had quickly earned a reputation in Hollywood as a hellraiser and the biggest shagger in town, played down rumours that it was much of anything: 'She's a sweet, sweet girl but there's nothing going on.' Britney, too, downplayed the rumours saying they had just kissed, adding, with a smile, that Farrell was such a 'bad boy'. His gentlemanly behaviour towards Britney was strangely at odds with the philosophy he expounded in *Playboy* magazine: 'I've always been a firm believer that casual sex is a fucking good thing. It's like ordering a fucking pizza.'

Farrell certainly played the acceptable Hollywood game of not kissing and telling regardless of what had been going on. Durst, perhaps because his feelings were hurt, did not toe the celebrity line. One of the more amusing extras in Britney's involvement with these two unsuitable men was the revelation that they had both bedded a Playboy Playmate called Nicole Narain who memorably said, 'This girl must be getting sick of having my seconds.'

These celebrity episodes were very inconsequential. Durst and Limp Bizkit announced a tour at the beginning of February 2003. Farrell was promoting both his film *The Recruit* and his own profile. Britney always attracted publicity. She may not have wanted to be portrayed in this way, but at least it was helping her brand to grow up without a huge marketing spend. One of the more interesting effects of the unwanted publicity was that this would be the last time, at least for the moment, when Britney was mentioned in connection with another famous person.

Celebrities always seem to date other celebrities. They are the only people they meet in the VIP area of parties. At various times throughout the last few years, Britney has been said to be getting close to Ben Affleck. She was also linked with Cameron Diaz's ex lover, Jared Leto, as well as an R'n'B singer called Thicke. Britney was soon to break that mould but, first, her general lifestyle was giving great cause for concern. On the surface, however, there was not that much to it. She was seen smoking a cigarette at the wheel of her Mercedes and knocking back vodkas in nightclubs – but, after all, the great majority of young women today would also be drinking on a Saturday night out.

A far more damaging allegation, however, linked Britney with cocaine use. The US magazine *Star* – part of the *National*

Enquirer stable – quoted an unnamed member of her entourage describing a night out with Britney the previous November in Crobar, a Miami nightclub. The male source said he and Britney were among four people who went into a small bathroom where the other man prepared some cocaine lines on a toilet seat. The description is slightly odd in that the source does not actually see Britney snort a line but hears her sniff while he is looking at her friend with raised eyebrows. The implication in the article is clear, however, when she tells her girlfriend to inspect her nose for any telltale signs with the words, 'Check me. Check me.'

Next day Britney answered the phone to an unidentified caller who appeared to be giving her a hard time. The source quotes Britney as saying, 'We didn't stay out that late. No, not really. I didn't do that much.' Britney allegedly got more upset and shouted, 'I can do what I want' before disappearing with the phone into her bedroom for an hour and a half.

Britney's lawyers wasted no time in threatening legal action although the story has been thoroughly aired in print since the initial allegations. A few days after they first appeared, the *New York Post* printed the following: 'Which navel-baring pop tart was less than discreet in a Miami nightclub? She allowed witnesses to see her snorting lines of cocaine.' In the end no legal action was taken.

Fred Durst, an unlikely Galahad, was asked if he had shared any 'nose candy' with Britney. He replied that he was drug free and that he had not seen Britney doing any drugs. Britney has only ever made one comment in an interview that implied she had tried drugs: 'Let's say that you reach a stage in your life where you are curious. And I was curious at one point. But I'm way too focused to let anything stop me. Was it a mistake? Yes.'

Allegations about sex and drugs always make for a good read, but the wider implications for Britney and for her record company, Jive, were that she was becoming more and more vulnerable and that a carefully crafted image was in serious danger of being dismantled. February 2003 must have seemed like the longest month of the year for Britney but at least her mother Lynne was not going to let scandalous headlines distract her from the really big story.

She wrote a Valentine message on the Net for Britney fans: 'We have all gone through the flu. Jamie Lynn was the first one to get it, then Bryan, Britney, then me. It went full circle because now Jamie Lynn has it again!' As for Britney's new album, she added, 'Brit's been recording and writing in the studio so much lately with some amazing producers. She is really lucky to work with people that she likes and collaborates with so well.'

Through thick and thin, Lynne always sticks to the party line that the Spears family are nice Southern folks. Although this health bulletin was unintentionally amusing, it did reveal that Lynne still had her eye very much on the ball. It was time to start mentioning the new album in the hope and expectation that it would refocus everybody's attention on Britney. The trouble with having promoted an image of general goodness and chastity is that indulging in the sort of behaviour which a million young people can relate to every day is easily construed as being bad.

Britney's year of unsuitable men continued with a friendship which was far more intriguing than any celebrity dalliance. She became very close to one of her dancers, a good-looking, cool young man called Columbus Short. Columbus is black and dating a coloured man would be an extremely big deal for someone brought up in the environs of Kentwood and McComb. Britney has always been very interested in the vibrant dance culture in Los Angeles and first saw Columbus dance at the Key Club on Sunset Strip. From a physical point of view she admires a typical dancer's lithe and athletic frame. From a professional point she has a practised eye in judging talent and whether a dancer has something to offer Britney Spears. Like Wade Robson before him, Columbus was a year younger than Britney and a dancer who had ambitions to make his mark as a choreographer. He was also friendly with another dancer called Kevin Federline who, the following year, would become much more significant in Britney's life.

Britney was searching for new talent for the stage show to accompany the album she was working on. The confident and extroverted Columbus Short was just the type she wanted. A friend of his explained, 'Britney was initially impressed by his dancing but his personality made a big impression too. He is a cocky kind of guy who girls really like. It's important you get on with your dancers because they have to spend so much time together on the road. Britney knew she could work with Columbus.' Britney was impressed enough to hire Columbus to work as a choreographer on her new show, a huge breakthrough for him.

Columbus offers a rare insight into what the real Britney was feeling at this time in her life. He has no hot and steamy tales of sex to narrate. Instead, he observes, 'Britney needed her confidence back. She was really insecure and out of shape. We would talk for hours. She needed someone to listen to her insecurities. *She* may have needed sex but that was not what *we* needed.'

For many months Britney had been clinging to the hope that she and Justin might get back together. Everybody who believed in happily ever after seemed to want it to happen. The media had chewed the bone to a mash months before, but still their relationship dominated stories about either of them. That changed in April 2003 when Justin met Cameron Diaz at the Nickelodeon Kids Awards in Los Angeles and asked her to go bowling. From that moment on Cameron replaced Britney both privately and publicly in Justin Timberlake's life.

Britney was at her most vulnerable when Columbus was a shoulder to cry on. He implies that she wanted a more intimate relationship. 'We never slept together,' stresses Columbus. You might ask "Who turns down Britney Spears?", but I respected her. I didn't see her as a sexual object. We may have had a conversation about it, but I don't crap where I eat!'

Britney and Columbus were first seen together outside a dance studio in Culver City. Nothing too much was made of it until he joined her in Rome in September, where she was filming a Pepsi commercial with Beyoncé and Pink. The trio had to dress as 'hot' gladiators and sing the Queen song 'We Will Rock You' while fighting to the death for the entertainment of the Emperor, played by Enrique Iglesias. Britney, meanwhile, was photographed standing next to Columbus wearing a very tight T-shirt bearing the slogan 'Miss B Haven'. They were seen making paper planes and kissing on the balcony of the Hotel Hassler and the press sniffed a big story, especially when it was revealed that Columbus already had a wife, Brandi, back home in LA. The storm raged more fiercely when it was revealed that Brandi was eight months pregnant with their first child.

They next showed up in New York, staying at the Trump International Hotel. They spent a couple of days shopping and sampling some fashionable bars and restaurants. Columbus was unprepared for the maelstrom that he was about to be caught up in. Britney, who had genuine affection for him, rallied round. He says, 'She helped me though it. She told me just how to ignore it and be really cool. She knew exactly how to play it and she showed me the way to handle it.' Meanwhile, back home, Mrs Brandi Short told reporters that she missed her husband but, as far as she was aware, his relationship with Britney was strictly professional.

Columbus and Brandi are now divorced, but he completely refutes the notion that Britney split them up, saying they were separated before he and Britney became close. He has only nice things to say about Britney, which must make a pleasant change for her. He has said that they did sleep in the same room one night but they were not alone. Both his personal and professional relationship with Britney was probably doomed as soon as the papers got hold of it.

The suggestion that Britney would have been willing if Columbus had weakened is backed up by a friend of both: 'Britney Spears is attracted to a black man. She likes the hipness and cool but, really, it's taboo for her. She was taking a big risk with the family!' Whether her family had any say in the development – or lack of it – of her relationship with Columbus Short is pure conjecture. His contract was not renewed for her 2005 dates.

The last time Columbus saw Britney was a few months later when she was rehearsing in the next studio to him in Burbank: 'I saw her in the car park and she came over and gave me the biggest hug. She was very sincere and said, "I miss you". It was definite closure for me.' Columbus is happy with the notion that Britney cared for him but, in retrospect, does not feel comfortable calling their relationship a romance. 'I don't think it was that,' he confides.

Candidly, Columbus explains that he could have taken advantage of Britney if he had wanted to at this time in her life: 'I could have milked the cow if you understand what I'm saying. Yea, I want a $19,000 shirt but I want to do it myself. I don't want to be defined from that Britney thing.' He has given up dancing altogether now, preferring to concentrate one hundred per cent on a burgeoning acting career.

When Britney released her fourth album, *In the Zone*, in November 2003, the sleeve notes contained the usual hello to her best girlfriends. Tacked on the end was the line 'Kevin and Columbus – we haven't even begun yet.' In Kevin's case that proved to be true, but not so with Columbus, which was about to end.

The obituary of Britney Spears's professional career was one written many times in 2003. She went from being named by *Forbes* magazine as the most powerful person in showbusiness in 2002 to being nowhere in its 2003 list. As the year drew to a close the jury remained out. Privately, the insecurity she was feeling, which Columbus had tried to ease, was still manifesting itself in surprising ways – especially in November, when she broke down while being interviewed by Diane Sawyer. A friend explains, 'It was just another fucking interview but then she touched a nerve. It snapped her out of the usual narcotic plateau of these things. I am sure Britney's tears were genuine.'

'I don't like people treating me like a little girl.'

SIXTEEN

Fifty-five Hours in Vegas

Britney, the lovely little girl with crucifix earrings, had reached rock bottom. She woke up in a Las Vegas hotel room married to a man she did not love and, in all honesty, barely knew.

It was the ultimate act of rebellion. All her life she had been crushed. The real Britney, a wonderful, warm and loving girl, had been the servant of the monstrous creation of Britney Spears, superstar. The values she held dear of family and marriage, of love and respect for her parents and the Church, were not bringing her happiness. Instead, her confidence and self-esteem had sunk to an all-time low. And, to make matters worse, her fall from grace had been in the full glare of public scrutiny. As the best-selling novelist Tony Parsons commented, 'We don't love celebrities, we hate them.'

The catalyst for Britney's now-notorious marriage to hometown boy Jason Alexander had little to do with a wild New Year in Vegas. It was triggered by a confrontation with her mother Lynne in Kentwood just before Christmas. Britney had flown home to Serenity in late December 2003 to spend the holiday with her family. She had known Jason, who was the same age, since they had been small children. In those days, Lynne ran a small kindergarten for pre-school-age children and both Britney and Jason were in the same class. He had known her before she became 'Britney Spears'.

They saw very little of each other over the years. Britney went to Parklane Academy in McComb while Jason went to school in the other direction at Oak Forest Academy in Amite, which Britney's cousin Laura Lynne also attended. Britney was away in New York and Orlando for large periods of time and when she came back as a teenager she went steady with Reg Jones. She mixed with a different circle of friends, although she would occasionally see Jason at parties and social events in and around Kentwood. They had shared a kiss and a cuddle a few months after she and Justin had broken up, but it was a just a little flirtation.

Jason always fancied Britney but had never had the opportunity to do anything about it. She was a glamorous celebrity enjoying the high life all over the world with Justin Timberlake. He was the son of a mechanic in Kentwood, still living at home. Reg Jones recalls how Jason and his friends were all jealous when he started dating their Kentwood girl: 'It kind of made them mad when I started dating her. One time for instance they came by my truck and they were cussing me so I chased them down and made them stop and pull over. I got up to the window and said what I had to say. Then I got the hell out of there!'

Jason had grown into the kind of brawny guy you would not want to meet in a fight. He was a man-mountain, very big and muscular – well over six feet tall and weighing in at seventeen stone, eight pounds. He had also become a star American football player at Southeastern Louisiana College in Hammond, about thirty miles south of Kentwood. He had the occasional run-in with the police in 2003, but nothing more serious than a young man out on the town having some high spirits. Two charges – for trespassing and simple battery – were dropped, while in October he pleaded guilty to disturbing the peace and was fined $105.

The battery was an incident in which he was alleged to have punched a man who was after his girlfriend. The breach of the peace charge followed a bar-room fight at the Extra Innings Bar in Hammond where Jason is a regular. Police were eventually called to break up proceedings when the brawl continued outside. The bar manager Brett Chatelain stuck up for Jason: 'He's a good guy. He's a little loud but he's got a good heart.'

The pre-Vegas party began when a group including Britney, her brother Bryan, Reg Jones and Jason met up at Serenity. Reg was still friendly with old pal Bryan and so occasionally would join up with him when he was at home. They moved on to Jason's house before ending up at the old family home on Highway 51. By this time Reg recalls that Britney was looking 'pretty wasted'. When the party eventually broke up, Bryan was asleep on the couch, Reg was slumped in a corner and Britney and Jason were wrapped around one another on the floor.

Britney had not told her mother where she was or what was going on and Lynne was very worried. In *Heart to Heart* Lynne revealed that Britney still had a curfew when she was staying at home because, while she was under Lynne's roof, her mother wanted to know she was safe. On this occasion she had no idea what was going on.

In the morning, some time after 6 a.m., Reg Jones woke up, crept past Jason and Britney still on the floor and went outside, where some of Jamie's workmates had arrived to start the day: 'Mister Jamie showed up and goes "Where's Britney?" and I said "Inside." He goes "Her mama's been looking for her." He walked in and saw her and Jason all cuddled up and he walked back outside and said "I'll be right back" and he went and called Miss Lynne. She came to the house raising hell. I wasn't close enough to hear what they were saying to each other but they were definitely having a row. Miss Lynne got Britney up and put her ass in the car and took her back to her house.'

Britney decided she did not want to spend New Year at home in Kentwood. She rang Jason and said, 'Let's go to Vegas.' He readily agreed and joined her and an entourage of girlfriends en route to Nevada. They checked into a $10,000 a night suite at the Palms Casino Hotel on New Years Eve, 2003. The Palms is owned by the Maloof family. One of the brothers, George, runs the hotel while another, Phil, was briefly linked with Britney after they were seen having dinner together on one of her previous visits to Las Vegas. At 11 p.m., Britney, in jeans and a black halter-neck top, led her friends to the hotel's nightclub, Rain, to see in the New Year. Unconfirmed reports say that Britney sank a string of vodkas and gave Jason a romantic Happy New Year kiss. They also suggested that she had to be carried out of the bar at 3.30 a.m. having seen out last orders. It was quite a party.

Jason Alexander later sold the story of his time with Britney in Vegas to the *News of the World*. He told the newspaper that it was after this night out that they made love for the first time, when they got back to her suite. It was an extremely lurid account, in which he claimed Britney performed oral sex on him in the shower before they had unprotected sex in every position.

The following day turned into a sex marathon, according to

Jason. It began when they woke up feeling horny and continued later in the bath tub when she climbed in. The wild and very physical sex continued on into 2 January with a bizarre interlude in which the couple went to the hotel's movie theatre for a screening of *Mona Lisa Smile* staring Julia Roberts, a girly picture if ever there was one, and not one readily associated with brawny football players.

The intriguing question is who exactly was sweeping who off their feet. In Jason Alexander's account, Britney comes across as Mae West's sex-crazed sister. It was after yet another bedroom session in the early hours of 3 January that Britney asked Jason to marry her. They had apparently been watching the romantic classic, *The Texas Chainsaw Massacre*. He said yes and that was all the encouragement she needed. At 3.30 a.m., they jumped into the hotel's lime green stretch limo and told the driver, who was also a bellman at the hotel, to take them to the nearest chapel because they were getting married. The bride to be was wearing torn blue jeans, a black top revealing the famous midriff, and a baseball cap. Her wedding shoes were sneakers. Jason recalled that she was not wearing any knickers.

The first two chapels they passed were closed but, pressing on, they discovered the ironically named Little White Wedding Chapel, which boasted a twenty-four-hour drive-up wedding window. When they arrived, they were directed to the twenty-four-hour courthouse, the Clark County Marriage Licence Bureau, where they paid $55 to purchase the marriage licence. They both had to sign – Jason, neat and on the line; Britney with a wild flourish that looked nothing like her old, tidy style. Back at the chapel, they bought a wedding package which included photographs, a video record, a piano player and a bouquet of pink roses. Britney was given a garter which she put on her left leg over her jeans. The limo driver/bell man stepped in to walk Britney down the aisle to the sound of 'Here Comes the Bride'. The room Britney was married in was the 'Michael Jordan Room', so called because the famous basketball player had married Juanita Vanoy there in 1989. It had white benches dotted with red velvet cushions. Bruce Willis and Demi Moore had also married at the chapel in 1987.

Britney Spears married for the first time at 5 a.m. in a seven-minute ceremony. The happy couple were 'smiling and laughing' said an unnamed eye witnesses.

Before the sun was up they were back at the hotel but, Jason recalled, none of Britney's other friends there congratulated them, even though she was saying how happy she was. The couple themselves celebrated with Cristal champagne and discussed where they should go on honeymoon.

In his account of the marriage, Jason said that he told Britney that her name was no longer Spears, it was Alexander. This was one of the unexpectedly humorous touches in the whole affair. Britney Alexander is the name of a well-known porn actress and the star of such classics as *I've Never Done That Before!* and *Bang My White Tight Ass*.

Another highly amusing sidebar to the unexpected Vegas wedding of Britney Spears is that when it became public knowledge everyone thought she had married *the* Jason Alexander, the short, balding co-star of *Seinfeld*. Lynne Spears did not find it the least amusing when Britney called her first thing in the morning and mother delivered a reality morning-after pill to daughter. Her brother Bryan was on the case immediately, telling Jason right from the beginning that there would be an annulment. Manager

Larry Rudolph allegedly sent her a wire: 'Congratulations, you just gave away half your money.'

The cavalry started flying in from all corners of the US to effect a damage-limitation exercise. Her close friends, Jansen and Cortney, were already at the hotel, but they too were taken completely by surprise by the bombshell breakfast news. They swiftly closed ranks around their beleaguered friend.

Britney and Jason spent one full day, 4 January, as a married couple. They made love for what would be the last time before having steaks at the hotel's steakhouse. It was not a romantic meal for two. Lynne had hopped on the first plane. Bryan was there. Larry Rudolph was there, as well as her friend George Maloof and an attorney, David Z. Chesnoff. Jason's account singled out Bryan as the driving force in sorting out the aftermath of their instant marriage. They were all of one mind – how to extricate the girl with a $100-million fortune out of this New Year disaster.

Jason was cajoled into signing papers agreeing to an annulment and at 12.24 p.m. on 5 January, Britney's first marriage was officially stamped into non-existence. The annulment papers cited a failure to 'know each other's likes and dislikes; each other's desires to have or not have children; and each other's desires as to state of residence'. The formal documents concluded, 'They are so incompatible that there was a want of understanding of each other's actions in entering into this marriage.'

The whole wild weekend was like something out of a Hollywood melodrama. Was it a comedy or a tragedy? Jason said he was handed an airplane ticket by Bryan Spears which turned out to be economy class. He was then driven to the airport and left there for four hours before his flight home to Kentwood. He claimed that he had to sign the annulment papers because they told him he was ruining Britney's career. She, he said, couldn't even look at him. The terms of their agreement remain a secret. He maintains he took no money. Other reports suggest he was paid half a million dollars. Clearly, Britney's purse got off lightly, whether there was a financial deal or not. If there was a deal, then why did Jason sell his account to the *News of the World*?

By the time Jason was back home in Kentwood, the world's press were going crazy trying to piece together a most astonishing showbiz story. Could this really be the ex-virgin Britney Spears? A popular theory was that she was reacting to the rumours that Justin Timberlake had just become engaged to Cameron Diaz. They turned out to be untrue. Back home, everyone was choking on their breakfast cereal. Reg Jones was in total shock: 'I could not believe it. I think she did it to show her mom "You don't tell me what to do."'

The general consensus was that it was a joke that went too far. Jason's mother, Doreen Seal, said, 'They weren't drunk. It's just a moment that got out of control and there was no one there to stop them. They made a mistake and then they fixed it.' Mrs Seal, who remarried after divorcing Jason's father Dennis, noted, 'Britney wants a normal life that she can't have.'

Justin Timberlake made no comment. He was enjoying a New Year break, skiing and snowboarding with Cameron Diaz in Vail, where he had previously spent a romantic Christmas with Britney. His grandmother Sadie did say that she thought Britney's 'marriage' was 'strange'. Justin's fellow 'N Sync-member Lance Bass, who is still on good terms with Britney, was in Vegas at the time and observed, 'Young people do stupid things every day.'

Britney's official website carried a message that it was all a joke. The attorney, David Z. Chesnoff, said, 'They are simply two young people who regret what they have done.' The best quote, however, came from the wedding chapel's owner, Charlotte Richards, who said, 'We do not marry anybody who is inebriated.'

Jason Alexander enjoyed his moment of fame. He was widely described as a churchgoer, which did not actually count for much. In the Deep South even mass murderers are churchgoers. He found himself a professional agent, did the rounds of talk shows, appeared in a reality TV show and bought a sports car. Friends in Kentwood say that much of the money he received has already gone. He told *In Touch* magazine: 'I'm more popular than ever and I'm divorced.' The reality for Jason is that he was swimming a little out of his depth. He had apparently finished with his high-school sweetheart, Corie Miller, the month before he married Britney. This may or may not have had something to do with Britney. The reports vary. It would not have been the first or the last time that Britney became involved with someone spoken for. Unnamed friends of Corie claimed she screamed out loud and burst into tears when she heard news of the wedding on TV.

In a spooky reminder of what happened to Reg Jones, Jason's next girlfriend after Britney Spears was also called Britney.

By a strange coincidence, Britney's life now seemed to be following the script of *Friends*. After 'The One where Rachel and Ross take a Break', she was now imitating the plot of 'The One in Vegas'. In this 1999 episode the on–off lovers got very drunk in a Las Vegas hotel and ended up getting married. It was quickly annulled after Rachel woke with the hangover from hell and was mortified when she realized what she had done. In real life, the actress Jennifer Aniston, who plays Rachel, told David Letterman, 'What was she [Britney] thinking? It's wild.'

The Vegas adventure probably did Britney very little harm. On top of all her other records, she could now lay claim to the shortest ever showbiz marriage.

The old virginity saga and break-up with Justin had run their course on a jaded public palate. This, however, transformed Britney into an off-the-wall rock chick, suggesting that maybe she actually was going to inherit Madonna's mantle. On a personal level she had made a big point to her family and, in particular, to her mother. Team Britney rallied round her in commendable fashion. The long-term effect drew the Spears family closer together than it had been for years. When the dust settled, Britney's love affair in Las Vegas was a life-changing mini-break.

'I had felt lost for so long.'

SEVENTEEN

Britney Against the Music

The rehearsal was not going well. Christina Aguilera was getting the hang of it but Britney, for once, was not entirely comfortable. In the end, an exasperated Madonna exclaimed, 'Kiss me, Britney, kiss me!'

Even the record company were worried. The sales of *Britney* would have been highly acceptable if it had been anybody else. The problem was the comparison with what had gone before. The first album . . . *Baby One More Time* sold more than 14 million copies, the second *Oops! I Did it Again* 10 million, but *Britney* only managed 4 million. This was perceived as a crisis, especially in the media, who talked of a 'waning' career. The fourth single from the album, 'Boys', peaked at number thirty-nine in the US charts despite featuring in the Austin Powers movie *Goldmember*. In the United Kingdom the situation was just as bad. *Britney* peaked at number four on the charts while two of the singles from it, 'Boys' and 'I Love Rock 'N' Roll', failed to make the top five. The latter only sold 45,000 copies in the UK.

Britney had not become unpopular and lost all her fans

overnight but the perception was that she would be unable to make the jump from teen star to fully fledged adult. A record company executive explains, 'A lot of people were down on her. It looked like the bubble was about to burst.' Things were even getting strained between her and Johnny Wright, described as 'some friction' by the record company insider. Wright was still the manager of Justin Timberlake, which did not help matters. Larry Rudolph, too, had moved to Los Angeles, where he had other commitments, like the enormously popular *Newlyweds* show starring Jessica Simpson. Britney was being looked after by Dan Dymtrow, one of Larry's team.

The music business moves so fast that you can be forgotten and part of a nostalgia tour in the blink of an eye. If the sales of her fourth album continued the downward progression and sold less than a million, then the likelihood was that it would be her last. Britney needed something special. She needed inspiration from her musical hero, Madonna. In an interview early in her pop career, Britney said, 'I hope to reinvent myself like Madonna does.'

Britney grew up pretending she was Madonna. Before the girl from Detroit became the world's biggest star, young white girls had no real aspirational figures in pop. The great female vocalists – Aretha Franklin, Tina Turner and Diana Ross – were black. And in the days before rock 'n' roll, the iconic figures were black singers like Billie Holiday, Ella Fitzgerald and Bessie Smith. Britney was never particularly exposed to country music, so popular in the South.

Her mother Lynne did not care for it so singers like Dolly Parton and Loretta Lynn were never role models. Instead, when she and little Britney headed off down the highway to dance classes, they would turn the radio up loud and sing along to Madonna. Other big stars of the mid eighties like Prince, Michael Jackson, Janet Jackson and Whitney Houston would also feature among young Britney's favourites but, when she was singing into her hairbrush in front of the bathroom mirror, she was pretending to be Madonna. When she sang 'Open Your Heart', Madonna's 1986 number one, at the start of *Crossroads* she was an eighteen-year-old bouncing around the bedroom. She was, in fact, recreating a scene from her home in Kentwood when she was five.

Madonna's name would be raised throughout Britney's career. Britney admired the way she was 'always four steps ahead of everyone'. There are two groups of female superstar, the singers and the dancers. The singers are led by Celine Dion, Whitney Houston and Mariah Carey; the dancers by Madonna, Janet Jackson and Jennifer Lopez. Britney would have to prove that she was more than just a teen artist to gain admission to this inner circle. Christina Aguilera was a candidate for the first group, Britney the second.

At the turn of the millennium Madonna's music was in the best shape it had been for years. The enormous success of the number one album *Ray of Light* was matched by her 2000 offering *Music*. The title track revealed an artist still fresh and contemporary after sixteen years at the pinnacle of pop.

Rumours first surfaced the following year that Madonna and Britney were considering a duet together which, at the time, seemed little more than publicity-machine flyers. One suggestion was that it would be a cover of the Serge Gainsbourg and Jane Birkin heavy breather 'Je T'aime . . . Moi Non Plus', which would have delighted all those who enjoy Sapphic undertones. Britney had only been at the top for three years but she was struggling.

Madonna did not need Britney Spears but something about her plight touched a nerve and, almost imperceptibly, she adopted the role of Britney's mentor. She seemed to resent the harsh attacks on Britney, taking them personally as an attack on womanhood in general: 'I find it really irritating that everyone beats up on Britney Spears. I want to do nothing but support her and praise her and wish her the best. I mean she's eighteen years old! It's just shocking. I wish I'd had my shit together when I was eighteen.'

The first indications that Britney might be receiving a welcome boost from Madonna came when the superstar started wearing Britney T-shirts. Madonna's defence of a potential rival was almost maternal and would have done Lynne Spears proud. She was, however, putting words into actions when she played a concert at the Roseland Ballroom in New York. She wore what was then her trademark cowboy hat and boots, leather trousers and a tight black T-shirt with the logo Britney Spears emblazoned across her chest. It was an advertiser's dream. Imagine what Coke or Nike would have paid the Queen of Pop for such an overt plug.

The evening improved still further for Britney when Madonna dedicated the ballad 'What it Feels Like For a Girl' to her new pet project. It may have been light-hearted and even ironic, but it was still publicity gold. Britney gushed afterwards, 'She's my idol. For her to dedicate – even ironically – my favourite song on *Music* is incredibly flattering and sweet.' Britney also responded by wearing, and being photographed wearing, a T-shirt bearing Madonna's name.

The mutual appreciation society even included wearing matching diamond necklaces worth $15,000 each. Madonna wore one with a letter M attached to it and then gave Britney one with a letter B attached. Britney said it inspired her and Madonna was someone she looked up to, especially now she was a mother. Madonna was actually old enough to *be* Britney's mother.

All the nice words, kind gestures and 'Aw shucks' responses would quickly become tiresome if there was nothing more concrete to back them up. Britney had been working hard on a new album as soon as she got bored with her six months off, which was very quickly. She had made some progress with *Britney* away from the Europop style that had served her so well at the launch of her career. Now, metaphorically speaking, it was time to put everybody who had been part of the old Britney Spears into a dustbin and start afresh. She needed the new album to do well, not just for her own professional success, but also as a response to the critical and commercial breakthrough Justin Timberlake had achieved with *Justified*.

Larry Rudolph first coined the phrase 'the Zone' to describe the impenetrable cocoon of concentration Britney wraps around her when she is in dance mode. She and her long-suffering dancers would literally practise a routine a hundred times before Britney would declare herself satisfied. 'In the Zone', she explained, meant 'Don't even try to talk to her now, she's in the Zone!' When Britney chose *In the Zone* as the title for her fourth album it was her private reaffirmation that she was fully committed to her professional career.

Britney is not at all sentimental where Britney Spears is concerned. A music business insider and keen Britney-watcher observes, 'She is very progressive in her thinking and is always bringing in new people. She is quite in control of her music and surrounds herself with a lot of great musicians.'

The idea that Britney can be influential in her own sound may seem absurd to those who cannot see past her diamond-encrusted navel. When artists are getting started, they tend to be manipulated like plasticine, moulded this way and that by Svengali-like managers and record company executives trying to find the all-important gap in the market in which to place a new signing. They will plane and sandpaper a square peg until he or she fits into a round hole. Justin Timberlake was in one of the blandest and most anaemic boy bands of them all but as he grew in confidence, he was able to surround himself by artists who could accept his ideas and enhance him musically. The result, *Justified*, is practically a classic. Robbie Williams was suppressed and depressed in Take That. When he turned solo he was a self-confessed drunk and drug addict who spent most of his early recording sessions slumped underneath the studio consul. Few, however, would doubt the extent of his input into his own music today.

For the first time, Max Martin was absent from a Britney Spears record. How would Britney cope without her musical 'dad'? It would be like leaving home for the first time to go to college. Acclaimed producers like The Neptunes and BT were also nowhere to be seen on *In the Zone*. Perhaps they had worked too closely with Justin Timberlake for Britney's current mood. He certainly had nothing to do with the album. In their place came another raft of cutting-edge music producers including Redstone and Penelope Magnet, Moby and The Matrix. Britney did not dispense with her own services. She co-wrote six songs on *Britney* but that number had risen to eight for *In the Zone*.

The key track, if by no means the best, was the opening 'Me Against the Music', which managed somehow to contrive a seven-strong songwriting credit suggesting committee-composing worthy of an American sitcom. But only one name really counted

– Madonna. Britney had originally recorded the track as a solo but Madonna came on board and made some changes to give it a 'Madonna touch', which is probably why it ended up with so many credits.

The result is a moody and throbbing dance track in which both singers sound eerily alike. If it wasn't for some helpful exchanges like 'Hey, Britney' it would be nearly impossible to tell them apart. Not all critics thought Madonna actually added anything to the track and that she was a distraction from the main event – Britney. It sounded more than a little like an extension of 'I'm a Slave for U' with a passing nod to Timberlake's 'Like I Love You', but musical criticism of the track was missing the point. Madonna was affording Britney a great opportunity to move forward – a get out of jailbait card. She needed to maximize the promotional possibilities.

Madonna was scheduled to appear at the twentieth annual MTV Video Awards at New York's Radio City Music Hall towards the end of August 2003. She approached Britney and Jennifer Lopez to appear with her in a special version of possibly her most memorable song, 'Like a Virgin'. Over lunch she explained the idea that the two younger women would wear wedding dresses similar to the one she wore in the original video that accompanied the song some twenty years earlier. Lopez declined to take part because she thought it inappropriate to wear a wedding dress so close to her wedding to Ben Affleck (which never happened). Christina Aguilera stepped into her stilettos. Madonna would now have two of the hottest young stars on stage with her. It never does any harm for a member of the older generation to put themselves next to the younger set. It gives everyone a boost, as was proven by the classic duet between Tom

Jones and Robbie Williams at the 1998 Brits. This collaboration had the added frisson of featuring Britney and Christina, whose rivalry had been built up by their publicity machines over the years.

The idea at these award ceremonies is to be the act that everyone is talking about for days – and hopefully weeks – afterwards. Britney had memorably achieved that with her snake dance two years earlier. The performance was billed as a celebration of Madonna's forty-fifth birthday so it was rumoured that she was planning something special. She was a mother of two young children, one of whom would be at the show with Madonna's second husband, Guy Ritchie, so it was assumed it would not be too outrageous. The number even began with Madonna's six-year-old daughter Lourdes walking on stage with another little girl, both dressed as flower girls at a wedding.

Britney then made her entrance, emerging from a giant white cake in full wedding dress, knee-length white boots and veil. She then launched into a few verses of 'Like a Virgin' before Christina came out from the cake and joined in, the pair of them soon gyrating suggestively on the stage in a most unvirginlike manner, having ripped off most of their bridal gowns. This was the first time the two had appeared together since the more innocent days of *The Mickey Mouse Club*. Then it was Madonna's turn. She was the groom, debonair in top hat, tails and black shiny boots. She sang her current release, 'Hollywood' – the old stuff is fun but you have to sell records – which she delivered in a smouldering, sexy manner before embarking on a dance interlude with her two virgin brides. As the whole world now knows, out of the blue, she gave Britney a classic French kiss, an open-mouthed snog. Immediately a camera settled on the face of Justin Timberlake watching from the audience and, it was noted, looking distinctly uncomfortable.

It was perfect show-stealing. Nobody recalls that Missy Elliott joined them on stage and sang 'Work it'. Nobody recalls the other artists that night, who included Avril Lavigne, 50 Cent, Eminem, Beyoncé and P Diddy. Even Christina Aguilera, who had also shared a kiss on stage with Madonna, was largely ignored in the aftermath. Christina's image was, after all, rather street slut so it did not seem such a big deal. For Britney, however, whose image was one built on a precarious alliance between innocence and knowing sex appeal, it was a major move.

Afterwards she was wide-eyed again: 'I've never kissed a woman before,' she announced demurely. What she said did not concur with what she did – the kiss was a declaration of mature sexuality. The schoolgirl/Lolita fantasy for middle-aged men was one that had to be kept inside a plain, brown paper wrapper. Madonna and Britney snogging was acceptable erotica for every age group. Not everyone, however, in the Bible Belt country was pleased. As one MTV producer observed, 'Middle America is not going to let this one go lightly.'

The reaction around the world achieved exactly the right result – people were talking about Britney Spears again. The timing was perfect in the build-up to a new album and tour. Even Christina found herself talking about Britney afterwards. She told the Access Hollywood online site that they had both practised kissing Madonna in rehearsal but that Britney had not been comfortable with it. Madonna, apparently, had to keep encouraging her. Christina thought that Britney needed to loosen up.

Britney's interview with *MTV News* was a masterclass in brand maintenance. Britney, it seemed, was just a fan of Madonna who had been granted a lucky break. She said that she had sung 'Like a Virgin' when she was three and that being in Madonna's presence was 'an honour'. She managed to make Madonna seem like an old maid without saying anything that was not entirely nice.

The interviewer, Gideon Yago, referring to the kiss, said, 'I just wanted to say thank you.'

'Well, thank you!' replied Britney.

The conversation coyly echoed the exchange of thanks she had shared with Reg Jones after her first serious kiss with a boy, when she really was an innocent teenager.

Madonna, having received a welcome boost for ''Hollywood', now returned the favour with 'Me Against the Music'. It was definitely Britney's song and only 'featured' Madonna, but it obviously had the groove of a Madonna dance track. The accompanying video, directed by the influential Paul Hunter, depicted Madonna tempting Britney into a maze-like underground club, only to disappear into thin air when Britney is about to reach out and touch her. The critics found it all quite symbolic – the passing of a pop baton – but that was a bit fanciful.

'Me Against the Music' performed surprisingly disappointingly when it was finally released, perhaps a victim of overhype. It was kept off the top spot in the UK by Busted's 'Crashed the Wedding'. In the US it peaked at number thirty-five but did reach number one in two dance charts which, these days, are almost as important as the overall singles list.

The *Guardian* labelled 'Me Against the Music' the only 'duff track' when the album was released in November 2003. It had provided the most publicity, but the CD was brimming with a fresh, invigorating sound. Best of all, lurking on the track list at number six was 'Toxic', a song that would become her biggest hit since 'Oops! . . . I Did It Again' and win her a host of new awards. Curiously, 'Toxic' was largely ignored when the album first came out. Critics still had plenty to say about Britney and Madonna and some of the more controversial lyrical content. But 'Toxic' was a good, almost old-fashioned dance track with multi hooks including a twangy guitar riff reminiscent of the master of the 'twang's the thang', Duane Eddy.

The woman behind 'Toxic' was the former dance darling Cathy Dennis, one of the most influential songwriters of modern times. In 2001, she had co-written the million-selling 'Can't Get You Out of My Head,' which was Kylie Minogue's biggest-ever hit. Cathy had a string of hits as a singer with a much-copied bob haircut in the early nineties. She was probably better known across the Atlantic, where her song '(Touch Me) All Night Long' reached number two. She never became a household name, which may have had something to do with her self-deprecatory style: 'It never even crossed my mind that I could be a pop star, because I come from Norwich.'

Unusually, she never thrived in the spotlight and by the end of the nineties had given it all up to be a full-time songwriter, promptly writing most of the S Club 7 hits, including the anthemic 'Reach'. She also co-wrote 'Anything is Possible', a million seller for Will Young. In some ways Cathy is the Britney antidote, displaying a healthy contempt for many artists: 'They're celebrities, not pop artists – if you asked them about music they wouldn't have a Scooby-doo.' She has become a very rich woman staying in the shadows.

If Britney had never recorded '. . . Baby One More Time', then 'Toxic' would have been *the* record that made her career. Instead, it probably transformed her musically into a credible artist. The track was produced by the relatively unheralded Bloodshy and Avant team, also responsible for the other Cathy Dennis track, 'Showdown'. Christian 'Bloodshy' Karlsson and Pontus 'Avant' Winnberg are both Swedish, emphasizing once more how much Britney owes to the unlikely Scandinavian musical hotbed. On release in March 2004 it made number one in the US, the UK and Canada. The track may not have been breathtakingly original but it did attract a more mature audience, topping dance and air-play charts. 'Toxic' quickly became a dance classic. For the first time the public were buying a Britney record because it was a great track and not because of the image that accompanied it. Cathy Dennis won a prestigious Ivor Novello award in 2004 for writing 'Toxic'. A year later the song would win a second Ivor, this time in the category of most performed work

At the time of the album's release, however, far more attention was given to two tracks, 'Breathe On Me' and 'Touch Of My Hand', because of the sexual content of the lyrics. The former was a seductive-voiced number which sounded more than a little like Donna Summer meets Kylie. The thinly veiled references to oral sex meant it garnered plenty of press coverage, as did the latter's obvious references to masturbation. They succeeded in promoting the image of Britney as a fully fledged sexual being, no longer a girl but all woman. That was exactly the plan. More true to life, and unintentionally funny, were the lyrics of 'Outrageous', an R Kelly song containing the lines 'Outrageous – my sex drive; Outrageous – my shopping sprees' which seemed to sum Britney up nicely. And on the intro to '(I Got That) Boom Boom', the Ying Yang twins declare, 'Let's all go to the club and get drunk with Britney!'

In the Zone went straight to number one in the US, selling more than 600,000 copies in the first week. The overall sales were slightly down on her previous albums but, considering the changing shape of the music business where sales in general have declined, it may be seen as a considerable success. The sales were more than enough to convince the world that Britney had, at least professionally, made the jump from teen queen to authentic artist.

'No one slipped anyone the tongue.'

EIGHTEEN

Britney Style

During filming for *Crossroads*, Britney and her co-star Taryn Manning both had matching tattoos of a Japanese word. Britney's decorated her hip. The word, they were told, meant mysterious – or at least it did until Taryn was in Japan and learnt that the lettering actually meant 'strange'.

When she was a young teenager in Kentwood, Britney just used to slob around in T-shirts and sweat pants. All her friends wore that sort of thing so she wore it too. Then she became Britney Spears and changed her style as often as if she were changing her underwear. She managed to get it wrong nine times out of ten, much to the delight of the bitchy world of professed style gurus. It was as if you could take the girl out of Wal-Mart but you couldn't take Wal-Mart out of the girl.

When she was in *The Mickey Mouse Club*, Britney was already wearing the crop tops which became her trademark and spawned a million young teenage imitators. Observers are wide of the target when they suggest she started this fashion in the video for '. . . Baby One More Time'. Her penchant for a bare midriff was born from going to dance classes in the Southern climate of home where in summer it was so sticky and hot that clothes would become drenched and Britney would try everything to try and keep cool. The crop top or the shirt tied up worked best, creating a draught as she back flipped across the floor.

Any girl from the age of eight upwards seemed to imitate this look. Chuck Yerger confirms that she always dressed like that during her time with Disney, well before she became aware of her own sexuality. While she was a fresh-faced teenager herself there was no problem. Every young girl could dress like Britney Spears. Years of family money worries had taken their toll and she would hesitate at spending more than $50 on a dress. She would wait, think about it for two weeks and then go back and buy the dress. She splashed out $70 at a XoXo store for an important showcase for Jive executives. It was a dress any girl might have bought in a shopping mall and Britney looked a million dollars wearing it. Her problems began when she actually had millions. As Dolly Parton famously said, 'It costs a lot of money to look this cheap.'

Fashion designers have much to answer for when dressing celebrities. Magazines like *heat* would be no more than a few pages each week without the gleeful depiction of the fashion disasters of the rich and beautiful. Britney established herself early as the Queen of Calamity. She was only sixth in the world-famous Mr Blackwell's list of the ten worst-dressed celebrities in 1999. He observed, 'This belly-baring songbird is better heard than seen.'

The following year she was number one, with the fashion guru declaring, 'Her bra-topped collection of Madonna rejects is pure fashion overkill.' It was ironic because Britney spent most of her time dressed in pyjamas while touring her stage shows. After a tiring show she would get up late – probably p.m. – and loaf about until it was time for hair, make-up and stage costume. The only time fashion critics have had a proper chance to judge her was when she turned up at the numerous award ceremonies she attended each year.

She lost her 'crown' the following year to Anne Robinson, but only by a slender margin. In 2002 she was given a reprieve before returning as second in 2003, tied with Madonna, a judgement on their notorious stage kiss: 'Kissin' cousins of couture crime,' said Mr Blackwell. In 2004, she was placed seventh as 'a clothes encounter of the catastrophic kind'. The charts are all very amusing but did reflect the view that Britney's fashion sense was not getting any better.

Mr Blackwell wasn't the only one to find fault. Ironically in the year she escaped his wrath the readers of *Prima* magazine stepped in to vote her the worst dressed of 2002. They were apparently appalled at the outfit she wore to the American Music Awards the previous year. She was dressed head to toe in denim, a weird long dress with a patchwork of different shades. She had a matching denim handbag and boyfriend Justin Timberlake was dressed in a denim suit with a denim Stetson. The outfits might have turned heads at a rodeo.

Fashion expert Zoë Aird of *Company* magazine observed, 'Britney tries to be sexy, but gets it wrong. It's not beads, it's beads *and* fringes *and* sequins. All subtlety goes out the window. Her look evolved from schoolgirl to pop starlet but now she's an adult, she finds it difficult to get her persona right.'

The denim ensemble seemed positively tasteful compared with some of her other creations. At one MTV Awards ceremony in New York she drew gasps when she arrived in what was described as a bondage-style outfit complete with unflattering lace-up boots which would have looked better on Russell Crowe in *Gladiator*. At another she wore a see-through top that left nothing to the imagination. At one premiere of *Crossroads* she was a vision in pink; at another she wore a severely slashed dress and thigh-high boots.

There was worse. On MTV's *Carson Daly Roast* in the summer of 2003, she wore a miniskirt, pop-art leggings, rhinestone bow tie, fedora and a cut and cropped T-shirt. Observers designated it a stripper's outfit. She had apparently bought the whole outfit on one mad shopping trip in New York.

The general thrust of criticism about Britney's outfits is that she needs to wear more clothes. Avril Lavigne, who may stick around long enough to be a Britney rival, said, 'I mean, the way she dresses, would you walk around the street in a fuckin' bra?' Britney herself has more of a sense of humour about what she wears. Her 'favourite' of her killer outfits was one she wore to a *Billboard* awards ceremony. The ensemble consisted of orange hot pants with fishnet stockings, an orange bra and an orange hat. To add extra oomph it was all tie-dyed. 'It was obnoxious,' said Britney. She explained at the time that she was feeling 'very orange'.

Britney uses stylists but accepts ultimate responsibility for everything she wears. The intriguing thing is that her outfits work beautifully on her videos, where she is playing a part for a particular story to accompany a song. They work less well when the edges become blurred between *the* Britney and the excited girl from Kentwood going to the Grammys. She is caught in a twilight zone. At what point is she Britney Spears? She still prefers to wear a favourite old top and some tracksuit bottoms when she goes out to buy cigarettes. Do we expect her to look like Britney Spears all the time?

Britney's taste is small town, parochial. Her favourite shop in McComb – other than Wal-Mart – is an unassuming, small boutique in the shopping mall, the sort of place that is ubiquitous in Oxford Street or in every provincial town across Britain. It's not Rodeo Drive. For the magazines and fashion commentators the answer is simple: she is always Britney Spears. If she looks a mess buying Kentucky Fried Chicken from a local fast-food joint in Malibu then she is Britney Spears and it's considered fair sport to sneer at her spots, her spreading waistline or the shapeless clothes she is wearing. Is that fair? She's not getting paid to entertain us when she's buying a packet of cigarettes.

Much was made of Britney's 'wedding' outfit when she married Jason Alexander in Las Vegas in the middle of the night. She had just got out of bed and had pulled on some torn jeans, sneakers and a baseball cap. It was not high fashion. She did, however, get it absolutely right for her wedding to Kevin Federline in Los Angeles. She wore a strapless white Monique Lhullier A-Line silk gown with a four-foot train and a row of pearly buttons down the back. She looked a million dollars. Her stiletto heels, which she needed, being so much shorter than Kevin, cost $1,000 from Sergio Rossi. They were silver sandals each trimmed with a crystal flower. She looked beautiful, surrounded by red and pink roses as well as pink and purple hydrangeas.

But this was her wedding, so it is hardly surprising that she looked terrific. The difficulty for Britney is that she is photographed absolutely everywhere and is roundly condemned for looking like an average girl just slobbing around. She told *Teen Hollywood*, 'I walk out of my house in my pyjamas, with no make-up on, and I just don't care because that's how I feel more comfortable. If you want me to wear fancy dress to go to Starbucks, then you are completely wrong.' Photographer Rupert Thorpe observes, 'Britney scrubs up well but she can also look spotty and baggy, chowing down on a bag of potato crisps.'

The dilemma over Britney's style was perfectly illustrated in an issue of *heat* magazine in February 2006. On the front cover there was a picture of Britney at the Screen Actors Guild Awards in Los Angeles looking fabulous with a short blonde bob haircut and wearing a blue silk minidress. The headline proclaimed, 'Wow! Britney's New Look!' Inside, on page 40, the enthusiasm was equally fervent 'Britney – You Look Great!' Further inside, however, on pages 92 and 93, there were no less than eleven pictures of braless Britney with the headline 'Put a Bra On!' Each picture was accompanied by an 'udder rating'.

The same month Mr Blackwell restored Britney to number one on his worst-dressed list, declaring that she looked like an 'over the hill Lolita'. He added, 'When it comes to couture, this Tacky Terror should take a bow.'

Britney's own take on her style is a resounding victory for the private Britney over the public one: 'I see my imperfections. I see my flaws. I just don't care.'

'I look like such a goob.'

NINETEEN

Mrs Federline

The long flight back from Europe to the US became a memorable one when Britney and Kevin became engaged. 'Will you marry me?' asked Britney.

Kevin Federline is a wigger, in LA slang – a black man who happens to be white. His former dancing friend Columbus Short acknowledges, 'Kevin Federline is the next best thing to a black guy. He has that hip-hop feel. He's so cool, edgy and funky.' The urban credibility of black culture was something Justin Timberlake had sought and successfully exploited in his music. Justin, however, was already a multi-millionaire when he eschewed the bland bubblegum of 'N Sync in favour of a more contemporary style. Kevin, as far as Britney Spears was concerned, was much more the real deal.

For all her money and trappings of success, Britney remained on the fringe of Hollywood life. The celebrity lifestyle did not sit easily with her now that she had overcome her initial sense of awe at being in close proximity to contemporary heroes. She still liked to read about the life in the pages of a glossy magazine rather than live it herself. Justin and his new partner Cameron Diaz were quickly established as Hollywood royalty but Britney preferred the company of dancers and people she met in nightclubs. She lived the celebrity lifestyle without the celebrities.

Britney had first met Kevin when she was eighteen and with Justin Timberlake. They remained friendly, but not in a dating sense. Kevin was part of the thriving dance scene in LA. He was with a group called LFO which, at one point, were on the road with Britney. He had two characteristics which set him apart from the others, at least as far as Britney was concerned. Firstly, he was very cool and unphased by her fame. Secondly, women were attracted to him like moths to a flame. Columbus Short explains the appeal, 'He is so the coolest – what you see is what you get. He is very much *not* Hollywood.' Britney echoes that view in an interview with *Details* magazine: 'He's not a shallow mother-fucker, Hollywood actor guy.'

Kevin had closer contact with Britney while her friendship with Columbus was developing. Columbus maintains that, while Kevin did not exactly give him advice where Britney was concerned, it was 'so funny' when they started dating. Britney could not have been at a lower ebb when she started going out with Kevin Federline. After her friendship with Columbus had stalled, she had ended up marrying Jason Alexander in a moment of madness. She desperately needed a greater stability in her private life. Kevin Federline, however, already had a partner, a young daughter and another baby on the way.

Despite his street credentials, Federline is from a comfortable background in Clovis, an unpretentious suburb in the northern Californian town of Fresno. He is a product of what is now fashionably termed a 'blended' family. His parents separated when Kevin was eight. Kevin was brought up by Mike, a mechanic (the same profession as Jason Alexander's father), and Collette, a banker. He has a brother, Chris, and two step-siblings, Dustin and Nicole.

It was a safe environment and, according to a neighbour, Kevin was a 'stable, everyday kind of guy'.

LA journalist Cliff Renfrew was impressed when he talked to old friends of Kevin in Clovis: 'None of them had a list of bad things to say about him. As a young guy he was pretty quiet. I think it helped that his father had a reputation for being very laid back and liberal. Kevin doesn't seem to have had too many rules to follow.'

Most yearbooks contain pictures of children smiling sweetly alongside captions which announce them as being the handsomest or most likely to succeed. Britney had been 'Most beautiful'. Justin Timberlake and Reg Jones both featured under flattering headlines in their respective school yearbooks. At the Tenaya Middle School in Clovis, Kevin Federline was named 'Most likely to be seen on "America's Most Wanted"'.

Kevin Federline was more wanted by the teenage girl population of Clovis than by the police. He started dating a local girl, Felicia Cabrero, when they were both just twelve. She recalled that in those days he would break-dance and do body-popping in the street but she introduced him to more serious dancing and encouraged him to go to a hip-hop class. Even at this young age, Kevin had the knack with the opposite sex. Felicia recalled how smooth he was, charming her by making her feel that 'my world was his'. He was her first love. The problems arose when

Felicia changed schools and word reached her that Kevin was seeing other girls. Kevin admitted it during a row and that was that.

When Felicia was interviewed about Kevin she explained that they had remained friends and that he had told her when he first met Britney and Justin. Her observations bode well for Britney's future: 'He had a lot of respect for her and didn't talk like "Oh, she's so hot". He said she was cool and down to earth and fun to hang out with.' Kevin, it seemed, had no difficulty separating the real Britney from 'Britney Spears'.

His growing reputation as a teenage womanizer, a love 'em and leave 'em guy, did not bode so well. His love of dancing provided him with the ideal setting in which to meet girls. When he was fourteen he walked into a local dance studio called D.A.N.C.E Empowerment run by dance teacher Duane Hurley. At first he was a 'typical fourteen year old with a chip on his shoulder', acting tough, an older version of Billy Elliott. After a while Duane persuaded him to join in: 'He was natural. He's got something girls just love.'

Kevin had two things going for him that 'girls just love'. Felicia Cabrero hinted at it, and another girlfriend, Amy Woody, confirmed it: 'He made me feel like I was the only girl in the world,' said Amy. She also declared him to be a 'great lover'. That opinion was shared by yet another girlfriend, Kerri Whittington, who said he was 'exciting and adventurous' in bed and confirmed that he was a 'babe magnet'. In others words, Kevin was an incurable romantic and a sex machine – an irresistible combination.

After dropping out of college in 1993, when he was just fifteen, Kevin passed the next few years in a series of dead-end jobs while honing his dancing skills at Dance Empowerment. He worked in a car wash and delivered pizza. Kevin was a popular figure at the dance classes, always fun and outgoing. Dance Empowerment is a non-profit-making academy which aims to keep children off the streets. Dance in the metropolitan areas of the US serves a similar purpose to football in Britain. It gives youngsters a sense of belonging and the opportunity to escape unhealthy environments of poverty and violence. It's like belonging to a gang without the side issues. Kevin was not an underprivileged child in any shape or form, but he was a high-school dropout with no discernable prospects and dancing did give him something better to do than hanging around on street corners looking tough. Duane Hurley observed, 'Kevin is very strong and intelligent. The dance programme made him what he is.'

In many ways Kevin was a typical suburban teenager. In his early teens he wore baggy clothes three sizes too big and hung out with his mates, smoking and skateboarding, and he wore his baseball cap back to front. Classmate Edwin McDonald recalled, 'He was in the raver circles, always wearing really big, baggy clothes.'

He had long hair and a small moustache, wore T-shirts and trainers and looked more like a roadie for The Eagles than a cutting-edge kind of guy. He was seventeen when he first became engaged to be married. Kerri Whitington revealed that he asked her to marry him after they had been going out for four months. He went down on one knee when they were sitting on a bench in a local park. It was a spot near where they first kissed and where they often made love outdoors. Kevin even bought a ring on hire purchase but the engagement did not survive more allegations of his wandering. Kerri had to deal with girls literally throwing themselves at him.

After drifting through his teenage years, ambition for something outside Fresno overtook Kevin. He shaved off his moustache, cut his hair and dyed it red, started wearing earrings and moved to Los Angeles to find fortune. He was now Kevin Federline, dancer. The girls he left behind still live in Fresno, but Kevin was to find a more exciting lifestyle in the clubs of LA where he started answering to the hip-hop name 'Too Daze'.

He met a head-turning, black former model and actress called Shar (Sharisse) Jackson and they quickly became an item. She revealed that she found him 'dynamite' in bed. Jackson was already a mother of two despite being in her mid twenties. She was well known for appearing on countless television shows, especially *Moesha*, a popular sitcom in the US in which she played a character called Niecy Jackson. It ran for five years from 1996 until 2001 and, while it did not exactly establish her as a household name, she was considerably better off than Kevin. He was enjoying some success as a backing dancer for Justin Timberlake and Pink, with whom he had toured for a year, but had yet to make a really substantial breakthrough.

They set up home together and Shar had their first baby, a daughter called Kori, in July 2002. Kevin had an instant family. The two older Jackson children at the time were seven and nine. She became pregnant with their second child in late 2003, at a time when Britney was being pictured with Columbus Short. The prospect of a fourth mouth to feed prompted Shar Jackson to suggest to Kevin that he should get back in the dance loop in LA. She was six months pregnant when she took the call in which Kevin revealed he was seeing someone in LA or 'hanging out with someone this week', as he put it. The someone was Britney.

Above Britney breaks down while talking about Justin on American television in November 2003.

Right Britney loves T-shirts, but the American Dream was turning into a nightmare.

Below Britney sought consolation in the arms of Jason Alexander, who she married for fifty-five hours in Las Vegas.

Above left So that's what Britney saw in Kevin Federline. He provides the crotch she needed on holiday in Hawaii.

Top right They scrub-up well for this wedding photo, which became their 2004 Christmas card.

Below Britney looks fabulous as an expectant mother. She is pictured here with Kevin and Jamie Lynn, attending the premiere of *Charlie and the Chocolate Factory* at Graumann's Chinese Theatre in Hollywood.

Every slip Britney has made as a mother has been pictured around the world. In May 2006 she appeared to need a bodyguard's helping hand to stop baby Preston sliding from her grasp.

Her close shave in February 2007 shocked the world into believing there was something seriously wrong with Britney.

Britney's frustration boiled over when she attacked a photographer's car with her umbrella outside Kevin's new home in February 2007.

Britney seeks divine intervention during her much scorned comeback appearance at the MTV Video Music Awards at The Palms Hotel in Las Vegas, September 2007.

Above The county court in Los Angeles became a second home to Britney after her split with Kevin. Here she is bustled into a hearing in January 2008, a month before her hospitalization.

Right A glimpse of Britney's agony. After a row with Sam Lutfi, Britney slipped outside her house with her Yorkshire terrier, London, for a quiet weep.

Left For the present at least, where father Jamie leads, Britney follows.

Below Not everybody liked Britney's appearance on the *X Factor* in November 2008 when she lip-synched to her number one hit 'Womanizer'. But twelve million were watching.

Opposite What a difference a year makes. Britney looks like her old radiant self at the MTV Video Music Awards at the Paramount Studios in Los Angeles, September 2008.

THE CIRCUS TOUR
March 2009

Britney is more
centrefold than Mona Lisa.
Pictured on stage
in Newark.

Miami Vice:
Officer Britney
performing in
Florida City.

Shar could not believe that Kevin would leave her when she was six months pregnant and admitted to being very hurt. She came out with some pricelessly sour comments: 'You both smoke, you both drink and you both cheated on significant others after three years.' She also called him a 'dirty dog'.

By the time Shar Jackson gave birth to Kevin's second child, a son called Kaleb, Kevin and Britney were engaged. A friend in Los Angeles observed, 'You don't leave your wife or partner when she is six months pregnant. It's a complete no-no. What on earth was Britney thinking?' The damning evidence as far as Britney is concerned was that it was perceived as not being the first time she had lured a man away from a woman expecting his child. Columbus Short's wife was also heavily pregnant when he was close to Britney, although he maintains they had already split up.

Britney, of course, was madly in love. Her most telling comment on Kevin leaving Shar reveals how her strong Christian moral upbringing had been turned inside out. She said, 'He did it for me.' It was as if this was the ultimate sacrifice a man could make for love.

By the time that Kaleb was born, Shar Jackson had calmed down considerably. She declared that she was not going to be 'the bitter baby mommy'. Rumours circulated that Britney had eased her financial burden, including one that she had bought her fiancé's ex a new house. Jackson strongly denied this, although the prospect of paternity payments being met on time had considerably improved. She and Kevin were both struggling financially when Britney arrived on the scene, with reports of non-payment of rent and problems with vehicle finance.

Jackson indicated that life was too short to hold grudges. Her state of mind was influenced by the ironic fact that her public humiliation had brought her back into the limelight at a time when her career was in the doldrums. She had four young children and was pushing thirty so getting back on the celebrity carousel would have been difficult. She revealed that job offers were flooding in within six weeks of giving birth: 'In a sick, twisted way the Britney thing has put my name back out there.' She said you should never blame the 'other woman' and also declared that she was determined to make the situation work because, when the public interest had long died down, she would still have Kevin's children to raise.

Shar Jackson did reveal what turned Kevin on in bed. She said he loved what she wore in a video for the Missy Elliott song 'One Minute Man'. Her outfit consisted of a black leather bustier and see-through net skirt with skimpy lace panties underneath; a pair of six-inch-heel patent black leather boots finished off the look. The joke was that the outfit sounded just like something Britney would wear on stage, especially for her 2004 *Onyx Hotel* tour.

The Onyx Hotel in question was a plush hotel in Boston. Lynne Spears designed a special 'Britney Spears room' at the hotel where guests could stay in a room that replicated her own bedroom in Serenity. The minibar was stocked with some of Britney's favourites, including Red Bull, Pepsi (naturally) and strawberry pop tarts. For relaxation there was *Crossroads* to watch on DVD. The room cost $349 to rent in high season but ten per cent of that went to the Britney Spears Foundation.

On 2 March Britney opened the tour in San Diego, singing 'Toxic', which would become number one in the UK just in time for the her concerts at Wembley. The tour proved that, despite the debacle of her private life and her fifty-five-hour nightmare in Las Vegas, she was still immensely popular. Her average gross on each of the first eleven dates was nearly $750,000. Gary Bongiovanni, editor of *Pollstar*, commented, 'Her moment in the sun isn't over yet. There aren't many acts out there who can sell 10,000 tickets per show.' Britney even managed to outperform the winners of *American Idol*, who were very much teen flavour of the month in the US. Ray Waddell of *Billboard* paid Britney the best professional compliment by observing 'She's transcended that teen-pop thing, and it looks like a lot of her fans are going with her.'

The American leg of the tour ended on 10 April, which gave Britney the chance to develop her relationship with Kevin and introduce him to the world's press. Practically every member of the paparazzi had been tipped off that Britney was the celebrity worth following on that particular spring day. Rupert Thorpe, one of the leading photographers in Los Angeles, recalls, 'She "introduced" him at the Beverly Hills Hotel. By that I mean she came out with him and we all took pictures. We didn't have a clue who he was although someone said he was a dancer.

'It was a crazy day. They drove off to go to the beach at Malibu and Santa Monica and we all followed. There were something like 15 big SUVs on Britney's tail. On the way they decided to pull over at Subway and buy a snack. She stayed in the car and he got out. What could we do? All the photographers just stopped their cars in the lanes of the freeway. Nobody could risk losing them so we just had to stop. The entire highway was blocked with traffic going crazy behind us while Britney stopped to buy a sandwich.'

Since that first day Britney and Kevin's life has been led at lens length. Everything they have done has been to the sound of a zoom and a shutter. Any nod to privacy has been ignored. Rupert

Thorpe adds, 'I couldn't believe how open she was, just walking down the beach with Kevin. There was none of that "Get out of my way" stuff.

'Britney is much more relaxed than Justin Timberlake and Cameron Diaz, who get so pissed off. They have a sixth sense when you are around and inevitably your picture has them giving you the finger in it.'

Britney's relaxed attitude towards the photogaphers who pursued her was not destined to last. Britney's private life was being conducted amid more publicity than her professional life as Britney Spears. In the aftermath of Las Vegas, 2004 proved to be just as momentous in her professional life as in her private life. Her brother Bryan left New York, where he had been living in Britney's penthouse, and moved into her ocean-front apartment, a few hundred yards from the Fairmont Miramar Hotel where he conducted most of his business meetings. Most days his black Mercedes, a gift from Britney, can be seen parked a few yards from the hotel entrance. He has taken charge of much of her personal management.

By the end of the year, neither Johnny Wright nor Larry Rudolph were involved. Britney parted company with Larry Rudolph, ostensibly in an amicable split. They had been together nine years. They both had nice things to say. Rudolph said, 'Britney and I simply realized that we have done all we can do together.' Britney said, 'We had a great run and I appreciate Larry's guidance over the years.'

The additional quotes were more illuminating, with Britney wishing Rudolph all the best while her now former manager was looking forward to 'new challenges'. The phrasing suggested that the impetus for the split was on Britney's side. After all, why would Rudolph give up his percentage of an income, estimated that year to be $40 million, to embark on fresh challenges? In his place Britney appointed Dan Dymtrow, twenty-nine, who had helped look after her when he worked for Rudolph in New York. He was a close friend of Bryan. Far from suffering from long-term contrition in the wake of her Vegas marriage, Britney seems to have become empowered by that adventure, seizing more control of her life. It would not, however, be the last of Larry Rudolph in Britney's story.

At the end of April, Britney flew to Europe for the European leg of the tour. Her concerts had become pretty scary affairs, in that huge cans of Pepsi were displayed on the giant video screens and very young fans were encouraged to chant 'Pepsi, Pepsi' incessantly as if they were extras in a sci-fi horror. Britney showed that she had lost none of her professionalism when it came to working an audience. 'There are a lot of cute guys in this audience,' she announced mid-set. 'I might marry one of you.' The man she wanted to marry was home in California at the time. But Britney had learnt from past mistakes, particularly with Justin and Reg Jones, that relying on the telephone to keep a relationship sweet was not a good idea. She flew Kevin out to join her, giving photographers in London and Stockholm the chance to earn a few pennies.

The media was in a frenzy over what Britney Spears could possibly see in a man like Kevin Federline. They made much of the fact that Kevin was penniless. In some ways that was part of the appeal for Britney. He was just an ordinary Joe, the sort of man she might have met in a store in the shopping mall searching for trainers. He shared her love of Big Macs and fried chicken. He smoked far too many Marlboro Lights and liked to drink and party. He wasn't bothered about ordering a double decaf latte with a twist. He preferred a beer or a slug of bourbon. And he was sensational between the sheets. One appreciative ex-girlfriend might be ignored but four perhaps suggested a pattern. When Britney grabbed his crotch for the benefit of the paparazzi, she resembled a girl on a hen night enjoying the forbidden fruits of the male entertainment.

In Ireland they had matching tattoos of lucky dice etched onto the insides of their wrists. It was a gesture for each other and was a little more tasteful (just) than having the name Kevin scratched on her body. Tattoos are an absolute must for anyone with pretensions to celebrity. Kevin also had an eagle on his left shoulder. Traditionally in the Deep South tattoos were strictly for rednecks, but that is no longer the case, although Britney kept the first time she went to a parlour – for an angel on her back – a secret from her mother. She also has two – a flower and a symbol – on her toes, which is a particularly painful place for a tattoo because the skin is so thin there. At the same time as the dice she had some Hebrew symbols drawn on to her neck which were a sign of her devotion to the religion of Kabbalah.

When she returned to Los Angeles after the annulment of her marriage, Britney sought consolation by attending a large Baptist church with a primarily black congregation in an unfashionable area of the city. For whatever reason she gave up attending and, instead, turned to the faith recommended by Madonna. Britney had been raised as a churchgoing Southern Baptist in a deeply God-fearing community. God and religion had been of immense importance to her growing up. She did not question her faith. To follow an entirely different one was a hugely significant step.

Kabbalah is a breakaway branch of the Jewish religion that can trace its origins to the first century AD when Isaac the Blind formed a group of like-minded scholars to explore the mystical traditions of their faith. The ultimate goal of Kabbalists, as devotees are called, is to reach a oneness with God, to arrive in a state of total knowledge of the universe through extensive meditation. An extensive range of teachings and books are available to help the follower on their quest. Madonna, raised a Catholic, has enthusiastically embraced Kabbalah, helping to finance centres around the world. Her passion has made Kabbalah a fashionable option for celebrities like Demi Moore, Ashton Kutcher and Paris Hilton. The badge of Kabbalah is a red string bracelet dangling from a follower's wrist. Britney has been pictured many times wearing hers. Even David Beckham has been seen with one. The string, which costs $26, can be purchased online and is said to deflect 'envious stares and looks of ill will'.

Britney has also been photographed carrying Kabbalah literature, but it is not known how much money she has spent on her new religious interest. Kabbalah requires a great deal of study and there is no way of knowing the extent of Britney's intellectual involvement. Critics worry about its entrepreneurial ways, but it offered a support system for Britney when she felt very isolated. It encouraged her to pray for something more substantial than a Grammy award (although she did win one of those too).

Britney explained the importance of Kabbalah to her in a message she wrote for fans: 'It [Kabbalah] has helped me get rid of a lot of negative influences that were guiding me down the wrong path. There came a point when not even my family or my advisors had the answers I needed. Through Kabbalah, I was able to look within myself, clear all the negative energy and turn my life around.'

Undoubtedly Britney had been very calm since the low point of Las Vegas, although that may have had more to do with Kevin than the other K. Britney's family closed ranks around her after Vegas. One of the most dramatic postscripts involved the rehabilitation of her father. Quietly his life, which had seemed out of control with reports of heavy drinking and partying in New York, was sorted out behind the scenes with a move to Los Angeles. He went into a rehab clinic in the summer of 2004 and emerged to start a new business in Venice Beach. He bought a sandwich and smoothie cafe called J. J. Chill which was soon thriving. Despite his very masculine image Jamie has always been the most adept of the Spears family in the kitchen. Reg Jones still talks of Jamie's prowess as a cook. Britney reveals his skill in the notes to her album *Britney* in which she declares 'Daddy – I love you so much, especially when you cook for me!' Then she thanks her mother for 'being the best role model in the world'. Lynne was spending more time in LA and friends observed that Jamie and Lynne were getting on better than they had for years. Lynne was still looking after Britney's sister Jamie Lynn, but her youngest daughter's career was thriving even more than Britney's was at a young age. Jamie Lynn, looking even more like a mini-Britney, was appearing in a Nickelodeon show called *Zoey 101* and was splitting her time between LA and McComb, where she still attended Parklane Academy.

Lynne had been horrified when Britney married Jason Alexander but had subsequently realized how important it was for Britney to be happy. She seemed readily to accept Kevin, perhaps falling for his obvious twinkle. An LA friend observes, 'Kevin is basically a nice guy. Britney's parents seem perfectly OK with him. They can see that's she's happy.'

On their way back from Europe, Britney and Kevin became engaged. Britney chose a $50,000 engagement ring from renowned jewellery designer Cynthia Wolff, which she paid for by a credit card. The media jumped all over the fact that Kevin did not even have the money to buy his own ring. Britney and her friends seemed much less concerned. Columbus Short says, 'They may not have equal bank accounts but I think they will make it.'

Soon after they became engaged, they were photographed strolling along the beach at Marina Del Rey. Britney was wearing a top bearing the slogan, 'I'm a Virgin'. It was an ironic joke especially as underneath it declared, 'But this is an old T-shirt'. The joke was even better for those who recalled the time she and Justin Timberlake strolled around Sunset Strip in the rain underneath an umbrella emblazoned with the word 'Virgin'. Britney wasn't then and she certainly wasn't now.

She seemed able to relax despite the constant scrutiny. For her brother Bryan's birthday at the Beverly Hills Hotel she hired an actress to come along and pretend to arrest him. Rupert Thorpe recalls, 'It was hilarious. They were in a private bungalow and suddenly Britney came running out screaming and then Bryan appeared being led away in handcuffs. It made a great picture.'

Britney, in a manner of speaking, had a lucky break before she was due to resume the rest of her *Onyx Hotel* world tour. She was filming a new video in New York when she slipped and suffered an injury similar to the one that had affected her at the start of her career. Another arthroscopic operation to remove a piece of floating cartilage forced the cancellation of the remaining thirty-five tour dates. Although she promised to reschedule the concerts – the enforced rest allowed her to stay with Kevin and not risk any separation dampening their enthusiasm for one another.

The wedding was expected before the end of 2004. In the meantime Britney did not stop working. She was putting together a Greatest Hits package for Christmas release and went into the studio to record 'My Prerogative', the old Bobby Brown hit, and two new songs, 'Do Somethin' and 'I've Just Begun'. All three were produced by Bloodshy and Avant who had done such a commercial job on 'Toxic'. 'My Prerogative', in particular, was a Madonna-like presentation of a famous track. The lyrics seemed made-to-order for the new version of Britney Spears, stating that she did not need permission to make her own decisions – 'Don't tell me what to do,' she growled, while asking why she couldn't just live her life.

The cover of the CD was almost ironic. Britney was pictured in miniscule black bra and briefs and an excuse for a fur jacket. Her hair was porn-star blonde and she looked as plastic as it was possible to look. She was the ultimate Sindy doll, a million miles from the fresh faced ingénue of . . . Baby One More Time. If the idea was to show the public that this is what they had made Britney Spears become then it was masterful. There were even Internet rumours that it wasn't Britney's body in the picture but that she had used a body double.

The conception that Britney was closing a chapter on her life was emphasized by the fact that when the album appeared on the shelves Britney Spears was a married woman. Nothing could top her Las Vegas wedding, but she still had a surprise or two in store with her marriage to Kevin. Much of the speculation beforehand had questioned whether she would opt for a Kabbalah ceremony.

More than 300 invitations were sent for the plush affair at the luxurious Bacara resort in Santa Barbara. This was going to be the spectacular wedding of Britney's dreams. The date was set as 16 October. Just over a month before the big day her plans were leaked to the tabloid press in the US prompting Britney and Kevin to think again. The last thing they wanted was their wedding vows drowned out by the noise of helicopters ferrying photographers with long lenses across the venue. They decided on Plan B – a much smaller, low-key affair in the backyard of their wedding planner's home in Studio City. The new ceremony would be kept entirely secret. On 14 September, the couple's closest friends and family gathered in Los Angeles for what everyone had been told was their engagement party. Only the wedding planner Alyson Fox, her husband Jeff, a fashion store owner, and Britney's trusted assistant Felicia Culotta knew what was about to happen. Not even Lynne was in on the secret.

Britney had never been to the Fox home before the day of the ceremony but was delighted when she saw what had been prepared on her behalf. As she stepped inside she was almost overwhelmed by the sweet fragrance of thousands of red roses. Lights in the trees lit up the garden, giving the proceedings a fairy-tale quality. When the guests arrived at the house that evening they were handed invitations which began 'Surprise!' It was certainly that for Lynne who complained she was not dressed for a wedding. Fortunately, everybody's outfits were ready for them upstairs.

The wedding may not have been the grand celebration they had originally planned – there were only twenty-seven guests –

but it had all the ingredients Britney had always wanted for her big day, which meant so much in her life. Her parents were there and her father gave her away. Her cousin Laura Lynne was her chief bridesmaid and gave a moving speech about her relationship with Britney and how much it meant to her. The other bridesmaids were her closest friends Cortney and Jansen and they were joined by Jamie Lynn and the ever loyal Fe, who caught the bridal bouquet. The bride looked radiant with a new chestnut-brown hairdo and her gown was traditional white. Her mother observed, 'She looked like an angel.'

The ceremony itself was brief with little religious overtone. There was a small drama when Laura Lynne handed Britney the wedding band for Kevin. She promptly dropped it, only to be told by the female minister that it was a good sign. Endearingly, Kevin became quite emotional when he declared in his vows that he was 'so proud to be your husband'. He touched Britney's face and told her he loved her. Kabbalah was not entirely forgotten. Each bridesmaid had received a wedding bag which contained a special cut-out of a Kabbalah word in Hebrew that symbolized the power to heal. The bag also contained designer jeans, a necklace, earrings, a picture frame and the pink sweatsuits for the post-wedding party. The drinks reception, including speeches, was held at the house. Britney changed from her demure, classical wedding gown into a white minidress that could have come from one of the raunchier numbers on stage and left little to the imagination.

Afterwards, the photographers who had realized what was going on snapped the couple as they left in a black SUV. Britney was screaming with happiness, while Kevin looked cool. The wedding party was held at the trendy Xes nightclub in Los

Angeles. The outfits for the bride and groom's supporters had already been chosen – white tracksuits with 'Pimps' emblazoned on the back of the men's and 'The Maids' on the back of the women's pink sweatsuits. Britney had changed again and was now wearing one bearing the logo 'Mrs Federline', while her husband's simply declared 'The Pimp'.

The whole proceedings were quite provincial. They ate ribs and chicken and Britney and Kevin's first dance was to the corny soft-rock tune 'Lights' by 1980s California band, Journey. They spent their wedding night at the Bel Air Hotel. Kevin revealed that he had to carry his new wife over the threshold. 'I carried her out of the club', he said, wryly.

His one disappointment on an 'awesome' day was that his two children, Kori and Kaleb, were not there. Kevin was caught out by changing the date of the wedding and the kids were already looking forward to a day with their mother at Disneyland, which had been planned well in advance. Kevin explained, 'I couldn't say they needed to be here because their daddy was getting married, so I left it.'

The story soon went round that the wedding was fake, but it was simply a case of missing paperwork. The whole thing had been organized so swiftly that the proper documentation had not been collated and that was sorted out quietly in the subsequent weeks. Britney was definitely Mrs Britney Federline, a name she likes.

'I've kissed a lot of frogs in my life and now I have my prince.'

TWENTY

A Chaotic Life

The good-looking, athletic young man ambled into the vast Wal-Mart superstore in McComb and looked around. It was late in the evening and only a few stragglers were left searching the aisles. An assistant, who recognized him as the new husband of Britney Spears, went over and asked what she could help him find. 'Pregnancy test,' said Kevin.

Britney was halfway to her personal dream of marriage and a house full of children. In these days of female empowerment it may seem slightly incongruous that here was an independent, rich, successful woman craving the same life goals as her friends and contemporaries back home in Kentwood and McComb. Surprisingly, for a twenty-two-year-old woman, she had felt that she was being left behind. In southern terms she was a bit of a slowcoach. On her regular trips home there always seemed to be a wedding and other happy 'family' announcements. When her friend Cindy Reed married, Britney broke the habit of a professional lifetime and sang a cappella at the wedding.

A month after her own wedding, Britney declared, 'Being

married is great, and I can't wait to start a family.' She was desperate to be a young mom and advised everyone to watch when she was twenty-three. That was a red rag for the media, who would speculate daily on whether she was getting fat because of all the junk food she was eating or if a bump could be detected as she lounged about in a bikini or went to the shops in a cut-off top.

The British press were the worst offenders. One newspaper declared that Britney was definitely pregnant when she and Kevin married and that was why the wedding was brought forward. It also claimed Britney was telling 'friends' that she was expecting. A 'source' close to the singer said, 'She has told only her family and closest circle that she is pregnant.' They were jumping the gun, of course, but, if they had fluked the truth, then a plethora of stories shouting 'You read it here first' would have followed so it was probably worth taking a flyer.

While Britney waited for biology to take effect she made a particular effort to bond with Kevin's daughter Kori. She took her shopping in Malibu, swimming at the hotel where she was staying while builders worked on her house, and even helped style the two-year-old's hair. Kori seemed to be spending more time in Britney's arms than her little dog, Bit Bit. She even wrote on her fan site that she had bought her stepdaughter the 'cutest dresses' before gushing that she loved buying children's clothes.

Kevin purchased the pregnancy test in Wal-Mart in February 2005 and the kit confirmed the news that Britney was desperate to hear. When the test returned positive, it became the worst kept secret. Britney gave up smoking and drinking and kept her natural brown hair colour to avoid exposing herself to the toxins in her hair dye. Britney and Kevin, however, refused to confirm the obvious and make an official announcement. Their hand was eventually forced when they travelled to Florida in April to stay at her luxury penthouse condominium in the resort of Destin. Britney had bought the $1.5 million penthouse in 2002. It was a change of scenery while they waited to move in to their new Malibu home.

The trip had started uneventfully, just an ordinary day shopping for furniture and a new dress, and eating buffalo wings, cheese dip and ice-cream sundaes. She even dragged Kevin along to the Charming Baby store where they looked at baby clothes. That night, however, Kevin rushed Britney to the local Sacred Heart Hospital in West Destin. They were worried she was losing the baby and Britney was seen to be crying. Kevin paced up and down outside. He called Lynne who got on the first plane to be at her daughter's side.

It turned out not to be the miscarriage everyone feared. The next day Britney, accompanied by Lynne, was transferred to the larger Fort Walton Beach Medical Centre where she registered under the name of Madison Lea, but everyone knew it was her. Further tests revealed that the baby was absolutely fine, but that she needed complete rest for a week. It was a minor scare, but that's still a scare.

Speculation that she had lost the baby brought about an announcement on her official website, Britneyspears.com: 'The time has finally come to share our wonderful news that we are expecting our first child together. There are reports that I was in the hospital this weekend. Kevin and I just want everybody to know that all is well. Thank you for your thoughts and prayers.'

Nobody was in the least bit surprised. The pregnancy allowed Britney a little breathing space as far as the media was concerned.

She was treated more kindly, even being paid compliments when she decided to have her hair cut short and dispense with the usual hair extensions. It made a change from being lambasted about her rotten fashions, scraggy hair and ridiculous little dogs.

The hospital scare gave her the excuse to put *the* Britney Spears on the back burner. At least she had a reason not to suffer the obligatory 3,000 sit-ups a day to keep in shape. Instead, all her favourite fat-laden food was allowed. Although 2005 was a year in which pregnancy dominated Britney's life, she did not completely disappear from view. She was busy earning her $12 million for launching the perfume *Curious*. This was the sort of work Britney enjoys. When she was in New Orleans for a promotional trip Lynne came along too and the pair, as ever, went shopping. They also stopped off at Starbucks, where Britney ate an entire roast beef sandwich while she waited at the counter to pay. It was just like at home in Malibu.

Another important launch came in April when the first episode of *Britney and Kevin – Chaotic* was shown on American television. A reality television show featuring Britney had been rumoured to be in the pipeline for several months. She had been impressed by the success Jessica Simpson had enjoyed in *Newlyweds*, a show in which her former manager Larry Rudolph had been a key figure. She hoped she could match it with her own real-life drama. The first series of five episodes had been filmed in 2004 and was a behind-the-scenes look at how her relationship with Kevin had evolved, beginning in episode one when she was on her *Onyx Hotel* tour in Europe and telling the camera that she had met a guy (Kevin) in Los Angeles who she could not get out of her head.

Britney also engaged in some playful sexual banter with Felicia

Culotta and with JC Chasez, her support act, whose favourite sexual position she demanded to know. She also asked bouncers, roadies and assorted crew about their sexual preferences. It was nothing too spicy but a million miles away from virginal Britney Spears. She herself protested that she could not answer because she was worried her family might be watching. The series revealed the couple's flirting, Britney's insecurities – including her nerves at Kevin seeing her perform live – their time in Paris, the engagement and realizing he was the one.

Chaotic did not impress the critics. The *Washington Post* described it an 'execrable mess by absolutely any standards' and a show that 'plumbed new depths of shallowness'. The reviewer, Tom Shales, thought Kevin had bad posture and no personality, and that Britney herself was a 'smutty-mouthed, pudgy-faced brat'. The *Parents Television Council* dubbed the show the 'worst of the week'. Their reviewer, Aubree Bowling, noted, 'It is especially revolting for viewers to note that during the time of the show's filming, Kevin's former girlfriend was home in California raising toddler daughter and pregnant with his second child.'

The series, which was shown on British television in August 2005, was strangely compelling. It was shown in the US on the relatively minor UPN network, which makes the initial viewing figures of 3.5 million a startling success. *Chaotic* is an interesting concept because the viewer never knows for sure how much acting is actually going on in this sort of show. Intriguingly, the show was originally titled *Can You Handle Our Truth?*, which indicates the intention of a warts and all documentary-style show. Britney had spent her whole life being two people, *the* Britney Spears, superstar, and Britney, ordinary southern girl from Kentwood, and *Chaotic* brought together elements of both – although it was still a performance for the cameras.

The final episode focused on their wedding day, a private event made public for millions of people. Punningly titled 'Veil of Secrecy', it revealed how they kept the big day a secret from their families. It provided a very rare glimpse of a celebrity wedding. Kevin came across as easygoing and intrinsically nice, while Britney was stunning and very much in love. The ceremony was revealed to be a relaxed and informal affair. Most of all, everybody looked happy – except perhaps Britney's father who appeared a bit grumpy.

Almost inevitably the 'Newlyweds', Jessica Simpson and Nick Lachey, announced they were splitting up in November 2005. Britney and Kevin's own marriage soon became the subject of daily gossip. From the outset there has been an element of 'it won't last' in how the relationship has been perceived by journalists. Kevin was certainly not given any preferential treatment by the press simply because his famous wife was expecting a baby. He had to suffer a plethora of stories suggesting that he had a personal hygiene problem. His former girlfriend Amy Woody, who had previously praised him as being a great lover, now popped up claiming, 'He wouldn't shower or brush his teeth at all so he'd stink. He didn't care.'

Worse was to come just a couple of weeks after the pregnancy was announced when a 'Vegas hooker' claimed in the pages of the *National Enquirer* that she had 'partied' with Kevin and passed out on a bed after sinking a cocktail of booze and Ecstasy. The woman – a private adult entertainer – alleged she had encountered Kevin over the previous few months during his trips

BRITNEY

to Las Vegas with a group of male friends. The story did not suggest that Kevin had cheated on Britney.

The veracity of the story is immaterial. The world, it seemed, was determined that Kevin was going to suffer death by a thousand small cuts, whether by a story comparing his wealth (nil) to his wife's ($100 million) or a website urging Britney to divorce him or pouring scorn on his efforts to make something of himself. He was in a no-win situation, although he did have the consolation of living in a palatial home and driving a Ferrari.

Moving into her $7.5 million mansion was becoming a priority for Britney. She had spent the past few months living primarily at the Fairmount Miramar Hotel in Santa Monica. Rooms were $300 a night while the little self-contained bungalows at the back, one of which Britney and Kevin occupied, cost $1,000 a night.

The hotel literature boasted an 'exquisite setting for privacy', but this proved not to be the case for Britney. Photographers found it easy to rent a third-floor room with a balcony overlooking the pool area, where Britney spent days lounging around in her favourite green bikini. The pool area was for guests only but it is very visible. One afternoon when Britney was there, a holidaymaker from Manchester was enjoying a dip with his family. His twelve-year-old son splashed over to Britney and, recognizing her, excitedly told his father, who was swimming nearby. His Dad didn't recognise her with her natural brown hair. 'That's not Britney Spears,' he told his son. 'Well, actually I am,' exclaimed Britney laughing.

Britney's new home had its own gigantic swimming pool, as well as a pool house, tennis court, guest accommodation and a trampoline in the back yard. Aerial photographs reveal a huge, white-stucco, two-storey complex set in 1.4 acres of wooded

266

hillside. The style, in the parlance of Hollywood estate agents, would be Spanish contemporary with eight bedrooms and eight bathrooms. The mansion – at the foot of a hillside – is in a gated community, where her nearest celebrity neighbour is Mel Gibson. Neither photographers nor members of the public can gain access to the house or grounds without permission so there is complete privacy and safety. Gated homes with guards and security patrols are increasingly popular with celebrities in California. Robbie Williams, for one, moved into a gated community so that when he opened his curtains in the morning he did not have a photographer snapping him in his boxer shorts. Britney and Kevin, preparing for a new arrival, fitted the perfect celebrity profile for a security-conscious home.

A couple of weeks before she was due to give birth, Britney was deeply upset by the impact of Hurricane Katrina on her home state of Louisiana, especially when the pictures of the floods in New Orleans were shown on television. Britney's brittle mood was not helped by being unable to contact Lynne or Jamie Lynn for several days because all the power in the Kentwood area was down. Since the devastating storm Britney has backed fundraisers to help rebuild the area by selling personal items online. A pair of jeans made $3000 and a tank top emblazoned with the words 'I have the golden ticket' made $1000. She also set up the Spears Family Hurricane Relief Foundation to help fund regeneration schemes in her home state. Unsurprisingly, she jumped at the chance of travelling to New Orleans for the 2006 Mardi Gras to try and bring some *joie de vivre* backed to the stricken region.

Britney's first baby, weighing 6 lbs 11 ounces, was born on 14 September 2005 at the UCLA Medical Centre in Santa Monica. It was a boy, much to the surprise of the newspapers who had predicted confidently that it would be a girl because Britney had decorated the nursery pink. She had in fact chosen soft green and yellows for her baby's room, with a little help from the Petit Tresor boutique in West Hollywood. The boutique's owner Nina Rioja remarked that Britney had been 'very spiritual' about it. The effect was finished off with a squeezy toy called Sophie the Giraffe. Ironically, the *National Enquirer*, Britney and Kevin's least favourite reading matter, was one of the few to correctly predict the baby's sex.

Kevin was at the hospital to support his wife, who had a caesarean section. They stayed in a private suite on the fifth floor, guarded by several burly minders. Every visitor had to have their bag searched. First through the doors were Lynne, Jamie and Bryan. They stayed for several hours with Lynne, in particular, keeping Britney's spirits up. Not surprisingly, she was more apprehensive than spiritual on the day. A nurse confided, 'Like all new moms Britney was very nervous and was constantly asking if the baby was OK. Fortunately, she had a lot of trust in the doctors and nurses and they were able to reassure her.'

Another medical source explained, 'Britney was really anxious about her son to the point where she couldn't get any sleep. But her mom was great and stayed very late with her daughter, watching the baby when Britney finally fell asleep. Despite the fact that both she and the baby were very healthy, Britney couldn't seem to get any peace of mind. It was only when her mom spoke to her and got both the nurses and doctors involved that she finally calmed down.'

When Britney returned home it soon became apparent that Lynne would have a pivotal role in getting her on the right track as a young mother. Their close relationship, which had all but disappeared during the Vegas marriage debacle, was rescued. Now Britney turned once again to her mother to settle her fears and misgivings. For starters, Lynne came to stay. She had already bought a west coast base for herself, a $1.5 million condominium at Marino Del Rey, where she could be closer to her first grandchild and also oversee the blossoming career of Jamie Lynn.

Lynne postponed a trip back home to Kentwood – to view the progress of the clean-up operation post Hurricane Katrina – to stay with her daughter. Britney did seem to be struggling. Kabbalah was not helping for once. During one private Kabbalah teaching session at her home, Britney burst into tears and had to be put into bed by her mother, who admitted to guests that her daughter was suffering from 'stress'. Britney and Kevin were rumoured to be bickering at each other, hardly surprising considering how much the dynamic of their lives had changed overnight.

Kevin was much more laid back than Britney and could not understand why she was getting upset about absolutely everything. Being rich and famous, however, does not make you immune from self doubt and Britney has always been refreshingly normal about things that worry her. Lynne, for instance, had to constantly reassure her daughter that the scar from her c-section would gradually fade.

Britney and Kevin needed to decide on a name for their baby. It seemed to take ages before they could agree. Britney reportedly favoured Charlie after the character in *Charlie and the Chocolate Factory*. Kevin, more prosaically, wanted Kevin Junior. In the end they chose Sean Preston. Behind the scenes, negotiations were going on to sell the first pictures of baby and proud parents for in excess of a million dollars. The British magazine *OK!* was in the running. In the end they went with *People* magazine in the US for a six-figure sum. The whole thing was dragged out to such an extent that some paparazzi shots were already in circulation, which took a little gloss from the official shoot. Britney became a lot less easygoing where the photographers were concerned and almost every event seemed to throw up controversy.

At Sean's baby shower one photographer was hit in the leg by what was thought to be a plastic bullet from a pellet gun in an incident that has never been properly explained. He was one of more than thirty paparazzi who had gathered at the foot of the gated driveway to Britney's Malibu home in the vain hope of getting some pictures of the event. The pack were also on hand to see Kevin's silver Ferrari being towed away, which led to a flurry of speculation that Britney had sent it back to the dealers as a punishment following a row. The reality was that it needed repairs and was being taken off to a garage.

Speculation about the state of Britney's marriage continued. At the beginning of December Kevin did leave the house for a few days and checked into the Beverly Hills Hotel. There, in the legendary Polo Lounge, where Hollywood greats like Jack Nicholson and Tom Cruise hold court, he could be seen sporting a baseball cap, smoking cigarettes and talking loudly into his mobile phone. An eyewitness said he seemed out of place and out of his depth.

After a few days he flew to Las Vegas, a city he particularly enjoys. On a night out at the Paradise Club he was reported as having spoken unguardedly to a journalist, whinging about Britney: 'She just wants to control me and live with her mother, and for them to tell me how to live my life . . . she just wants me at her beck and call as a little house husband.' A spokesman for Kevin subsequently denied that the conversation took place.

Kevin's biggest challenge, other than keeping Britney happy, was trying to find something to do. *Chaotic* didn't turn him into a star so he decided to promote himself as a rap artist. He began his own website and released his first record called 'PopoZao', which failed to make waves. PopoZao means big fat bottom or something similar in Brazilian/Portuguese slang. Kevin released it on his own K-Fed productions label. A record business insider explains, 'Kevin lacks credibility because he comes from a nice Fresno family and has a very rich wife. There's only one great white rapper, Eminem, who came up from a trailer park. He's the Mozart of rap, Kevin isn't.'

On another occasion, photographers followed Britney and her baby on a completely random visit to the Malibu Hindu Temple, where she sought spiritual guidance. Britney was out driving in the beautiful Calabasis Mountains above her home when she spotted a ceremony being conducted in the grounds of the Temple and, intrigued, decided to taker a closer look.

Refreshingly, the Temple's minister of religion, Samudrala Krishna Ma Charyulu, did not have a clue who she was until another visitor told him. He was, however, used to celebrities, having prayed with George Harrison as well as members of the Beach Boys, and realized what was happening when a posse of photographers started to get out of their cars.

He invited Britney to remove her shoes and take part in some prayers celebrating the Makara Sankaranthi festival, which marks the changing position of the sun. Samudrala wrapped some Hindu cloth around both Britney and her son and gave them flowers to wear as part of the ceremony. Britney also placed a red dot on her forehead, the Hindu practice which enables the wearer to obtain increased spirituality and happiness by means of a 'third eye'. Samudrala recalls, 'Britney started to cry a little afterwards and then she was smiling, but the whole time she was very humble and respectful.'

In another temple there were more prayers and Samudrala blessed both mother and child, remarking how happy and attentive Britney now appeared. She left after an hour, tracked down the mountain by her paparazzi shadows in their SUVs.

'I love little ones.'

TWENTY-ONE

Losing Control

The paparazzi wearily taking yet more pictures of Britney wearing a very short black mini dress couldn't believe their luck. As she hitched up the dress to get out of Paris Hilton's sports car she gave everyone a flash of what she had on underneath. Nothing.

Britney did not plan to fall pregnant again so quickly. She was still getting used to being a mother to Preston, as she now called her first born. Lynne revealed in her memoir, *Through The Storm*, that 'It was a big surprise.' She gave Britney some homespun advice: 'Surprise babies are the ones you know are supposed to be here. They are the Lord's Plan, not ours.' The world now had two things on which to speculate where Britney was concerned. Was her marriage to Kevin heading for the rocks and, secondly, was she expecting again so soon after giving birth? For once, the rumours proved to be right on both counts.

There is little doubt that Britney and Kevin rowed a lot. A source said, 'They fight about dumb stuff and they make up.' Media reports made it appear that Kevin was dividing his time between playing golf with his buddies and continuing to try and make it as a rap artist. He seemed undaunted by the poor reception for 'PopoZao' and was busy recording his debut album. Britney would later complain that she never saw him.

The newly pregnant Britney started 2006 with some bad publicity about her abilities as a mother. She was photographed with four-month-old Preston on her lap while she was driving her SUV back from Starbucks in Malibu. The baby was not in his car seat. When pictures of the incident appeared they made front pages all over the world and Britney was branded an irresponsible mother.

Britney's own explanation was that she had driven to Starbucks with a bodyguard in the passenger seat and Preston strapped into his baby seat in the back. When the minder went inside to get their order she took Preston out of the car seat to play with him. While they waited, she claimed that photographers approached the car and behaved in an aggressive manner. When the bodyguard returned, Britney drove straight off with Preston still on her lap.

In an exclusive statement to *People* magazine, Britney said, 'Today I had a horrifying, frightful encounter with the paparazzi while I was with my baby. Because of a recent incident when I was trapped in my car, without my baby, by a throng of paparazzi, I was terrified that this time the physically aggressive paparazzi would put both me and my baby in danger. I instinctively took measures to get my baby and me out of harm's way but the paparazzi continued to stalk us, and took photos of us, which were sold to the media. I love my child and would do anything to protect him.' Nobody realised it at the time but the most significant aspect of this sorry incident would later turn out to be Britney's lack of a valid driver's licence.

The family headed off to Maui, Hawaii, later in February 2006 as Britney wanted to work on some new music at a studio there. It did not prove to be a happy family break. Britney and Kevin had a big fight and he spent three nights with his entourage at one hotel while Britney, Preston and the nanny were at another. Kevin's enjoyment of the company of his dancer friends was a considerable source of tension between him and his wife. But Britney, too, seemed to flourish in the company of her girlfriends. What's interesting about Britney and Kevin after the birth of their son is that neither of them seemed to change their lifestyles to accommodate being parents. They both still acted as if they were single and neither spent time with couples who had children. They also appeared to be spending less and less time with each other and the trip to Maui had not improved things.

The impression that Britney was in some way cavalier with the safety of her baby is one the media would continue to cultivate. In April, Preston needed an X-ray after he bruised his head in a fall at home. He was being lifted out of a high chair by his nanny when he slipped from her grasp. Neither Britney nor Kevin were involved, but one could almost hear the tut-tuts of the moral majority proclaiming 'that poor child'. The critics were out in force again the next month when she was pictured in New York carrying a glass in one hand while holding Preston. She slipped and almost dropped the child. The episode lasted a second but the pictures were scutinised in newspapers and magazines worldwide. They were only minor incidents but when such things happen in normal families they are not plastered all over the world's newspapers and magazines, and the scrutiny must have been hard to swallow.

Jayden James was born on 14 September 2006, just two days

before his elder brother's first birthday. He was Kevin's fourth child. Kevin had driven Britney to the UCLA medical centre in Santa Monica where she had her second caesarean birth. Her mother and her sister were there to give support. Afterwards the media said the child was called Sutton Pierce, which turned out to be completely wrong. They did not release any happy snaps of their new baby although Kevin said they would be doing so in the future. In the meantime, they wanted some 'private time' with their son. At this stage there was no indication of the storm to come. It's impossible to know just how much the birth and associated emotional fragility contributed to what happened next, but within two months Britney and Kevin's marriage was over. The final straw was apparently Kevin's decision to go to Las Vegas three weeks after the birth for the first anniversary party of the nightclub Tao, leaving Britney home alone. A short time later he reportedly moved out of the Malibu mansion and stayed with friends in the San Fernando Valley. Britney had been expected to throw her weight behind the release of Kevin's album, *Playing With Fire*, but she failed to show at many of the promotional events.

Kevin's album was released at the end of October and was panned by the critics. Chris Wilman in *Entertainment Weekly* called it a 'concept album about squandering Britney's fortune'. Kevin O'Donnell of *Rolling Stone* referred to it as 'poison'. It was a complete flop, selling only 16,000 copies and reaching number 151 in the US chart. Kevin did his best, performing some concert dates before half empty auditoriums but the album spelled the end of his musical ambitions.

Britney and Kevin both arrived in New York at the beginning of November but, by all accounts, managed to avoid each other, staying at separate hotels. Kevin reportedly stood his wife up when she was seen dining alone at the Regency Hotel. She missed a promotional party for *Playing With Fire* at the Stereo Club and, the following night, Kevin's sparsely attended gig at Webster Hall. He then went on to Toronto alone while she appeared on *The Late Show With David Letterman*, sporting a new short blonde bob and a slim figure. Immediately after the recording she faxed her signature to her lawyers in LA and went ice skating. The very next day, 7 November, her lawyers filed divorce papers at the LA County Supreme Court, citing 'irreconcilable difficulties'. Britney asked for both legal and physical custody of the two boys, with Kevin getting reasonable visitation rights. Friends of Britney believe this was a final throw of the dice – with her trying to shock Kevin into being her ideal husband. If it was a bluff, and, as some suggested, she did not really want a divorce, then it backfired disastrously. Twenty-four hours later it became clear what Kevin was going to do. He filed for sole custody of Preston and Jayden. Her naive picture of how her married life would be, with a dutiful husband at her side, was in tatters.

The prospect of losing her children, however remote at this time, combined with the reality of losing her husband, proved too much for Britney. Her reaction was extreme. In public at least, she seemed to be having a whale of a time, hitting the LA nightspots with her two new best friends, heiress Paris Hilton and actress Lindsay Lohan. They may both have been A-list party girls but, in comparison to Britney, their achievements were very slim. The unlikely threesome seemed to be out on the town every night. Each time Britney was pictured she seemed dishevelled and wearing fewer clothes. On a trip to the fashionable Hyde Lounge in West Hollywood, she wore what observers described as a 'green skimpy frock which bore a striking resemblance to a fig leaf and covered little more than the real thing'. The dress was slashed to the waist at the front and Britney was struggling to keep everything from spilling out. Paris looked demure by comparison. When they left in the small hours, Britney was clutching a can of Red Bull, a packet of cigarettes and her mobile phone – all a girl needs for a night out on the town. Most notoriously, twice within a week Britney was photographed with no underwear, revealing all to the world. Psychologists enjoyed deliberating on her mental state. One, Linda Papadopoulos, told *Closer* magazine, 'She can't deal with going from being an incredibly desirable woman to a mom of two whose life's in a mess. She thinks that she can fix everything if she's seen as a sex object again.'

But Britney herself did not see it that way. She did want to go back in time but not to a place where she was necessarily a sex object. She just wanted to be 'cool' again. She blamed the paparazzi: 'I used to be a cool chick but I feel the paparazzi has taken the whole cool side away from me.' She perhaps also did not realise that most Britney fans considered Hilton and Lohan anything but cool.

The public Britney appeared to be a mess. The private one was faring no better. A couple of weeks after she filed for divorce, she met a woman called Kalie Machado who was working for a celebrity hair stylist. The two women got chatting while Britney was having her hair extensions done for a party. It's a laborious job which takes a few days to complete and, on the last day, Britney invited Kalie to come along to the party. They had fun and really hit off. Kalie recalled, 'After two weeks with me being with her she asked me to work full time. I ended up staying with her for three months without going home.'

Kalie would later provide heartbreaking observations of what Britney was really going through. She revealed to the *Daily Mirror* that Britney was still hoping to win Kevin back, was 'incredibly sad and lonely' and would burst into tears when he wouldn't return her calls. Kalie recalled, 'She'd cry at night a lot. She would sob, "Why isn't he calling me back". She'd look at the boys and say, "Where's your daddy? I need help."' Kalie also said that Britney's house was almost a shrine to her marriage. She kept all of Kevin's clothes and would wander into his wardrobe to look at them. Most tellingly, she kept her wedding dress in a glass case in the hallway.

At Christmas time, Britney faced the grim truth of a future apart from Kevin. While he was in Miami, she was in Malibu with Preston and Jayden. 'There were a lot of tears around then,' said Kalie. Many of the tears were for her beloved aunt Sandra, who was dying from cancer. Lynne's elder sister was the mother of Britney's closest childhood friend, her cousin Laura Lynne. She died in January. Britney went to the funeral back home in rural Louisiana and, for once, not one photographer accompanied her. It was a very sad day for Britney.

While Britney was being portrayed in the media as being on a permanent hen night, Kalie insisted that she was a sweet, loving girl who doted on her children. Her parents, however, were becoming increasingly worried by her partying lifestyle. *US* magazine reported that Lynne was threatening to get emergency custody unless the singer went into rehab. Reluctantly, Britney buckled under the pressure and flew to the beautiful Caribbean island of Antigua to stay at the Crossroads clinic, which had been founded by legendary guitarist Eric Clapton as a refuge of tranquillity and peace. Britney flew back to Los Angeles after only a day.

'I never really faced it and I just ran.'

TWENTY-TWO

A Piece of Britney

Britney wandered into the fashionable Mondrian Hotel in West Hollywood and attempted to book a room with no money and no credit card. She tried to offer staff a piece of paper with a partial credit card number on. One of many witnesses said 'She was crying and kept saying "Nobody wants me anymore".'

Sometimes you just want to look away and pretend you didn't see it. When Britney, accompanied as ever by her paparazzi posse, wandered in to an unassuming hair salon in the San Fernando Valley and sat down in a chair, no one could have predicted what would happen next. While the staff, pleased to have such a famous celebrity on the premises, fussed about making sure she had everything she wanted, Britney simply grabbed a pair of clippers and shaved off all her hair. The waiting photographers could not believe their luck at being presented with such a million-dollar opportunity and gleefully snapped away, capturing the deeply shocking episode.

The salon staff looked on in horror as Britney transformed herself into GI Jane and stared wild eyed at her new self in the mirror. By this time a large crowd had gathered outside the window as word spread at what was unfolding inside. The scene was like an accident where motorists slow down to sneak a closer look. Britney, oblivious to the onlookers, started to weep and said, 'Oh my God I shaved it all off. My mom is going to be so upset.' The salon's owner, Esther Tognozzi, observed that Britney was 'just there in body and not really emotionally there.'

Esther also said, 'I thought she had everything going for her. Why does she have to do this? Was it for attention?' Esther's question was one posed by many psychiatric experts over the following days. Psychotherapists queued up to have their say. One of them, Phillip Hodson, pointed out that Britney's hair was a symbol of sexual glamour and that shaving one's head was a de-sexing gesture. He added, 'This is a woman deep in crisis and it's imperative she thinks about getting help before events take a potentially tragic turn.' Meanwhile, Britney had left the salon and gone to a tattoo parlour.

The hair shaving incident did focus everyone's attention on the need for Britney to get some help. Celebrities seem to check in and out of rehab centres all the time so it's sometimes hard to know who really needs care. Here was a woman no longer on the verge or the edge. She appeared to have fallen into the abyss. At the time, she apparently told another customer at the tattoo parlour why she had shaved her hair. She said, bizarrely, that she was tired of having 'things plugged into her' and didn't want anyone to touch her.'

Taken in isolation, the head shaving incident remains the single most shocking event in Britney's emotional decline. It was scary stuff. In reality, it was one of a series of events highlighting her unhappiness after Kevin had left. 'He had just left me and I was devastated', she said in her MTV documentary, *Britney For The Record*. She described the shaving as a 'little bit of rebellion, feeling free, shedding stuff.'

Perhaps the most poignant comments about Britney's state of mind at the time came from her long standing friend and chaperone Felicia Culotta: 'There is just so much you can do to help a person. I cannot love her enough for the both of us. I cannot convince her in any way to love herself. I cannot save her from herself, nor can I commit her to any type of treatment against her wishes and will.'

After reportedly getting three new tattoos Britney returned to her Malibu home where worried staff managed to persuade her to go and see a doctor to get something to calm her down. Britney, wearing a long dark wig, was driven to the Cedars Sinai Medical Centre in Beverly Hills where she asked for help. After spending an hour with a concerned doctor she left and returned home. Her assistant, Kalie Machado, who had not been with her at the salon, later revealed that Britney had talked before of shaving her head. She said she had no idea why Britney had done it but added that it was very difficult to say no to her when she had decided what she was going to do.

The next day Lynne Spears left Kentwood to fly to Los Angeles to try and help. She recalled in her memoir, 'That day I was devastated, broken by what had happened to my child.' Britney would later admit it should have been the other way round, saying 'I should have gone home to Louisiana.'

Britney's father, Jamie, was trying to help. He joined Britney for dinner at a restaurant in Encino, north of Los Angeles, and urged her to get some professional help. He hadn't had a drink himself for three years but at this stage was unable to persuade his daughter to stop drinking. Instead, wearing a platinum blonde wig and pink tinted sunglasses, Britney headed off to the Roxy on Sunset Strip where she sang karaoke with some girl friends until the DJ cheekily put '. . . Baby One More Time' on the turntable. Britney was not amused and abruptly adjourned to the famous Polo Lounge at the Beverly Hills Hotel. Pictures from the evening show Britney looking flushed and bloated – the effect of too much partying. Just four months earlier she had looked a million dollars when she was interviewed by David Letterman, but partying was taking its toll as her skin suffered and she put on weight.

Her family, supported by Larry Rudolph, who she had reappointed, continued to press Britney to go back to rehab after the abortive trip to Antigua. She agreed to go into the Promises centre in Malibu. Kevin, too, was pressing her to get professional help. She still had joint custody of the boys but agreed that they should live with Kevin while she received treatment. Larry Rudolph issued a statement: 'Britney Spears has voluntarily checked herself into an undisclosed rehab facility today. We ask that the media respect her privacy as well as that of her family and friends at this time.'

Promises is used to the rich and famous, having previously played host to Mel Gibson, Ben Affleck, Charlie Sheen and Robert Downey Jnr. It's not cheap, costing nearly £1,000 a night. The 'guests' begin their mornings at 7 a.m. with meditation before embarking on a day of various treatments including yoga, acupuncture and art therapy, all punctuated by group therapy sessions for coping with alcohol or narcotics abuse and one-to-one meetings with a psychiatrist. They are also set various tasks or chores to do. But Britney was not in the right frame of mind to help herself, and her spell in rehab again lasted just a day. She checked out at 4 a.m. on Wednesday 21 February 2007 and went home. The problem was that the house in Malibu did not feel like home without her two children there. Preston was just eighteen months old while Jayden was only seven months. As Britney explained, 'My babies represented home.' After a fitful sleep Britney went to a meeting with her lawyers where she learnt the full extent of her ex husband's plans.

Britney did not want to go back to Malibu alone so booked herself in to the Bel Air Hotel. She seemed to prefer hotels to home but, on this occasion, could not settle. Instead she was driven round to Kevin's house where she tried desperately to see her sons by reportedly ringing the doorbell for a full fifteen minutes. Kevin refused to open the door and a frustrated Britney took out her anger and desperation on the paparazzi still stalking her. She attacked one of the photographer's cars with a turquoise umbrella, screaming, 'F*** off, you motherf***er. Stop following me, leave me be. I just want to see my kids.' The images of a demented-looking Britney sold around the world.

The next day Britney went back to Promises. Her 'first' husband, Jason Alexander, took the opportunity for another few minutes of fame by telling all to the *Sunday Mirror* newspaper. Britney, he alleged, had taken a pure form of ecstasy and indulged in some exotic sex games during their weekend in Las Vegas. The timing of sex and drugs revelations was not ideal for a mother facing a legal challenge to her rights to her children.

At least her father Jamie showed signs of stepping up to the plate. He said, 'We've got a sick little girl – we're just trying to take care of her.' The old 'Team Britney' of her parents and Larry Rudolph tried to form a security blanket around the star. One of the first things that happened was the ejection from her inner circle of her latest personal assistant, Kalie Machado. Lynne had apparently accused the PA of being an 'enabler' who accompanied her daughter to parties – a suggestion which Kalie strongly denied.

This time Britney stayed in rehab for several weeks. Larry Rudolph issued another statement: 'Britney has been released by the Promises Malibu Treatment Centre after successfully completing their programme.' It sounded as if Britney had been in prison. Nobody realised it fully at the time but Britney was extremely resentful of, as she saw it, being forced in to rehab. Kalie Machado observed, 'It didn't help – it made things worse. Being forced into rehab made her crazier.'

At the time perhaps, everyone was looking at the obvious signs of an emotional decline, namely drink, drugs and partying rather than the root causes of her problems. She was a lonely and lost young woman struggling to cope with a marriage break-up and the destruction of the family home which had left her bereft. Britney was convinced that she was being ganged up on and was determined to fight back. She started by firing Larry Rudolph in April 2007. She also thought her mother was siding with Kevin and refused to speak to her for seven months.

The nadir of her relationship with her mother came in June 2007 when Lynne was visiting Jamie Lynn, who was filming TV series *Zoey 101* in Valencia, north of Los Angeles. Britney arrived on set, marched up to her sister's trailer and 'served' Lynne a bitter letter in which she said she wanted to be left alone. She allegedly wrote 'I hate you Momma'. Lynne was reportedly devastated. As a final coup de grace when she left, Britney told waiting reporters, 'I'm praying for her right now,' clearly mocking her mother's strongly held religious views.

The rift with her family continued when Jamie gave a state-

ment to the press in which he apologised to Larry Rudolph for
his daughter's treatment of her ex-manager: 'When Larry talked
Britney into rehab, he was doing what her mother, father and a
team of professionals with over one hundred years of experience
knew needed to be done. She was out of control. Larry was the
one chosen by the team to roll up his sleeves and deliver the
message to help save her life . . . unfortunately she blames him
and her family for where she is today with her kids and career.'

Britney needed to focus on something that wasn't being lonely
and lost. Fortunately she still had an album to finish. Despite her
personal problems, Britney retained the ability to keep working.
Her professionalism was so deeply ingrained that it came naturally to her. Work also acted as a safe haven, perhaps just as
valuable to her as any spell in rehab might be.

The new album was scheduled for release in the autumn of
2007. Progress was good and Britney agreed to a daring promotional launch pad – a star appearance at the MTV Video Music
Awards in Las Vegas in September. It was the perfect setting for
The Big Comeback as the media called it. Celebrity writer Cliff
Renfrew observed, 'Everybody wants Britney to do well. They
feel quite protective towards her, and recognise that she has had
a really tough time.'

The lady herself flew into Las Vegas with an entourage that
included her new personal assistant, Alli Sims, her brother Bryan
and her friend, illusionist, Criss Angel. Britney, it seemed, was
determined to have fun that weekend. The trips to rehab earlier
in the year were forgotten as she continued in restless party mode.
The first night she and Criss ended up at a party hosted by P
Diddy at the Pure nightclub in Caesars Palace where, according
to reports, she 'guzzled champagne' while being introduced by

the host: 'Listen up, we have Miss Britney Spears in the crowd!' P Diddy was again on the scene the next night when Britney and three girlfriends joined him for drinks at Tao nightclub before they headed to other clubs, finishing up at the Revolution Lounge where Britney partied and danced on the furniture. She wasn't driven back to her suite at the Palms Casino Resort until 4.00 a.m. It was hardly good training for the key performance of the year which would begin at 6 p.m. the following day.

The portents were not good when the VMA host, comedienne Sarah Silverman, referred to Britney's children as 'the most adorable mistakes you'll ever see'. Britney was the opening act, performing her new single, 'Gimme More'. From the opening bars it was clear the performance was going to be a disaster. Britney seemed chronically underprepared as she drifted through the routine as if she was taking part in a casual rehearsal. She was out of time with her lip synching and lethargic with her dancing. Some unsubstantiated reports suggest that Britney was so nervous she had taken antidepressants to calm her down. In some ways it was as shocking as the hair-shaving. Britney was always such a consummate professional so it was a total surprise to see her struggling with this side of her life as well. Afterwards, commentators fell over themselves to bury Britney. The unkindest observed that the woman who had given birth to two children within the previous two years was not as 'toned' as she used to be. Her outfit, in fairness, was probably ill judged – a black sequined, studded bikini with fishnet stockings and knee-high boots – and seemed to have strayed from a burlesque show.

Celebrity gossip blogger, Perez Hilton, wrote, 'It was so bad, it was embarrassing'. Even Simon Cowell observed, 'If she had given that performance in the X Factor auditions, I wouldn't have put her through. She may have killed her career.' For once, though, Cowell's famous judgement would fail him.

Britney, however, probably would have agreed with him when she came off stage and burst into tears, complaining she looked fat. One ingredient the numerous critics, columnists and armchair observers missed was Britney's own state of mind. It had been assumed that she was fully recovered from what ailed her and that rehab had done the trick. That was not the case and while she partied in Las Vegas, she was painfully aware that she was missing the birthday party for both of her baby boys. Kevin threw the party at his new house in Tanzana, in the San Fernando Valley, and both Lynne and Jamie were there to give presents and be doting grandparents. Only their mother was missing. Britney hated the fact that her parents seemed to be siding with Kevin.

Her ex-husband was playing a very smart hand in the run-up to the crucial custody hearing, which was due to take place just a week after the VMA debacle. He appeared to have been well-advised by his lawyers because the man who had lived life in the fast lane during his marriage now appeared to be in the crawler lane, providing a good home for his children, keeping his head down, getting on well with Lynne and generally being beyond reproach.

The prospects for the court hearing looked bleak when word reached Britney's camp that a mystery witness had come forward with damning evidence regarding the singer's lifestyle and parental fitness. It highlighted just how vulnerable Britney was without the ring of steel which had protected her so resolutely throughout her career – Lynne, Larry, Jamie and Felicia were nowhere to be seen. They had been replaced by a man called Sam Lutfi, an enigmatic character, sometimes described as a film producer, who had managed to inveigle his way into Britney's life at a time when her defences were weakened. When Samson allowed his hair to be cut off in the biblical story, he lost his legendary strength. In a curious way, the same thing had happened to Britney.

Several versions exist of how Sam Lutfi met Britney. He said it was at a party, and that at least was probably true. He was almost certainly introduced to the vulnerable star by her friend and new personal assistant Alli Sims. Lutfi, however, had been trying to get close to Britney for a while and in a number of different ways. Those allegedly included posing as a private detective when he contacted former assistant Kalie Machado and trying to interest Lynne in a scheme to sell jewellery on a shopping channel. Whatever his exact means of fashioning an introduction to Britney, he did not waste the opportunity. Lynne explained in *Through The Storm* that within a month or so of meeting her daughter, Sam was in complete control of her life, 'labelling himself her friend, her manager, her life coach'. According to Lynne, 'He appointed himself as her gatekeeper, and there was no one he wanted to keep the gate closed to more than Britney's family.'

The mystery witness for the custody hearing turned out to be a bodyguard called Tony Biretta, who had worked for Britney for three months until he was fired the previous May. He was not called to give evidence at the hearing on 18 September 2007 but his signed written testimony was damning. Judge Scott Gordon told Britney some harsh truths, 'Based on evidence presented, the court finds that there is habitual, frequent and continuous use of controlled substances and alcohol . . .'

Both Britney and Kevin were banned from drinking and taking drugs while looking after their boys or for twelve hours beforehand. They were also instructed to attend classes entitled 'Parenting Without Conflict' and banned from driving the children unless they had a valid Californian driving licence. But, most humiliatingly for Britney, she was ordered to face random alcohol and drug testing twice a week, as well as being observed by a parenting coach when she visited the children. Judge Gordon set a deadline of 26 November for a final decision on whether Britney retained joint custody of the children.

Britney 'celebrated' Judge Scott's damning instructions by going to a bar with best friend and new assistant Alli Sims and pop star Avril Lavigne. Later, at the Hyde Lounge she astounded onlookers by dancing on a table with a sock on her head. At least nobody pictured her drinking, even though she was surrounded by booze. She was seen heading home at about 1.40 a.m. to get some sleep before Kevin dropped the children off at 10 a.m. the following morning.

The day provided another opportunity for Britney's paparazzi following when she wandered down Robertson Boulevard with Preston in her arms. She was wearing sensible specs, a demure grey cardi, practical jeans and little make-up. She looked for all the world like a responsible mum looking after her kids, but, sadly for Britney, nobody believed what they were seeing. It appeared contrived. One observer remarked, 'She just doesn't get it. You can't go out on the town and try and be supermom the next day. Nobody believes it.'

Britney's week did not get any better when she was charged with two driving offences resulting from a car park prang in August. She had clipped a parked car with her Mercedes but had not stopped to leave her details or try and contact the owner. She apparently had been trying to park her car while holding her new puppy, a Yorkshire terrier. Her paparazzi pursuers had helpfully contacted the owner, correctly sensing another Britney escapade. She was subsequently charged with hit and run and not having a valid Californian drivers licence. She had taken a California driving test earlier in the year but had failed. Britney and cars did not have a happy relationship.

Tony Biretta, known as Fat Tony, may not have had his say in court but he had a big day, nevertheless, in the following Sunday's *News of the World*. Under the banner *Bodyguard Tells All* the front page promised 'Britney Laid Bare' and then proceeded to reveal Britney's mad world over four pages of the newspaper. In the context of her custody predicament, his allegations about her behaviour were very bad news. He claimed she had gone on a drug binge with a rock singer called Howie Day who she had met in rehab. Tony recalled, 'She was in a terrible state, just sweating and shaking.'

He also alleged she snorted a white powder in a nightclub, drank Jack Daniels from polysterene cups pretending it was coffee and, most damagingly, appeared to be 'under the influence' near her children. At her mansion, he claimed, Britney would have hot tub parties for her girlfriends where she would strip off. She would also parade nude around the house. 'I must have seen her naked dozens of times and each time I've been extremely embarrassed', said Tony.

The bodyguard's last word on Britney was, 'All I want is for her to be a success and a good mom.'

While Tony's revelations, which also appeared in the *Mail on Sunday*, are obviously made to appear as sensational as possible, they do provide fascinating insights into Britney's rudderless life in 2007. Her daily routine when she got up at one or two in the afternoon was to drink a Starbucks coffee (a vanilla latte or a mocha frappuccino), go to tanning shop Epitome in Bel Air, where she would lie on a sunbed for ten minutes, and then have a manicure. Her first meal of the day in mid-afternoon would be a plate of sushi. She would then return to the house where she would swim, relax in her bedroom and snack on Special K cereal and Red Bull until it was time to go out for dinner and on to a club.

He also offered a glimpse into one of the unsavoury aspects of being a star of Britney's magnitude. As well as dealing with her ever growing paparazzi posse, Britney attracted some 'pretty sick types'. Tony said Britney would receive two letters a day from stalkers and that 'some of them were way out there'.

The bodyguard did offer some good advice: 'What she needs more than anything is her family around her,' though Britney would not have agreed with that at the time. Instead she had Alli and Sam Lutfi, who allegedly had a deal with an agency allowing its photographers access to Britney at times when she could have expected privacy. He was apparently buzzing paparazzi in to her gated estate.

Within a week Britney had completely lost her children. Kevin's lawyer had gone back to court as soon as pictures surfaced of Britney driving her boys in flagrant contradiction of the order not to drive them without a valid licence. The judge had little alternative than to hand the children to Kevin who was to 'retain physical custody of the minor children until further order of the court'. Britney, it was claimed, had also failed to submit to the random drug testing or enrol in the required parenting classes. She appeared stunned and numb at the ruling, almost failing to register any emotion as she handed the children over. She then spent the day at the tanning salon before dinner at Nobu in Malibu and checking in for the night at the Peninsula Hotel in Beverly Hills. It seemed that the last thing she wanted to do was go home. At least she went to the Motor Vehicles Department to apply for a driving licence. After all her irrational behaviour, Britney's downfall in the custody battle had been her lack of a valid drivers licence. While she appeared to be carrying on normally, her mother Lynne said, 'We are all fearing for Britney and this will be the final straw for her.' Meanwhile, a desperately worried Lynne phoned Britney's father to persuade him that they needed to be united to get Britney back on track.

While it had been widely assumed in the media that Britney's new album and the first single from it, 'Gimme More', would bomb, that proved not to be the case. Britney has such a strong fan base that her shambling performance in Las Vegas was not the final nail in the coffin for her career. Ironically, being so awful once again ensured that Britney was the only story in town following an MTV awards night. The song itself may not have been another 'Toxic' but it grabbed the attention from its opening line, 'It's Britney, bitch.' 'Gimme More' was the first collaboration between Britney and techno pop wizard Nate Hills, better known in music circles as renowned producer Danja. He was raised in Virginia but had caught the attention of Timbaland and had worked alongside the legendary producer at his studios in Miami.

When Britney met him in Los Angeles in the summer of 2006 he was only twenty four – five months younger than her. He co-produced Justin Timberlake's international hit 'SexyBack' which was released in July of that year and became the singer's biggest hit to date, reaching number one in the UK and the US. Britney did not follow Justin sheep-like where music was concerned but she has always been shrewd enough to recognise that her former boyfriend knows what he is doing when it comes to producers.

'Gimme More' was not 'SexyBack' or a classic like the Danja produced 'Say It Right', a US number one for Nelly Furtado, but it was highly skilful techno pop that set the tone for the album to follow. In some ways it was a retro disco number reminiscent of Donna Summer, especially in the way it repeated the word 'Gimme' about a hundred times during the song. It reached number three in the UK charts and number two on the US *Billboard* charts, eventually selling more than 1,300,000 copies – hardly a flop. The album *Blackout* had been scheduled for a November release but was brought forward to October because Jive were concerned at the number of online leaks. Reviews were generally positive, although Melissa Maerz in *Rolling Stone* pointed out that the lyrical content was a little over the top for someone concerned with their child visitation rights. One line, for instance, exclaimed, 'I'm as crazy as a motherfucker'. Melissa thought the stand-out tracks were 'Freakshow' and 'Piece of Me', both hard edged commentaries on Britney's life. Both were written and produced by Bloodshy and Avant who had done so much work for 'In The Zone' and were very effective rants against those who treated Britney as a commodity.

The influential website *popjustice* thought it the best album of Britney's career: 'It's modern sounding and brilliantly produced, but still absolutely pop.' Alex Petridis in The *Guardian* described it as a 'bold, exciting album', although he also said that the timing of the album's release might, in the end, prove its biggest problem, having to compete for attention in a Britney crowded market place where every minute of her life was picked over by glossy magazines. He wrote, 'It's a bold, exciting album. The question is whether anyone will be able to hear its content over the deafening roar of tittle-tattle.'

Britney did no promotional work whatsoever for the album. She was totally preoccupied with her custody battle and perhaps suffering a reaction from the VMA awards. Despite that, it only just missed entering the US charts at number one and also reached number two in the UK. Because of the timing of its release, *Blackout* is in danger of unjustly becoming Britney's lost album. The final track of the album 'Why Should I Be Sad' was interpreted as a goodbye to Kevin, especially with the reference to not worrying about 'their little angels'. It was a mellow end to a generally aggressive track list and could have stepped straight out of a Justin Timberlake album. Unsurprisingly, the song was written by Justin's friend and collaborator Pharrell Williams who had co-produced much of his first solo album, *Justified*.

But Britney had more than enough reason to be sad. The unthinkable happened and by the end of the year she had not just lost custody of her two boys but her visits now had to be supervised by a court appointed monitor, who would observe and report on her parenting skills. She was allowed two per week: one afternoon and one overnight.

'I confess, I was so lost.'

TWENTY-THREE

Circus

An unhappy looking figure slunk out of the house wearing a tartan hat and clutching a small Yorkshire terrier. She kicked off her shoes, sat on a wall and started sobbing. When a female reporter approached her to see if she was alright, Britney said she was 'just sitting for once having a nice time with my dog'.

Britney was linked with various men after Kevin. Nothing much came of them, although there were untrue but widespread rumours in December 2007 that she was pregnant by record producer JR Rotem. The boyfriend who caught the public imagination, however, was a thirty-five-year-old swarthy Asian man called Adnan Ghalib. He had been brought up in Birmingham but had settled in LA in the mid nineties. Her relationship with him amazed the world because he was one of the paparazzi who had made her life miserable for so long. He had been ever present for five years when one day she asked for his help in escaping the pursuing pack. A little light flirtation became the real thing over Christmas 2007 when he stayed in her suite at the Peninsula Hotel.

The new relationship, however, could only partially distract her from her problems, and 3 January 2008 began like many other days for Britney in these troubled times. She had to go to a legal meeting to answers questions about her parental abilities. She was particularly upset by what she considered to be an intrusion and spent the hours brooding over it before convincing herself that Kevin was not going to let her see her beloved children again. The boys were at her house that evening for a supervised visit and when Kevin's bodyguard came over to collect them at 8 p.m., she simply refused to hand them over. The monitor helped pass Preston to the minder but could not prevent Britney locking herself in the bathroom with Jayden.

Alarm bells immediately started ringing, and Kevin and his lawyer were informed. It was like a movie. Ten police cars raced to the scene, police and TV helicopters hovered overhead and paramedics and fire crews stood by to help. Sam, who was in the house, rang Lynne. She was back in Louisiana supporting her youngest daughter, Jamie-Lynn, who had shocked the family herself by announcing she was pregnant at sixteen. Lynne could do nothing more than watch the incredible events unfold on television. The on-the-spot news reports said that Britney had taken Jayden 'hostage'. The exact set of circumstances of that dramatic night may never be made public. Some sources suggest that Alli Sims eventually smashed the door down. Others suggest Britney opened the door of her own accord, and then sat huddled in a corner, sobbing and laughing uncontrollably.

Britney was clearly distraught and for her own safety was strapped to an ambulance trolley by her left ankle. She was driven, perhaps over dramatically, under police escort with sirens blaring to Cedars-Sinai hospital, where she was admitted to a psychiatric ward under section 5150, which enabled doctors to hold her for three days while they made an evaluation of her mental state.

Britney did not stay in hospital for the full three days, discharging herself to spend time with Adnan. They drove to Mexico and checked into a cheap hotel in a village just south of the US border. When they returned they were conveniently pictured shopping for a pregnancy test kit in a store in Studio City. The test proved negative, although Adnan gave a television interview to *Entertainment Tonight* where he talked of the pregnancy scare. Behind the scenes, however, her parents were desperately trying to work out ways they could wrest control of Britney's life back from the men they saw as ruining it – Sam and, to a lesser extent, Adnan. For the first time there began to emerge a different explanation for Britney's erratic behaviour – she was taking prescription medication for a bi-polar condition, more commonly known as manic depression. It was reported that Britney was diagnosed as 'suspected bi-polar' when she attended the Promises rehab centre almost a year before.

Suddenly much of Britney's behaviour seemed to fall into place. If she was a manic depressive then her constant mood swings and erratic behaviour were not down to drink and drugs but to a medical condition which could be controlled with the proper medication. Television doctor Dr Mark Porter explained that mood swings could last for weeks and months. He said that during a manic phase the sufferer would need little sleep and cast aside inhibitions and caution. He added that they would be capable of spending vast amounts of money, would dress outrageously and may be sexually promiscuous, all of which seemed to describe Britney's recent behaviour perfectly.

During her spell in the hospital, a judge suspended all her visitation rights and gave sole custody of the boys to Kevin. Over the coming weeks Britney's condition would continue to worsen while her mother and father were engaged in a power struggle with Sam Lutfi. Her parents needed to challenge Britney's decision to allow Sam control over her medical treatment. Ironically, while this tug of war was going on, the song 'Piece of Me' was released in the UK as the second single from *Blackout* and reached number two in the charts.

The battle for Britney came to a head on 31 January when she became the subject of a large police operation to get her back into hospital for proper treatment. Eye witnesses said Sam and Britney's father almost came to blows, so tense was the atmosphere. Some reports suggested Britney had not slept for five days and had been upset following fierce rows with Sam.

A presidential style cavalcade of a dozen motorbikes, two cars and a helicopter swept a bewildered Britney to the UCLA hospital. She appeared to have no idea of what was about to happen to her. Nor, apparently, did her parents, who believed Sam engineered the whole thing in order to regain full control over Britney and her affairs. Britney was sectioned, again under a 5150 order, and taken to a psychiatric wing. According to Lynne, the admission slip said that Britney had been driving recklessly, not taking her medication as directed and wasn't sleeping properly. Lynne recalled, 'Aha, I thought. No one could know that except Sam. Later, I found out that he had been working in conjunction with the Smart Team, a branch of the police force that watches for reckless drivers.'

At the hospital Britney was held for seventy-two hours, the maximum allowed under the order, while Jamie went into court.

In a closed hearing at the LA Superior Court, the judge, commissioner Reva Goetz, granted Jamie a temporary conservatorship which would allow him to control Britney's life. Her parents also successfully obtained a restraining order against Sam Lutfi and were given permission to change the locks on her estate and remove anyone from there.

Sam's reaction to the order which prevented him from going within 250 yards of Britney or her home was to say, 'It won't last.' The temporary conservatorship was made permanent in October 2008 and the restraining orders issued against Sam and one subsequently issued against Adnan were still in force when Britney left Los Angeles to begin touring the UK in the summer of 2009. Lynne was very outspoken about Sam Lutfi and the role he played in Britney's life in her memoir *Through The Storm*. He strongly rejected her claims and it was reported that in February 2009 he sued Britney, Lynne and Jamie for defamation. He claimed that since the book's publication he has been 'subjected to unfathomable amounts of ridicule and public scorn'.

The conservatorship handed control to Jamie over all aspects of Britney's life. He moved into her home and put the ground rules for her recovery on the fridge door. She had to be in bed by ten every night. No alcohol and no stimulating drinks were allowed in the house. Jamie, an accomplished chef, would do all the cooking and Britney's principle visitors would be those hired to do her hair and nails. Jamie was determined to get rid of all the hangers-on in her life. At first Adnan had been allowed to visit Britney, but that changed when Jamie heard that he and Sam planned to challenge the conservatorship.

Neither her parents nor Britney have ever revealed the full story of her medical condition, and they have never confirmed that she is bi-polar. A source, however, said 'It's one hundred per cent certain that Britney is bi-polar and what she needed most of all was the correct medication for her condition.'

The new regime proved to be a godsend for Britney. Within a couple of months she was planning a new album with a tour to follow. While it may seem hasty to start work again so soon after such dramatic upheaval in her life, the music business is an extremely fickle one and Britney still had contractual obligations to fulfil. Britney also became the subject of a full length documentary film, *Britney For The Record*, which provided a fascinating look at the world of Britney as she recovered her health. She was living a life which she described in the film as '*Groundhog Day* every day'.

Jamie drifts in and out, fixing cheese grits, a southern favourite, for his 'little girl'; Larry Rudolph is back; and Britney seems to get on well with her latest personal assistant, Brett Miller. Lynne is not in the film. Britney smiles and generally seems happy, although prone to periods of sad reflection: 'You do something wrong and you learn from it. You move on but I am having to pay for it for a really long time . . . Even when you go to jail, there's always the time when you know you are going to get out.'

She seemed fragile and uncertain. She said to the camera, 'There's a lot people don't know about me that I want them to know.'

Britney does not name the people she considered to have been bad influences on her. All she says is that she had allowed 'bad people' into her life and that she had been taken advantage of.

While the private Britney admitted to having good and bad days, the public Britney Spears was clearly getting her strength back. Keeping away from the limelight, she recorded her new album and started rehearsals for her tour. As she rehearsed, choreographer Andre Fuentes said he could see the fire back in her eyes. And Jamie agreed: 'She's in her element. She's in her world. I like to go fishing – she likes to sing and dance.'

A year is a long time in Britney's world and the debacle of her shambolic appearance at the 2007 VMA awards was completely forgotten when she marched on stage at the beginning of September to open the 2008 awards at the Paramount Studios in Los Angeles. She looked blonde and fabulous in a shimmering silver dress and was given a standing ovation, just for being there, just for being Britney. 'Thank you so much. Thank you for all the love.' To improve matters even more, Britney won three awards including Best Female Video for 'Piece of Me'. She thanked God and her two sons, who she said inspired her every day. It was the perfect start for reintroducing Britney the artist to the world. Larry Rudolph called it the beginning of the comeback. A live performance would wait for another day.

The first single from the new album is one of the most memorable of all Britney songs. 'Womanizer' was also one of the most successful, becoming her first single to top the US *Billboard* charts since her debut, '. . . Baby One More Time'. Yet again, Britney and her musical advisors struck gold when they chose an unknown production duo from Atlanta, The Outsyders (Nikesha Briscoe and Rafael Akinyemi), to write and produce the key track on Britney's sixth studio album. It was hypnotically catchy, repeating the word 'Womanizer' incessantly. Everybody seemed to be singing the chorus.

Britney flew into London in November to perform the song on the *X Factor*, where she had to endure the usual criticism for lip synching while she danced. In reality it was mission accomplished. It was Britney week on the *X Factor* so all the remaining contestants sang a Britney song. Simon Cowell gave her a standing ovation and the audience viewing figures for the week were more than 12 million. The purpose was to sell records and publicise Britney's 2009 British tour and it achieved both those aims. 'Womanizer' sold more than 250,000 copies in the UK.

Columnist Polly Hudson, however, tried to catch a glimpse of the private Britney peeping out from behind the glitz and the glamour. She did not like what she saw: 'I hated it because the spark had gone from her eyes.'

Britney's second album within little more than a year, *Circus*, was released in December 2008 and went straight to number one in the US. While almost certainly not as daring as *Blackout*, there was a reassuring symmetry about *Circus*. Britney embraced new talents like The Outsyders, but familiar producers like Bloodshy and Avant and Danja were also back. Most interestingly, Britney had turned once again to Max Martin, who had been so important in the launch of her career when he wrote '. . . Baby One More Time'. He wrote and produced probably the best track on the album, 'If U Seek Amy'. Gordon Smart in the *Sun* described it a stomping robopop number, although he did not comment on the lyrical content of the chorus – 'All the girls and all the boys want to f*** me' – a sentiment which would have had all the Baptist folk in Kentwood spluttering into their tea.

Circus was really a statement that normal Britney service was being resumed, after the edgy, unpredictability of *Blackout*. She explained, '*Circus* is a little bit lighter than *Blackout*, when I was going through a really dark phase in my life, so a lot of the songs reflected that.' In the sleeve notes for *Blackout*, Britney didn't thank a single person. For *Circus*, however, she thanked her mom and dad, brother Bryan, Jamie Lynn and her niece Maddie, who had been born in June 2008. She thanked Larry Rudolph who was one of the executive producers on the album. Even Clive Calder, the boss of Jive Records, got a special mention. It was a return to the complete professionalism, and family values, of old.

Britney combined the two albums to make up the majority of the set list for her world tour which opened in New Orleans in March 2009, just over a year after she was sectioned. While the gruelling stage show revealed Britney Spears to be in rude professional health once again, privately progress was slower. She did, however, buy a new $9 million dollar mansion in rural Calabasas, about ten miles from where Kevin and her boys were living in Tarzana. There was nothing country cottage about the property which offered much greater privacy than she had before. Britney's new home was in a private, gated community with armed guards patrolling a main gate and making sure no unwanted visitors could sneak in.

Britney started a new relationship with her agent, Jason Trawick, who works for the famous William Morris Agency. Trawick was first noticed with her when the tour began but by then, he had already accompanied her on holiday to Costa Rica where they were guests of Mel Gibson who has a home there. A colleague said, 'Jason is a very solid guy.' He is also nearly ten years older than Britney, offering some stability in her life. Most importantly, he has the approval of Jamie Spears. Rumours are already circulating that he has asked Britney to marry him.

In the meantime Britney is gradually gaining more access to her children, just as her parents promised she would when they took control of her life. Kevin still has full custody but her visitation rights have been upped to fifty per cent while she is on tour. Kevin, who receives monthly child support of $20,000, was awarded an extra $4,000 a month for accompanying them when she's performing.

The boys were with her in London in June 2009 when she took to the stage for a series of concerts in the UK. She took them out to McDonald's and to the zoo, just like any ordinary mom. She was photographed, of course, but at least the days of parenting mishaps were long forgotten. Then, she set aside the private woman and was driven to the O2 arena where more than 20,000 expectant fans were waiting. She didn't disappoint them as, once again, she became *the* Britney Spears for the night.

'I'm not perfect, I'm human.'

Britney at the O2, London, 11 June 2009

There's a buzz in the O2 even where I am sitting. I am so high up they should have supplied me with an oxygen mask at the door. It's all too much for a girl in the centre of my row who feels sick and giddy and has to be helped very slowly down the steps. I feel a bit nervous myself. I SO don't want this to be a disappointing concert. I remember being told in Los Angeles earlier in the year that everybody wants Britney to do well. There remains a genuine affection for her.

The critics never get that. I've read reviews of the Circus tour and every single one of them bangs on about her lip-synching. They don't seem to realise that nobody cares. This is a show, not a concert. The thousands of fans packed in to the O2 want to see Britney alive and well, in the flesh. All around, a mixture of male and female fans are excited and greet the warm-up circus routines involving clowns and acrobats with much laughter and sharp intakes of breath as a tumbler performs yet another amazing somersault.

The cheers at the opening bars of 'Circus' are quite the most deafening I have heard in years. A young guy of about sixteen is straight out of his seat and proceeds to dance through the entire show. The first number sets the tone for what follows. It's all sex from start to finish. The opening routine is very S&M and to my mind perfectly reflects the paradox of Britney Spears. Since she first teased us in a school uniform singing '. . . Baby One More Time', Britney has mixed the childish with strictly adult themes. At first the contrast existed because of Britney's age and sweetly innocent look. Now that she is a mother of two, a twice divorced woman of twenty-seven, the effect is reached by putting her into an environment we associate with childhood – namely, a circus complete with clowns and stilts, acrobats and magic tricks.

The sexual imagery continues apace with Britney in a cage for 'Piece Of Me'. This is one of my favourite Britney songs because I think it says so much about her life. The song is usually interpreted as a rant against the paparazzi who have made her so miserable over the years. For me, it's only partly about the photographer posse. It's actually about all of us and the fact that we are obsessed with every detail about her and what she is going to do next. There's something neatly symbolic about Britney performing this concert in the round. She is in the middle and we all sit round gazing intently down on her. When I first wrote about Britney in 2005, I thought she was striving to find her own identity when everybody thinks they own a piece of you. It was true then and I believe it's still true.

'What do you think?' I ask the girl on my right as we pause for breath while Britney launches into 'Radar'. 'It's high class porn,' she says, which, on reflection, it is. There's nothing too subtle about the gymnastics going on with her well-muscled dancers. Kevin Federline was a dancer and it's easy to see how sexual sparks might fly with this sort of high energy circulating among people working in such close proximity every night. Britney's dancing seems faultless from my vantage point and there's no question of her not being fit enough as she gyrates about the stage. She always seems most 'in the zone' as a dancer. This show is more about Britney the dancer than Britney the singer.

The clowns and acrobats are still darting here and there and Britney even slots in the old magician's trick of blades through the box. The songs merge into one another, although 'If U Seek Amy' gets everyone up and dancing. I feel that the tracks from the *Blackout* album are more exciting than the ones from the more recent *Circus*. 'Get Naked' is about as raunchy as you can get on stage without needing a special adult licence.

Finally Britney speaks: 'What's Up London?', which does not exactly qualify as interacting with the audience. The only time she does connect is during the one song which she sings live, the classic, plaintive ballad, 'Everytime'. Barbara Ellen in The *Observer* said it was 'breathless, cracked imperfect but somehow exquisite' and I can't better that description. Britney does have a good voice, but it is so produced these days that a well pro-grammed robot could produce the same effect.

When Britney finishes the show with her twin peaks – '. . . Baby One More Time' and 'Toxic' – I started wondering where she would be in ten years time. Professionally I think she is morphing into Madonna. The Princess of Pop is becoming the Queen of Pop. Madonna is becoming the Queen Mum of Pop. This is a show which Madonna herself might have put together twenty years ago. Madonna has been cutting edge for so many years, it's easy to forget how little girly she was when she started with 'Holiday'. Britney is still at the pointy bra stage of Madonna's career, but if she continues to use the cream of production talent then her music will remain current. For her encore she performs 'Womanizer' dressed in the sort of policeman's outfit, complete with truncheon, that a stripper might wear at a stag party.

Britney does not use any 'live' video so we can't see the expressions on her face or her skill at lip-synching. More pertinently, I wanted to see her eyes and if they still had the fire for performing.

I've always had a soft spot for Britney, an intrinsically nice person in a cynical, hard-nosed business. The crunch will come when she regains control of her life and, in particular, her vast fortune. I am sure that will happen in the future. I hope it coincides with a stable and flourishing relationship with her sons in which she feels she is the good mother she wants to be.

This final piece in the book is entitled 'Last Impressions' but really I should have called it 'Last Impressions *for the moment*', because I am convinced I will have much more to write about Britney Spears in the future.

Life and Times

2 December 1981 *

Britney Jean Spears born in a maternity hospital in McComb, Mississippi, near family home in Kentwood, Louisiana. Her father, Jamie, is a building contractor, and her mother, Lynne, an elementary schoolteacher. Elder brother Bryan is four.

December 1985 *

Sings 'What Child Is This' during pre-school Christmas concert at First Baptist Church in Kentwood – her first public performance – and is the hit of the show. Has already been taking dancing lessons for a year at Renee Donewar School of Dance.

June 1988 *

Wins her first talent contest at Kentwood Dairy Festival.

January 1990 *

Auditions in Atlanta for *The Mickey Mouse Club* but is turned down for being too young.

January 1991 *

Jamie Spears writes to New York agent Nancy Carson seeking advice and asking her to look at a video of his daughter singing 'Shine on Harvest Moon' and 'Nothing Compares 2 U'. Nancy suggests the family come and see her.

4 April 1991 *

Younger sister Jamie Lynn Spears born in McComb. The following month Lynne takes Britney and her new daughter to New York for the summer to give Britney her first taste of real showbusiness. Appears in commercials for cars and barbecue sauce.

April 1992 *

Reaches finals of TV talent contest *Star Search* in Los Angeles. Sings power ballad 'Love Can Build A Bridge' but is pipped by another of Nancy Carson's young clients, Marty Thomas, by a quarter of a point. Collapses in tears backstage.

May 1992 *

Is understudy to lead role in musical *Ruthless!* which opens off-Broadway at Players Theatre. Plays little girl who kills rival to secure star role in school play. Attends Professional Performing Arts School on West 48th Street and takes classes at Broadway Dance Centre.

December 1992 ✳

Quits *Ruthless!* to spend Christmas back home in Kentwood. Meets Reg Jones, a friend of her elder brother, for first time.

April 1993 ✳

Kentwood declares 24 April Britney Spears Day in honour of Britney's achievement in winning a place on *The Mickey Mouse Club*. Lynne and Jamie Lynn travel with her to Orlando, Florida, to begin filming. Meets fellow Mouseketeers Justin Timberlake and Christina Aguilera.

February 1995 ✳

The Mickey Mouse Club is cancelled and Britney returns to Parklane Academy, a private Christian school in McComb, where she leads the life of an ordinary schoolgirl for two years.

September 1995 ✳

Attends Homecoming Dance at Parklane with first boyfriend Reg Jones.

June 1997 ✳

New York entertainment lawyer Larry Rudolph sets up six auditions for Britney at record companies in New York, singing a cappella. Jive Records take an interest.

September 1997 ✳

Lynne Spears calls Felicia Culotta and asks if she would like to be her fifteen-year-old daughter's chaperone when she moves to New York and Stockholm. She and Britney move into penthouse apartment on Upper East Side in Manhattan.

July 1998 ✳

Years of financial strain finally overwhelm Spears family and Lynne and Jamie file for bankruptcy with debts of $190,000.

August 1998 ✳

Shoots famous video for '. . . Baby One More Time' at Venice High School in California. Cousin Chad Spears plays love interest and Felicia Culotta is featured as teacher.

October 1998 ✳

'. . . Baby One More Time' is released on 23 October. Single takes more than two months to reach number one on Billboard chart, reaching top spot on 30 January and staying there for two weeks.

November 1998 ✳

Begins three-month tour as opening act for 'N Sync on their *Back II None* tour. Within a few weeks rumours start that she is dating Justin Timberlake and the denials begin.

February 1999 ✳

Breaks first-week sales record for debut act in UK when '. . . Baby One More Time' sells 464,000 copies. Single eventually sells 1,450,154 copies, with Britney becoming youngest female to top a million sales in UK. Becomes youngest solo performer ever to have simultaneous number one US album and single.

March 1999 ✳

Undergoes surgery to remove piece of loose cartilage from left knee. Flies home to Kentwood to recuperate.

April 1999 ✳

Adorns cover of *Rolling Stone* magazine for first time, stirring up controversy over her apparently much larger breasts.

May 1999 ✳

Dons black wig to look like Cher when she performs the diva's hit 'And the Beat Goes On' at World Music Awards in Monte Carlo.

September 1999 ✳

Plays herself in episode of *Sabrina, the Teenage Witch* starring her old friend from Orlando, Melissa Joan Hart.

February 2000 ✳

Performs '. . . Baby One More Time' and 'From The Bottom Of My Broken Heart' at Grammy Awards. Is nominated for Best

Female Pop Vocal Performance and Best New Artist but goes home empty-handed. Christina Aguilera picks up newcomer award.

March 2000 ✳

During filming for video of 'Oops! . . . I Did It Again', is accidentally hit on head by part of camera. Needs four stitches in wound.

May 2000 ✳

Hosts *Saturday Night Live*. Pokes fun at breast implant rumours by wearing huge set of false boobs while introducing show. Runner-up to boyfriend Justin in *People* magazine's online poll of the Most Beautiful People in the World. *Heart to Heart*, a book of Britney memoirs co-written with her mother, is published.

June 2000 ✳

First-week US sales of second album *Oops! . . . I Did It Again* total 1.3 million, the biggest first-week sales by female artist. Britney Spears exhibit opens at Kentwood Museum and includes replica of her childhood bedroom complete with dolls and bears. Shoots McDonald's commercial with Justin and 'N Sync.

December 2000 ✳

Justin orders twenty-six dozen roses to adorn Britney's hotel room in Palm Springs as a surprise on her nineteenth birthday. Petals from another ten dozen roses are scattered around the room.

January 2001 *

Britney and Justin fly to Rio de Janeiro for Rock in Rio Festival and spend three nights in suite at Intercontinental Hotel. Britney orders fried chicken, chips and cans of cola.

April 2001 *

Lynne and Britney's first novel, *A Mother's Gift*, published. Tells story of teenage singer from the Deep South who must leave her mother behind in her search for success.

May 2001 *

Tells *US Weekly* magazine she is finding it harder and harder to remain a virgin.

June 2001 *

Jive Records officially deny 'spoof' report on radio show that Britney and Justin have been killed in car crash.

September 2001 *

Steals show at MTV awards in New York when she performs 'I'm A Slave 4 U' with a seven-foot-long albino python draped around her neck. The following week she is on a flight bound for Sydney, Australia when the September 11 attacks unfold in New York.

November 2001 ✳

Third album, *Britney*, debuts at number one in US, knocking Michael Jackson's *Invincible* off top spot. Tells *News of the World* she and Justin are going to get married, perhaps in 2002.

January 2002 ✳

Tells *CD-UK* host Cat Deeley she will marry Justin some time in the future but not in 2002.

February 2002 ✳

Crossroads opens in US to poor reviews but good box office, taking more than $17 million in first week.

March 2002 ✳

Denies split with Justin during television interview with MTV. Is booed at British premiere of *Crossroads* when she ignores 3,000 fans who had waited more than an hour to see her.

April 2002 ✳

Justin's mother tells *People* magazine her son's relationship has hit a rough spot.

May 2002 ✳

Britney's parents divorce. Lynne is living in Serenity, the $4.5-million house Britney had built for her in Kentwood, while Jamie is back at the old family home a few miles away. Britney buys Lynne $62,000 Lexus car as Mother's Day gift.

June 2002 ✳

Named world's most powerful celebrity by *Forbes* magazine ahead of Tiger Woods, Steven Spielberg, Madonna, U2 and Justin Timberlake's group, 'N Sync.

July 2002 ✳

Gives the finger to photographers at Toluca airport in Mexico. Five days later walks off stage in Mexico City during fifth number, leaving angry crowd behind her, and flies home.

August 2002 ✳

Announces she is taking six months off.

November 2002 ✳

Declares she was shocked to s**t when she sees video for 'Cry Me A River', which features Justin getting his own back on a Britney lookalike after she apparently cheats on him.

December 2002 ✳

Horrid year ends with Britney terminating association with her New York restaurant Nyla after six-month period punctuated by bad press and falling custom.

January 2003 ✳

Gains restraining order against Japanese fan she claims has been stalking her for four months, both in California and in Louisiana.

March 2003 *

For performance in *Crossroads*, ties with Madonna for Worst Actress at twenty-third annual Golden Raspberry Awards in Santa Monica.

September 2003 *

Admits she slept with Justin but only because she thought they would marry. Tells *GQ* magazine, 'Just because I've admitted to having sex doesn't make me a bad person, does it?' Kisses Madonna on lips during performance at MTV Video Music Awards in New York.

November 2003 *

Breaks down in tears when television interviewer Diane Sawyer asks about her split from Justin. Receives star on Hollywood Walk of Fame. Her fourth album, *In The Zone*, emulates her first three by making its US chart debut at number one.

January 2004 *

Marries Jason Alexander, who she knew as a boy in Kentwood, at Little White Wedding Chapel in Las Vegas. Wears torn jeans, black top and baseball cap. Marriage lasts fifty-five hours before it is annulled.

March 2004 *

Onyx Hotel Tour opens in San Diego with 'Toxic' as first number.

April 2004 *

Is photographed for first time with new boyfriend Kevin Feder-line, a dancer from Fresno, California and father of two. They drive to a beach in Malibu, stopping traffic when they pop into Subway to buy a sandwich.

May 2004 *

Is number one in *FHM*'s 100 Sexiest Women in the World 2004. Kevin joins her on the European leg of the tour and they have matching tattoos of lucky dice etched onto the insides of their wrists.

June 2004 *

Injures knee filming video for 'Outrageous' and has arthroscopic surgery for second time. Cancels remaining dates of *Onyx Hotel* Tour. Announces engagement to Kevin Federline.

September 2004 *

Becomes Mrs Federline in surprise ceremony in the garden of her wedding planner's home in Studio City. Even her mother was kept in the dark. Wears stunning white strapless gown designed by Monique L'Huillier. Couple honeymoon in Kentwood before flying to Fiji.

October 2004 *

Parts company with long-standing manager Larry Rudolph, who says it is all amicable. Buys new home in gated community in Malibu for $7.5 million.

January 2005 ✳

Kevin Federline makes late-night shopping trip to Wal-Mart in McComb to buy pregnancy test for Britney.

February 2005 ✳

At last, wins coveted Grammy when 'Toxic' is named best dance record. Releases 'Do Somethin', her eighteenth UK single. Launches own brand of perfume, *Curious*, which tempts the senses with 'fragrant blooms of Louisiana magnolia touched with golden Anjou pear and dewy lotus flower'. In just five weeks it becomes the top-selling brand in US department stores.

March 2005 ✳

Writes on her website that she has turned her life around through Kabbalah, the cult religion she was introduced to by Madonna.

April 2005 ✳

It is official. After weeks of media speculation, Britney announces on her website that she is expecting her first child at the age of twenty-three.

August 2005 ✳

Chaotic, a reality show featuring the lives of Britney and Kevin, begins on British television.

322

September 2005 ✳

Sean Preston, her first baby, is born at the UCLA Medical Centre in Santa Monica. Kevin is present for the birth and the new family of three spends the night in a luxury suite on the fifth floor.

December 2005 ✳

For the third time in four years Britney is the most searched for name on the net according to Yahoo's annual list.

January 2006 ✳

Tops Mr Blackwell's worst dressed list for 2005. Looks a million dollars at the Screen Actors Guild Awards in Los Angeles, sporting a new blonde bob and blue silk dress. Kevin wears a tie.

February 2006 ✳

The police interview Britney after she is pictured behind the wheel of her SUV with four-month-old Preston, as she liked to call her son, on her lap. She blames 'a horrifying, frightful encounter with the paparazzi'.

April 2006 ✳

Preston is X-rayed after he bruises his head in a fall at home. He was being lifted out of a high chair by his nanny when he slipped from her grasp. The Department of Children and Family Services determined that neither Kevin nor Britney was involved in the incident.

LIFE AND TIMES

September 2006 ✳

Britney's second son is born. The media is convinced he is called Sutton Pierce but, six weeks later, Kevin and Britney reveal they have named him Jayden James.

November 2006 ✳

Just eight weeks after the birth, Britney files for divorce from Kevin, citing 'irreconcilable differences'. She faxes her lawyers her signature after appearing on *The Late Show with David Letterman* in New York. She asks for sole custody with visitation rights for Kevin. The next day he counters by seeking sole custody for himself. Britney is pictured getting out of a car wearing no knickers.

February 2007 ✳

Britney flies to a rehab centre in Antigua but only lasts a day. On her return to LA she visits a salon and shaves off all her hair. She later calls it 'a little bit of rebellion'. Goes to rehab centre in Malibu but again only lasts a day.

March 2007 ✳

Attacks a paparazzo's car with an umbrella. Goes back into rehab in Malibu for three weeks. Her father Jamie says, 'We've got a sick little girl here'.

June 2007 ✳

Is filmed delivering a hand-written letter to her mother in which she reportedly tells her she wants to be left alone.

September 2007 *

Opens the show at the MTV Video Music Awards with her new single 'Gimme More' but the critics hate it and Simon Cowell says she may have killed her career. The judge at a custody hearing in LA says, 'There is habitual, frequent and continuous use of controlled substances and alcohol.' Britney is ordered to face random alcohol and drug testing twice a week.

October 2007 *

'Gimme More' reaches number three in the UK charts. New album *Blackout* makes number two despite Britney doing no promotion whatsoever.

December 2007 *

Sister Jamie Lynn reveals she is pregnant at sixteen.

January 2008 *

Police are called to her home when Britney refuses to hand children back to Kevin's bodyguard and locks herself in the bathroom with Jayden. She loses visiting rights. Goes to Mexico with boyfriend Adnan Ghalib after discharging herself from hospital. Rumours begin that Britney is bi-polar. On 31 January, Britney is detained in hospital under section 5150 while doctors evaluate her mental condition.

February 2008 *

Her father Jamie is given temporary conservatorship of her affairs. He is granted a restraining order against her manager, Sam Lutfi.

September 2008 ✳

What a difference a year makes! Looks fabulous in a silver dress and wins three awards at the MTV video music awards.

November 2008 ✳

New single 'Womanizer' becomes Britney's first US number one since her debut single '. . . Baby One More Time' ten years earlier.

December 2008 ✳

Reveals on MTV documentary *Britney For The Record* that she should never have married Kevin Federline. Releases sixth studio album, *Circus*, and announces 2009 world tour.

March 2009 ✳

First night of the *Circus* tour in New Orleans. The *Daily Mirror* describes her performance as 'sizzling and sexy'.

June 2009 ✳

Plays eight nights at the O2 arena in London. She is photographed taking Preston and Jayden to the zoo. She announces plans to take the tour to Australia and play a further twenty-two dates across North America. Britney Spears is predicted to be the highest grossing live act of 2009.

UK Discography

Release Date	Title	Highest UK Chart Position
8 March 1999	... Baby One More Time UK Sales: 1,110,000 ... Baby One More Time; (You Drive Me) Crazy; Sometimes; Soda Pop; Born To Make You Happy; From The Bottom Of My Broken Heart; I Will Be There; I Will Still Love You (Duet with Don Phillips); Deep In My Heart; Thinkin' About You; E-Mail My Heart; And The Beat Goes On	2
15 May 2000	Oops! ... I Did It Again UK Sales: 910,000 Oops! ... I Did It Again; Stronger; Don't Go Knockin' On My Door; (I Can't Get No) Satisfaction;	2

Release Date	Title	Highest UK Chart Position
	Don't Let Me Be The Last To Know; What U See (Is What U Get); Lucky; One Kiss From You; Where Are You Now; Can't Make You Love Me; When Your Eyes Say It; Girl In The Mirror; Dear Diary	
5 November 2001	Britney UK Sales: 460,000 I'm A Slave 4 U; Overprotected; Lonely; I'm Not A Girl, Not Yet A Woman; Boys; Anticipating; I Love Rock 'N' Roll; Cinderella; Let Me Be; Bombastic Love; That's Where You Take Me; When I Found You; Before The Goodbye; What It's Like To Be Me	4
15 November 2003	In The Zone UK Sales: 492,000 Me Against The Music (Feat. Madonna); (I Got That) Boom Boom (Feat. The Ying Yang Twins); Showdown; Breathe On Me; Early Morning; Toxic; Outrageous; Touch of My Hand; The Hook Up; Shadow; Brave New Girl; Everytime; Me Against The Music (Feat. Madonna's Rishi Rich's Desi Kulcha Remix); The Answer (Bonus Track); Don't Hang Up (Bonus Track)	13

Release Date	Title	Highest UK Chart Position
8 November 2004	*Greatest Hits: My Prerogative* (Limited Edition 2 CD Set) UK Sales: 750,000	2

Disc 1

My Prerogative; Toxic; I'm A Slave 4 U; Oops! . . . I Did It Again; Me Against The Music (Feat. Madonna); Stronger; Everytime; . . . Baby One More Time; (You Drive Me) Crazy (The Stop! Remix); Boys (Co-ed Remix Feat. Pharrell Williams); Sometimes; Overprotected; Lucky; Outrageous; Don't Let Me Be The Last To Know; Born To Make You Happy; I Love Rock 'N' Roll; I'm Not A Girl, Not Yet A Woman; I've Just Begun (Having My Fun); Do Somethin'

Bonus Remix CD

Toxic (Armand Van Helden Club Remix); Everytime (Valentin Remix); Breath On Me (Jacques Lu Cont Remix); Outrageous (Junkie XL's Dancehall Mix); Stronger (Miguel 'Migs' Vocal Mix); I'm A Slave For You (Thunderpuss Club Mix); Chris Cox Megamix (without Outrageous)

(Disc 1 also released without Bonus Remix CD)

Release Date	Title	Highest UK Chart Position
29 October 2007	Blackout UK Sales: 260,000 Gimme More; Piece Of Me; Radar; Break The Ice; Heaven On Earth; Get Naked (I Got A Plan); , Freakshow; Toy Soldier; Hot As Ice; Ooh Ooh Baby; Perfect Lover; Why Should I Be Sad?	2
1 December 2008	Circus UK Sales: 210,000 Womanizer; Circus; Out From Under; Kill The Lights; Shattered Glass; If U Seek Amy; Unusual You; Blur; Mmm Papi; Mannequin; Lace & Leather; My Baby; Radar; Amnesia	4

✻ SINGLES ✻

Release Date	Title	Highest UK Chart Position
15 February 1999	… Baby One More Time UK Sales: 1,445,000	1
14 June 1999	Sometimes UK Sales: 414,000	3
20 September 1999	(You Drive Me) Crazy UK Sales: 257,000	5
17 January 2000	Born to Make You Happy UK Sales: 305,000	1

UK DISCOGRAPHY

Release Date	Title	Highest UK Chart Position
1 May 2000	Oops! ... I Did It Again UK Sales: 423,000	1
4 August 2000	Lucky UK Sales: 203,000	5
4 December 2000	Stronger UK Sales: 163,000	7
26 March 2001	Don't Let Me Be the Last To Know UK Sales: 67,000	12
15 October 2001	I'm A Slave 4 U UK Sales: 149,000	4
21 January 2002	Overprotected UK Sales: 124,000	4
1 April 2002	I'm Not A Girl, Not Yet A Woman UK Sales: 125,000	2
21 July 2002	Boys UK Sales: 74,000	7
4 November 2002	I Love Rock 'N' Roll UK Sales: 51,000	13
10 November 2003	Me Against The Music (Feat. Madonna) UK Sales: 122,000	2
1 March 2004	Toxic UK Sales: 268,000	1
14 June 2004	Everytime UK Sales: 196,000	1

UK DISCOGRAPHY

Release Date	Title	Highest UK Chart Position
1 November 2004	My Prerogative UK Sales: 180,000	3
28 February 2005	Do Somethin' UK Sales: 90,000	6
22 October 2007	Gimme More UK Sales: 135,000	3
14 January 2008	Piece of Me UK Sales: 210,000	2
14 April 2008	Break the Ice UK Sales: 78,000	15
17 November 2008	Womanizer UK Sales: 250,000	3
16 February 2009	Circus UK Sales: 130,000	13
4 May 2009	If You Seek Amy UK Sales:—	20

Index

INDEX

INDEX

INDEX

INDEX

INDEX

INDEX

Acknowledgements

Going backwards and forwards across the United States provided me with a wonderful opportunity to experience the different cultures throughout that vast country. Along the way I met many people who have helped to enrich this book. I would like to thank them all for making *Britney: The Biography* such a memorable book to research and write.

Firstly, my sincere thanks to Reg Jones, a gentleman and a fine companion with whom to enjoy a beer. I would also like to give a special mention to Chuck Yerger and Veronica Finn for kindly agreeing to help me for the second time. I am grateful to everyone who shared their thoughts and memories of Britney Spears and enabled me to build a picture of the real person behind the image. They include: Gay Austin, Kelly Burch, Nancy Carson, Dale Godboldo, Darlene Hughes, F. A. Jackson, Tony Lucca, Lindey Hughes Magee, Columbus Short, Rupert Thorpe, Jodie Wasserman and Sherry Yerger.

I would also like to mention the helpful staff at the McComb public library, even if they didn't stock any of my books! The waitresses at Ruby Tuesday's are the best in town. The Kentwood

ACKNOWLEDGEMENTS

Museum is an excellent place to while-away an hour. I must mention the Snap and Scrap store in Main Street, McComb, a very friendly place and a 'very cool scrapbook store'. I was made very welcome there by Lindey Magee and her assistant Maureen Wilson.

My old friends Richard Mineards and Gill Pringle were enormously helpful in Los Angeles. Thanks, too, to Cliff Renfrew for showing me round with such good humour. Lizzie Clachan did another brilliant job as my principal researcher. Adele's Typing Works were, as usual, fantastic in transcribing all my tapes.

I would also like to thank Ingrid Connell for commissioning this biography, my editor Jacqui Butler for her tireless efforts on this book's behalf, and the rest of the great team at Pan Macmillan.

Picture Acknowledgements

Section 1

Page 1: top © *News of the World*; bottom © Sherry Yerger. Page 2: top © Blue Wave Productions; bottom left and right © Reg Jones. Page 3: all © Reg Jones. Page 4: top © Reg Jones; bottom © Veronica Finn. Page 5: top left © Alex Lloyd Gross/Star File; top right © Gary Lewis/Camera Press; bottom © wireimage.com. Page 6: top left © wireimage.com; top right © Reuters/CORBIS; bottom left © Rex Features; bottom right © wireimage.com. Page 7: top left © Reuters/Ferran Paredes; top right © bigpicturesphoto.com; bottom © Reuters/CORBIS. Page 8: top © Reuters/Win Mcnamee; bottom © Reuters/CORBIS.

Section 2

Page 1: top and bottom right © Rex Features; bottom left © *News of the World*. Page 2: top left © Bauergriffin Agency; top right and bottom © bigpicturesphoto.com. Page 3: top © Rex Features; bottom © X17online.com. Page 4: top © X17online.com; bottom © Getty Images. Page 5: top © Getty Images; bottom © X17online.com. Page 6: top © Splash News; bottom © Rex Features. Page 7: © wireimage.com. Page 8: both © wireimage.com.